CONSECRATED PHRASES

Consecrated Phrases

A Latin Theological Dictionary

*Latin Expressions Commonly Found
in Theological Writings*

THIRD EDITION

James T. Bretzke, SJ

A Michael Glazier Book

LITURGICAL PRESS

Collegeville, Minnesota

www.litpress.org

A Michael Glazier Book published by Liturgical Press

3rd edition

Cover design by Ann Blattner.

ISBN 978-0-8146-8503-7 (paperback)

Library of Congress Cataloging-in-Publication Data

Bretzke, James T., 1952–
    Consecrated phrases : a Latin theological dictionary : Latin
expressions commonly found in theological writings / James T. Bretzke,
SJ. — 3rd edition.
        pages   cm
    "A Michael Glazier book."
    ISBN 978-0-8146-8214-2 — ISBN 978-0-8146-8239-5 (e-book)
    1. Catholic Church—Terminology.   2. Theology—Terminology.   3. Latin
language—Church Latin—Terms and phrases.   I. Title.

BX841.B68   2013
230.03—dc23   2012047221

To My Students

Contents

Preface to the Third Edition

Quidquid latine dictum sit altum videtur (That which may be said in Latin seems deep) was one page in a "Latin Phrase-a-Day" I received some time ago as a gift. To the best of my knowledge, though, this is *not* a "consecrated phrase," as I have never seen it used in any other context. Humorous to be sure, it also touches on an aspect of the rest of the Latin phrases contained in this third edition: all of them represent a good deal of wisdom in the Western classical tradition. This third edition contains 50 percent of new entries from the second edition, and many of the entries in the earlier editions likewise have been expanded and extensively cross-referenced so that the resulting volume not only functions better as a guide to translation of these phrases but also helps delve more deeply into the tradition out of which the consecrated phrases arose. The third edition contains a good deal of entries from canon and civil law, as well as terms from philosophy and theology. While Latin has often been called a "dead language," I believe this book shows convincingly that the tradition continues not only to live but to thrive and will aid generations yet to come in understanding, appropriating, and developing the best of that tradition.

I would like to thank in a special way Rev. Mark Massa, SJ, my academic dean at the Boston College School of Theology and Ministry, who supported my sabbatical application, which allowed completion of this project, as well as the Jesuit Community of Marquette University in Milwaukee, Wisconsin, who hosted me while I finished this volume.

Finally, I would like to thank all of my students over the last two decades who have supported this ongoing project and to whom I gratefully rededicate this volume.

31 July 2012
Solemnity of St. Ignatius Loyola
Founder of the Society of Jesus
Chestnut Hill, Massachusetts

Introductory Note
and Preface to the First Edition

A *consecrated phrase* refers to an expression that is used, often in a shorthand manner, to express a certain theological position or thought, such as *ex opere operato*, which expresses a significant position of Roman Catholic sacramental theology as defined at the Council of Trent, or *finis operantis*, which refers to the importance of the intention of the person (the "agent") in evaluating moral actions. Often these terms appear simply in a given theological text and no, or little, effort is made either to translate or explain such terms. The aim of this dictionary is to compile, translate, and briefly explain these Latin consecrated phrases, which are found with some frequency in theological writings and canon law and which therefore may puzzle readers unfamiliar with Latin and/or the theological meaning and nuances of these terms. For example, someone familiar with Latin may be able to translate each of the words *ex opere operato* ("by the work performed") but still be in some doubt as to precisely what this term means in theological usage. Each entry in this dictionary gives first a rather literal translation of the Latin term or phrase and then in most cases a brief gloss on the theological meaning and/or significance of the term. However, this dictionary is designed primarily for quick consultation in order to give the reader a general idea of what might otherwise be a puzzling expression. Other dictionaries or encyclopedias of theology should be consulted if one wishes a fuller theological and/or historical discussion of the term in question. While most of the entries contain theological, liturgical, canonical, and/or philosophical terms primarily from the Roman Catholic tradition, important expressions in the various Protestant traditions are also included, as well as a number of common classical aphorisms, such as *In vino veritas* ("In wine there is truth").

Latin titles of many church documents are also included and are further indicated as being a title by being printed in **bold type**, such as ***Gaudium et spes***. Since such document titles are derived from the opening words of the given document itself, the literal translation of a given document ("Joy and hope," in this case) does not always indicate clearly what the document concerns. In most cases an English subtitle is supplied, which is a better guide to the nature and content of the document in question.

Entries are listed according to the form most likely to be used in the expressions themselves as found in theological writings or references. Thus, the nominative singular of nouns or the infinitive form of verbs normally would not necessarily be the usual entry form. For example, the Latin word for "God" is *Deus*, and yet many other common expressions involving the use of "God" occur in the other grammatical cases, such as *Dei* (genitive, used in the possessive sense), *Deo* (dative or ablative, used as indirect objects and/or with certain prepositions) and *Deum* (accusative, used as a direct object). While efforts have been made to cross-referencing the entries as much as possible, given the fluidity of Latin word order not every possible grammatical form has been entered. Thus, if one is looking for *non licet* ("not legal") and cannot find this term listed under the letter "N," one might try looking for *licet* under the letter "L" (which will yield a better result). Similarly, since word order can be easily varied in Latin one might try looking for the meaning of the phrase by taking the last word instead of the first or some other word in the phrase. Thus, if one cannot find *Amor vincit omnia* under the letter "A," a second search under the letter "O" might produce *Omnia vincit amor* ("Love conquers all").

Finally, some common scholarly abbreviations and terms, such as *ibid.* (*ibidem*), *i.e.* (*id est*), *q.v.* (*quod vide* ["which see"]), etc., are also included.

Most of the entries contained in this dictionary have come from my own reading of various theological texts, and thus the dictionary makes no pretensions to be exhaustive and complete. I would be grateful if readers suggest other entries for this dictionary, especially for items which are used in theological writings and left untranslated in the given text. Finally, recognizing the basic truth of the adage *errare humanum est* ("to err is human"), I would also be grateful if one comes across typographical and/or grammatical errors as well as any other inaccuracies or unclear and/or misleading definitions in these listings.

I would like to express my gratitude first and foremost to the late John Wright, SJ, who read, corrected, and made many helpful suggestions to virtually the entire 1st edition manuscript. I would also like to thank several others who have given helpful input to this dictionary, especially John Donahue, SJ, Mary Ann Donovan, SC, and Michael Hilbert, SJ. Their input has improved this dictionary greatly; its remaining errors, deficiencies, and infelicities of idiom remain my own responsibility. A final note of thanks to Thomas Buckley, SJ, who suggested that the traditional expression "consecrated phrases" would serve well as the title for this dictionary.

James T. Bretzke, SJ
Berkeley, California
Solemnity of Christ the King, 1996

A

A
> From, away from, after, by, because of

Common Latin preposition.

A capella
> In the chapel (mode)

Refers to music that is sung without accompaniment, such as plain chant or Gregorian chant.

A cruce salus
> Salvation comes from the Cross

Salvation comes from Christ's death on the cross, and therefore for human individuals this salvation comes from belief in Christianity. See also *Extra ecclesia nulla salus, Ecclesia militans, Extra pauper nulla salus*, and *Limbus*.

A divinis
> From the holy (divine) service

Refers to the ecclesiastical canonical penalty of suspension ("suspension *a divinis*") in which a cleric is forbidden by his competent ecclesiastical authority (such as his bishop) from exercising the powers of orders, such as presiding at the Eucharist, hearing confessions, and administering the other sacraments. See also *Cessatio a divinis*.

A fortiori
> With stronger reason

Common expression, used in the sense of "all the more." Thus, for example, if someone should prepare the readings assigned for a given class, then *a fortiori* (all the more) she or he should prepare for the exam at the end of the semester.

A posteriori
> From that which comes after (i.e., the effect)

E.g., reasoning *a posteriori* is inductive reasoning, working back from the observed experiential effects to the formulation of a generalization or principle understood to express causality. Cf. *a priori* for the opposite approach.

A priori
> From that which comes before (i.e., the principle or cause)

For example, reasoning *a priori* is deductive reasoning, working from a general principle forward to judgment of consequences assumed from the given principle. Cf. *a posteriori* for the opposite approach. *A priori* can also refer to that which precedes, or is independent of, sense experience, whereas *a posteriori* refers to that which is dependent upon, or follows from, sense experience.

A quo
From which/whom

A tergo
From behind

Usually refers to the position in sexual intercourse in which the male lies behind the female.

Ab
From, away from, after, by, because of

Common Latin preposition.

Ab abusu ad usum non valet consequentia
From abuses to use (of something) (bad) consequences are not determinative (literally, "valid")

See the fuller discussion under *Abusus non tollit usum*. See also *Optimus interpres rerum usus*.

Ab extra
From outside

E.g., something that comes from outside of the entity under discussion. Thus, artificial insemination by a donor (AID) other than the husband is said to be fecundation *ab extra* and is therefore condemned in the traditional Roman Catholic view since it involves the introduction of a third party into the procreative process.

Ab initio
From the beginning

This expression is often used in the context of making a clean break and starting over from scratch, or to refer to the earliest moment of the historical development of whatever topic is being treated. See also *Ab ovo* and *De novo*.

Ab intra
From the inside

E.g., the insider's role in an event or process is *ab intra*. The opposite of *ab extra*.

Ab ovo
From the egg

From the very beginning (such as the egg that produces the chicken), i.e., a thoroughgoing analysis and/or construction and, in this sense, quite similar to *ab initio* (*q.v.*). See also *De novo*.

Ab urbe condita
From the City (Rome) being founded

This expression was used to denote linear time in ancient Rome and was abbreviated *a.u.c.*, much the way that we might use BC or AD. See also *Caput mundi*.

Absit invidia
Let no ill will be present

Expression similar to the wish that "no offense" be taken by one's words or actions.

Absolutus sententia judicis praseumitur innocens
Innocence is presumed if so found through a legal sentence/judgment

Legal aphorism that is usually understood as "innocent until proven guilty," though in this expression it means more literally that upon a judicial judgment of innocence the party should be in fact presumed innocent. See also *Actori incumbit onus probandi*; *Allegatio contra factum non est admittenda*; *Da mihi factum, dabo tibi ius*; *Facta non praesumuntur sed probantur*; *Onus probandi*; *Res iudicata pro veritate accipitur*; *Testis in uno falsus in nullo fidem meretur*; and *Ubi non est culpa, ibi non est delictum.*

Absolvitur ambulando
Wandering absolved (penitent)

Refers to the early Christian practice of undertaking a pilgrimage as part of one's penance for the absolution of sins. This expression seems to be derived from the philosophical phrase *solvitur ambulando* ("solved walking"), which indicated the instance of walking as an instance that would resolve Zeno's paradox against the possibility of local motion.

Abundans cautela non nocet
An abundance of caution does not injure

Principle of prudential judgment which indicates that, as a general rule, exercising caution rather than the opposite generally is to be preferred. The colloquial English expression "You can never be too careful" would capture the same idea. See also *Ad cautelam.*

Abusus non tollit usum
Abuse does not abolish use

The fact that a thing may be abused or improperly used from a moral point of view does not justify its destruction, nonuse, or non-application. Thus, the presence of medical equipment in an abortion clinic (equipment which could be used for a variety of legitimate purposes) would not of itself morally justify the destruction of such equipment in that particular location. In the same vein, the fact that a certain right might be abused by some would not justify its being withheld from others. Rights remain rights, even if and when they are abused. A related pair of axioms used in law are *ab abusu ad usum non valet consequentia,* which could be freely translated as "from abuses to use (of something) (bad) consequences are not determinative (literally, 'valid')" and *ex abusu non est argumentum ad desuetudinem,* namely "abuse (of a law) does not argue for (the law) falling into desuetude (disuse or nonobservance)." See also *Optimus interpres rerum usus.*

Accelaratio partus
Acceleration of parturition (i.e., birth)

In the moral tradition, this would refer to something done to hasten birth before the completion of the normal nine-month gestation period. Generally this term was understood to refer to those actions that had morally illicit abortion as the intended effect and thus should *not* be taken to refer to medical interventions, such as inducing labor or caesarean section, which have as their intended effect the well-being of the mother and child. The application of this moral term involves a careful discernment of the goal of the action in light of the concrete circumstances. See also in this regard *Finis operis, Finis operantis, Licet cor-*

rigere defectus naturae, *Obiectum actus,* and *Voluntarium directum/indirectum.*

Accidens
Accident

Important concept in scholastic philosophy and theology which refers to a nonessential property, attribute, or quality of a given entity. An "accident" is something which can only exist in another being and therefore cannot exist by and of itself. That which can exist in and of itself is called a substance. In regards to the being, in which an "accident" belongs or pertains, the "accident" is not necessary for the entity's existence as that particular entity. Thus, for example, hair color is an "accident" of a human person and not part of a human being's "essence" as a human being; even those who are totally bald are still considered to be human beings totally and essentially. See also *Ens*, *Ens ut ens*, *Ens ut sic*, *Essentia*, *In se*, *Per accidens*, *Per se*, and *Suppositum.*

Acta
Acts

Usually understood as the formal records or proceedings of something like a convention, meeting, council, or court case. See below for some common examples.

Acta Apolostolicae Sedis
"Acts of the Apostolic See"

Commonly abbreviated in scholarly references as **AAS**. The *Acta Apolostolicae Sedis* is the official publication of the Vatican which contains important documents, such as encyclicals, letters, and addresses of the pope, as well as decrees and decisions of the various congregations of the Roman Curia. The first volume appeared in 1909, and issues come out on a monthly basis. Not every document of the Holy See appears in the **AAS**, so its inclusion in this collection gives the document added extrinsic authority, and/or its date of publication may indicate when the legislation takes effect. See also *Vacatio legis.*

Acta causae
Acts of the case

I.e., the records or proceedings and relevant materials of a court case or canonical action.

Acta Romana (Societatis Iesu)
Roman Acts of the Society of Jesus

Collection of official documents of the Society of Jesus whose international headquarters are located in Rome, issued on an annual basis. Letters of the superior general to the whole Society, as well as other important talks and documents, are contained in this collection.

Acta Sanctorum
Acts (deeds) of the saints

Usually refers to a collection of the lives of the martyrs and saints, especially the series of scholarly works undertaken by the Bollandists, the group of scholars who devote themselves to the historically accurate treatment of the lives of the saints. Originally, members of this group were Jesuits, and the name comes from Jean Bolland or Bollandus (1596–1665).

Actori incumbit onus probandi
The plaintiff ("actor") has the burden of proof

Legal aphorism that one who brings a charge has the greater responsibility to prove the assertion, not the one named in the charge. See also *Absolutus sententia judicis praseumitur innocens*, *Allegatio contra factum non est admittenda*, and *Onus probandi*.

Actus essendi
Act of being

Refers to the fact of being. See also *Esse*, *Essentia*, and *Suppositum*.

Actus existentis
Act of existence

That is, an act related to the existence of an individual being. Eating would be such an act. Compare and contrast this term with any of the several other terms which begin with *actus* in order to see the differences in nuance. Not every *actus existentis* would be a truly "human act" (*actus humanus, q.v.*) in the sense of a "moral" act.

Actus hominis
Act of a human person (*without* a moral dimension)

Classical scholastic expression, usually translated as "act of man," and which is used to make a distinction from *Actus humanus (q.v.)*, which in turn is usually translated as "human act." Therefore, it is difficult to translate this term into in-clusive language. The *actus hominis* refers to an action performed by a human person but which may in itself have no *moral* significance, because it does not involve the use of moral reason, intention, and will. Digesting food or growing fingernails are examples of an *actus hominis*. While they are clearly activities related to a human person, they have no clear moral dimension. This distinction can also be helpful in assessing moral responsibility (or lack thereof) in cases that at first glance may seem to involve more personal responsibility. Thus, if my brakes fail (through no fault of my own) and my car hits a pedestrian, I am not *morally* guilty of a crime, as this would be an *actus hominis* and **not** an *actus humanus*. See *Actus humanus* (below) and *Voluntarium directum/indirectum*.

Actus humanus
Act of the human person (act *with* a moral dimension)

Distinguished from *actus hominis (q.v.)*, the *actus humanus* refers to the moral dimension, responsibility, etc., for one's actions. The use of deliberative reason that aims at a moral purpose proper to the human person provides the key to making an act a genuine *actus humanus* and thus a "moral" act. Cf. St. Thomas Aquinas, **Summa Theologiae** I–II, q. 1, a. 3, for his discussion of this point. See *Actus hominis* above as well as *Ea (eorum) quae sunt ad finem*; *Finis operis*; *Finis operantis*; *In necessariis unitas, in dubiis libertas, in omnibus caritas*; *Libertas est inaestimabilis*; *Obiectum actus*; and *Voluntarium directum/ indirectum*.

Actus judicialis
Judicial act

Refers to a juridical act (e.g., a judgment on a disputed point) performed by a judge in a trial or proceeding. See also *Actus juridicus*.

Actus juridicus
Juridic act

Refers to a formal legal act which has an *effect*, such as a formal decree of nullity in a marriage case. See also *Actus judicialis*.

Actus naturae
Natural act

Traditional moral norm, based on a physicalist paradigm, which held that an act (e.g., sexual acts) must be performed in a "natural" way in order to be considered moral. Cf. *Natura actus* and *Actus personae*.

Actus non facit reum,
nisi mens sit rea
The act itself does not constitute a crime, unless the intent be criminal

In moral theology this maxim notes the importance of bad intention for a morally bad action. Thus, an action that may appear "bad" or "evil" in itself, if it lacks a "bad" intention or was in fact done from a good intention, would not be judged to be "criminal," i.e., bad in its totality. In this moral context, see also *Fontes moralitatis* and *In se sed non propter se*. This phrase also enunciates a basic principle of criminal law which requires proof of an evil intent (*mens rea*, q.v.) to establish culpability for a crime. In this context, see also *Ab-solutus sententia judicis praseumitur innocens*; *Actus reus*; *Onus probandi*; *Nulla poena sine culpa*; *Sententia facit ius*; *Sententia incerta non valet*; *Sine culpa*; and *Ubi non est culpa, ibi non est delictum*.

Actus personae
Act of the person

Consideration of the moral nature of an act in terms of how it relates to the whole of the human person. This development is especially important in sexual ethics, as it moves away from physicalist conceptions of evaluation of conjugal acts (cf. *actus naturae* and *natura actus*). **Gaudium et spes**, Vatican II's Pastoral Constitution on the Church in the Modern World, uses this understanding of *actus personae* in its teaching on marriage (cf. **GS** #51).

Actus specificatur ab obiecto
The act is specified by its object (of choice)

The moral meaning of an act is determined by the object which is involved in the choice that lays behind the act, i.e., in choosing to do good one chooses God and in choosing to do evil one rejects God. See also *Ea (eorum) quae sunt ad finem*, *Finis operis*, *Finis operantis*, *Obiectum actus*, and *Voluntarium directum/indirectum*.

Ad
To, toward, at, near, for, as far as

Common Latin preposition.

Ad absurdum
To (the point of) absurdity

Taking an argument to its extreme point as a means of discrediting the argument itself. See also *reductio ad absurdum.*

Ad alterum/ad me
To (or for) another / to (or for) myself

Expression often paired with *ad me* to indicate something done for others as well as (or in distinction) with something done for myself. Thus, the virtue of temperance is something that is done *ad me*, for myself, but also is done *ad alterum*, for others. Other virtues, such as justice, are understood as being primarily directed toward society and others and thus are considered chiefly *ad alterum* rather than *ad me*—though of course when I practice the virtue of justice this also benefits myself.

Ad arbitrium
By one's will

Something done of one's own free will or by one's own authority. Similar to *arbitrio suo*. See also *Liberum arbitrium.*

Ad astra per aspera
Through adversity to the stars

Aphorism that indicates that only through trials and tribulations will one succeed to a worthwhile goal. This saying or its most common variant, *Per ardua ad astra*, is often employed as a motto by a number of institutions, branches of the armed forces, and so on.

Ad cautelam
With due caution

Principle of prudential judgment that indicates that a decision or application of some aspect of law (for example, a dispensation) should be done cautiously so as not to produce scandal or call respect for the law into question. For example, a teacher may grant permission for a student to turn an assignment in late (for just cause) but would want to grant this dispensation *ad cautelam* so that the other students would not take unjustified advantage of this dispensation and fail to turn in their assignments. In canon law, this principle is used to help guide those who can give dispensations so that they exercise this administrative power prudently. See also *Abundans cautela non nocet.*

Ad experimentum
For an experiment

Usually refers to something given provisional approval on an "experimental" basis, such as a new liturgical rite, in order to gauge how well the matter in question will function in actual practice. For example, the various Eucharistic Prayers for Masses for Children were first introduced in the United States *ad experimentum* and then after a period of trial use were given final and definitive approval to be used on a regular basis.

Ad extra/intra
To the outside/inside

Expression used primarily to indicate one's orientation, e.g., whether to the outside world or focused more internally. In this sense, it was remarked that Pope John Paul II was an *ad extra* pope since he undertook so many visits to foreign countries, etc.

Ad fontes
> (back) to the sources (fonts)

See *Recursus ad fontes*

Ad gentes
> To the peoples

Vatican II's Decree on the Church's Missionary Activity (1965).

Ad hoc
> For this (purpose, reason)

For example, an *ad hoc* solution is one devised for a particular, individual situation and need not be understood as establishing a general norm or precedent. In the same way, an *ad hoc* committee is one established for a particular need or project that would go out of existence once that project has been completed (in distinction to a "standing" committee).

Ad hominem
> Against the person

A fallacious, though common, type of argumentation in which the opponent's character, etc., are attacked rather than the merits of the opposing argument as such. An example would be labeling and summarily dismissing the arguments of moralists with whom one disagrees as "dissenters" or "traditionalists" rather than considering and answering the arguments themselves proposed by these individuals. See also *ad rem*.

Ad infinitum
> To infinity

Refers to something done or held forever, endlessly, and can also be used to indicate an exaggeration of detail. See also *Ad nauseam*.

Ad libitum
> At one's pleasure/choice

In theological usage this phrase is found in liturgical books, such as the *Ordo* and/or *Tabula dierum liturgicorum* (*q.v.*), indicating that no particular Mass text is prescribed for a certain day (such as a feast or non-optional memorial), and therefore the choice of the Mass text celebrated is up to the presider, who is to take into consideration the spiritual needs of the faithful in making the appropriate choice. The English expression *ad lib*, which means to speak extemporaneously, comes from the abbreviation of this Latin phrase.

Ad limina (apostolorum)
> To the threshold (of the apostles)

To the highest ecclesiastical authority, i.e., to the successor of Peter, the head of the apostles (namely, the pope). More commonly, this phrase is used in the expression "*ad limina* visit," which designates the required visit a bishop must make once every five years to Rome, during which he meets with the Holy Father one-on-one (for about fifteen minutes) and during which occasion other meetings are arranged with the various Vatican offices (such as the Congregation for the Doctrine of the Faith). *Ad limina* visits are normally organized geographically and linguistically. Therefore, a number of bishops from the same country, ecclesiastical province, or geographical region within a country generally makes the *ad limina* visit to Rome at the same time.

Ad literam
>   Literally, to the letter (of the law or text)

Expression usually applied in a negative sense, such as "we are following the spirit of the law (or policy), but we are not following each provision *ad literam* in precise detail." Thus, this adage also points to the tradition of the process of hermeneutics and the necessity of interpretation even of otherwise quite clear statutes, provisions, laws, etc. In Scripture, this expression is also used to refer to the "literal" or supposedly "plain" sense of Scripture that holds that the biblical texts need not be exegeted and interpreted, but rather simply applied and followed, i.e., *Sola scriptura (q.v.)*. See also *Cessante fine cessat lex*; *Consuetudo optima legum interpres*; *Lex valet ut in pluribus*; *Odia restringi, et favores convenit ampliari*; *Sensum, non verba spectamus*; and *Statuta sunt stricte interpretanda*.

Ad maiorem Dei gloriam (A.M.D.G.)
>   For the greater glory of God

Motto of the Society of Jesus (Jesuits) and a principle of apostolic discernment in which one is to choose that which would give God the greater glory. This principle is often referred to as the *magis (q.v.*, "the greater"). See also *Caritas Christi urget nos*, *Curet primo Deum*, and *Soli Deo gloria*.

Ad me
>   To (or for) myself

See the fuller discussion under *Ad alterum/ad me*.

Ad multos annos
>   For many years

Common form of congratulatory greeting, e.g., for birthdays, used in circles in which Latin might be known (such as communities of religious), similar to "many happy returns."

Ad nauseam
>   To (the point of) nausea

Something done or repeated endlessly to the point in which it causes or provokes extreme boredom or revulsion. See also *Ad infinitum*.

Ad orientem
>   To the east

Expression used primarily in a recent liturgical dispute surrounding the "proper" direction that the eucharistic presider and people should face during the Eucharist. Certain "traditionalists," such as those allied with Mother Angelica's Eternal Word Television (EWTN) network, based in the diocese of Birmingham, Alabama, claimed that the only "true" tradition in the church was for both the presider and the people alike to face toward the east in celebrating the Eucharist, rather than toward the people (*versus populum, q.v.*), as is the current practice under the post–Vatican II liturgy, the so-called *Novus Ordo (q.v.*). This would have the effect of returning to the pre–Vatican II liturgical practice in which the presider kept his back to the people. The bishop of Birmingham, David E. Foley, petitioned for a judgment from the Congregation for Divine Worship and the Sacraments, and in February 2000 this congregation rejected the traditionalists' claims, along with their further claims that only the First Eucharistic Prayer was truly traditional and should therefore be given preference in eucharistic celebrations. The Congregation's Prefect, Cardinal Jorge Medina Estévez, wrote that it is "incorrect and indeed quite unacceptable" that anyone should claim that to celebrate toward the apse is a more orthodox choice for the presider. See also *Coetus fidelium*, *Forma extraordinaria*, *Missale Romanum*, *Novus ordo*, **Summorum Pontificum**, **Universae Ecclesiae**, and *Versus populum*.

Ad quem
For/to which/whom

Ad rem
To the thing (at hand)

A relevant observation, application, argument, etc. An *ad rem* argument would contrast with one that was *ad hominem* (*q.v.*) or that simply would be extraneous or irrelevant to the issue at hand.

Ad tuendam fidem
To defend the faith

Motu Proprio (*q.v.*) of Pope John Paul II, dated 18 May 1998 and released on 30 June 1998. The English text can be found in *Origins* 28 (16 July 1998): 113, 115–16. The Cardinal Prefect of the Congregation for the Doctrine of the Faith (CDF), Joseph Cardinal Ratzinger (later Pope Benedict XVI), also released at the same time a *Commentary on Profession of Faith's Concluding Paragraphs*, which is found in the same issue of *Origins*, pp. 116–19. As a *Motu proprio*, *Ad tudendam fidem* both ex-

plains certain technical aspects of the *Professio Fidei*, *q.v.*, the 1989 Profession of Faith established by the CDF which is to be taken by teachers of theology, and also incorporates certain changes into the Code of Canon Law of both the Latin Rite and the Eastern Rite of the Catholic Church in order to specify in proper legal form, e.g., penalties for non-adherence to those things covered by the *Professio fidei*. The document *Ad tuendam fidem* itself does not specify exactly which articles of the faith, dogmas, and doctrines are included, while Cardinal Ratzinger's *Commentary* does give both fuller descriptions of what is meant by sorts of things governed by the *Professio* as well as some concrete examples (such as papal infallibility, priestly ordination being reserved to men alone, and the moral illicitness of fornication). However, it should be noted that Cardinal Ratzinger's *Commentary* does not carry the same legal or magisterial authority of the pope's *Motu proprio*. The *Commentary* was not adopted by the pope *in forma specifica* (*q.v.*) and so is not of itself a papal act but retains the authority of the Roman Congregation.

Ad validitatem
[Required] for validity (e.g., the valid administration of a sacrament)

Concept tied to scholastic sacramental theology which required that there must be a certain necessary order, matter, or form for the internal validity or efficacy of a sacrament. Thus, for the valid celebration (confection) of the Eucharist the presider must be ordained. Another example, in sacramental confession the priest had to use the formula "*Ego te absolvo . . .*" ("I absolve you [from your sins in the name of the Father, Son, and Holy Spirit"]). Manuals of moral theology would debate just how much of this formula had to be said for "validity" and a minimalist opinion held that "*Te absolvo*" ("I absolve you") would suffice. The concept of validity was foundational since it established the grounds for the efficacious celebration of the sacrament itself. Validity is therefore distinguished from liceity, which latter term refers to the "legal" provisions which should be followed. However, one could have a defect in liceity and still have a valid reception of the sacrament. See also *Ecclesia supplet*, *Ego te absolvo*, and *Res et sacramentum*.

Ad vitam (aut culpam)
For life (or until fault)

Used generally to refer to the election or appointment of someone to a post for life (such as pope or superior general of the Society of Jesus) to indicate a job or assignment that has no set time or term limit. Federal judges serve *ad vitam aut culpam* once their nomination has been confirmed by the Senate and until they either die, voluntarily retire, or are impeached due to serious misconduct. Bishops and cardinals remain such *ad vitam*, but bishops must resign their pastoral office on their seventy-fifth birthday and cardinals over the age of eighty may no longer participate in a papal conclave (though they could still be elected pope).

Adonai
Lord (in Hebrew)

This is the vocalization devout Jews will use when "reading" the Tetragrammaton, the four Hebrew consonants *YHWH* (*Yawheh*) used first by God speaking to Moses in Exodus 3:13-15 to designate God's own name. Since *Yahweh* is the holy name of God, the Jewish tradition respects this holiness by never vocalizing the name, using *Adonai* instead. In Latin usage the term *Adonai* occurs as the second of the seven "O Antiphons" in the octave of anticipation for Christmas. On this usage, see the fuller discussion under *O Adonai*.

Adsum
I am here

Formal reply to a roll-call type summons, similar to responding "present" in English. In the ordination rite in the Latin Church, when the candidate's name is called the reply in Latin would be *adsum*, though in contemporary English this is usually rendered as "I am ready and willing."

Adventus
Coming [of the Savior Emmanuel]

Latin term to express the period of waiting for the coming of the Messiah, the Christ, which the church celebrates liturgically each year in the four weeks prior to Christmas. See also *Adventus medius* and *Gaudete*.

Adventus medius
Intermediate coming

Expression attributed to St. Bernard of Clairvaux which speaks of Christ's periodic renewal of the church in the intermediate period between His original coming as man in Bethlehem and His second and final coming at the end of the world. See also *Adventus*.

Adversus solem ne loquitor
Don't speak against the sun

In other words, do not cling to a position that is obviously in error or counter to plain facts. See also *Allegatio contra factum non est admittenda*.

Aeterni Patris
(Of the) Eternal Father

Encyclical of Pope Leo XIII (1879) mandating the study of the philosophy of St. Thomas Aquinas, which led to a (forced) revival of scholastic philosophy and theology in seminaries.

Affectio commodi
Affection for the helpful

Refers to the capacity of the human will to love or desire those things which are helpful to the human person, in other words, for their "instrumentality" or as an aid as a means to some good end, i.e., a natural desire for a useful good. This desire is distinguished from *Affectio iustitiae* and *bonum honestum* (*q.v.*). See also *Bonum utile*.

Affectio iustitiae
Affection for justice

Refers to the capacity of the human will to love goods in such a way that respects their inherent goodness (rather than only as a means to some other end). See also *Affectio commodi* and *Bonum honestum*.

Affinitas non parit affinitatem
Affinity does not beget affinity

Affinity is an important concept in the canon law of marriage since it can constitute an impediment of marriage between certain parties if they themselves are blood relatives of one or another spouse in a marriage already ratified. Affinity is held between the husband and blood relatives of his wife and vice versa. However, this relationship of affinity between the blood relatives of the husband and the blood relatives of the wife (*affinitas non parit affinitatem*). Thus, while a widow could not marry her deceased husband's brother, the brother of the same husband (whether or not he were still alive) *could* marry the sister of the wife, and so on. Further aspects connected with affinity and consanguinity are covered in some detail in canon law. See also **Codex Iuris Canonici**, *Ligamen*, and *Ratum et consummatum*.

Africae munus
Africa's commitment (to the Lord Jesus Christ)

Opening words and title of the postsynodal apostolic exhortation of Pope Benedict XVI, promulgated in Benin on the occasion of his apostolic visit to Africa on 19 November 2011.

Age quod agis
Do what you are doing

Usually understood as an exhortation to do well whatever one has undertaken to do and thus is often used as a motto for educational enterprises.

Agere contra
To act against

Principle in spirituality, especially Ignatian spirituality, of overcoming some aversion or reluctance by acting directly against said difficulty. Thus, if one has an aversion to serving by way of manual labor, following the principle of *agere contra* one would directly involve oneself in just such labor in order to overcome the aversion and gain greater freedom.

Agere sequitur (esse)
Action follows being

Important metaphysical and moral principle in which one's moral duties, possibilities, etc., are grounded in one's being. Thus, the moral "ought" is founded on the "is," the given reality of the individual. This principle indicates the inseparable connection among ontology, obligation, and ethics. See also *Deus impossibilia non iubet*; *Humano modo*; *Lex sequitur esse; Lex spectat naturae ordinem*; *Modus operandi sequitur modum essendi*; *Operari sequitur esse*; *Qualis modus essendi, talis modus operandi*; *Quidquid percipitur ad modum percipientis percipitur*; and *Quidquid recipitur ad modum recipientis recipitur*.

Agere sequitur credere
Action follows belief

We act according to what we believe (ourselves to be). This expression should not be understood as a form of biological determinism but rather as a conscious moral choice to live according to our self-understanding of our moral being.

Agnus Dei
Lamb of God

First words of the prayer recited by the whole congregation in the Eucharist following the recitation of the *Pater Noster* (*q.v.*) and before reception of Holy Communion. The entire prayer is *Agnus Dei qui tollis peccata mundi, miserere nobis* ("Lamb of God who takes away the sins of the world, have mercy on us" [said twice]) and concludes with *Agnus Dei qui tollis peccata mundi, dona nobis pacem* ("Lamb of God who takes away the sins of the world, grant us peace").

Aliqualiter
In some manner (or other)

Refers to something unspecified or not in an entirely precisely stated fashion.

Aliquid
Something, to some extent

Refers to something somewhat indeterminate and therefore can be used as a pronoun. As an adverb it can be translated as "to some extent" or "at all."

Aliquo modo/Aliqua cognitio
In some manner or other

Indefinite adverbial expression that allows for a wide latitude of application. Often this expression is teamed with a general principle which is followed, leaving it up to the individual in the concrete situation to determine the best precise means of applying the principle. To some extent, the English expression "by hook or crook" gets at the same idea, though the Latin would not include the nuance of anything illegal or immoral. See also *Quaecumque ea sit* (whatever they may be). Versions of *aliquo* (some) can be used to modify other words to give similar "indefinite" expressions, such as *aliqua cognitio* (some knowledge) to indicate a certain minimum threshold required for something else. For example, it is sufficient that children, in order to make their First Communion, have a basic knowledge that the eucharistic host is "different" or "more special" than ordinary bread, but it is not required of them that they have a fuller knowledge of eucharistic theology or be able to explain the doctrine of the Real Presence and so on.

Allegatio contra factum non est admittenda

An allegation against the facts of a matter cannot be admitted

Legal aphorism that indicates that the simple making of an allegation is insufficient (i.e., inadmissible) in law to indicate the "proof" of the allegation. See also *Actori incumbit onus probandi*; *Adversus solem ne loquitor*; *Da mihi factum, dabo tibi ius;* and *Onus probandi.*

Alter Christus
Another Christ

Theological expression that the priest acts for the Christian community, especially in the celebration of the Eucharist, as *alter Christus*, "another Christ." This expression also figures in some of the theological reasoning behind the restriction of ordination to men alone, since—the argument runs—it would be more difficult, if not impossible, for women to "image" Christ in this way. See also *In persona Christi*, **Inter insigniores**, and **Ordinatio sacerdotalis**.

Altum dominium
Supreme (highest) dominion

In civil law, this is what gives the State the right to acquire property for the common good even if held privately by others (i.e., the right of eminent domain). In the ecclesiastical arena, this same concept gives the pope the ultimate power of administration over ecclesiastical property. See also *Prima sedes a nemine iudicatur*; *Quod in necessitate sunt omnia communia*; *Rex non potest peccare*; *Summa iustitia in se*; and *Summum ius, summa iniuria.*

A.M.D.G.
See *Ad majorem Dei gloriam*

Ama et quod vis fac
Love and do what you will

This should *not* be understood as a principle license but rather as direction. In other words, if one truly loves, then one's will will be properly oriented to do or choose the right and loving thing. See also *Dilige et quod vis fac.*

Amicus curiae
Friend of the court

Refers to one who is not party to a certain litigation and yet who is invited to give advice or render a legal opinion on the matter before the court, e.g., in the form of an *amicus curiae* brief. An example might be a legal brief outlining some expert testimony in an area or aspect involved in the case, e.g., a scientific report on the effects of secondhand smoke in a lawsuit against smoking in public places.

Amor Dei
Love of God

Refers to the proper end of the human person and the highest form of love. Sometimes other "loves" are contrasted with this proper love. For example, see *Amor mortis*.

Amor Dei usque ad contemptum sui
The love of God (that leads) even to contempt of self

Expression of St. Augustine of Hippo, which can be interpreted as the basic dynamic involved in a positive (or good) stance toward God as the one who gives the individual a genuine sense of perspective about his or her moral goodness by relating this to God's infinite goodness and love. In a certain sense this same idea is related also to St. Ignatius of Loyola's First Principle and Foundation and the Three Degrees of Humility found in the latter's Spiritual Exercises. See also *Usque ad*.

Amor mortis
Love of death

This expression is used to refer to the nature of sin, i.e., that which ultimately is death-dealing and perverts human beings from their proper end, which could be expressed as *Amor Dei* (love of God, *q.v.*).

Amor sui usque ad contemptum Dei
The love of self (that leads) even to contempt of God

Expression of St. Augustine of Hippo, which can be interpreted as the basic dynamic involved in a negative (or bad) fundamental option stance. See also *Amor Dei usque ad contemptum sui* and *Usque ad*.

Amor vincit omnia
Love conquers all

A play on Virgil's expression, *Labor vincit omnia* ("Labor conquers all," *q.v.*), used by Chaucer in his *The Canterbury Tales* and widely used ever since. True love will prevail ultimately against any and all adversities.

Amplexus reservatus
Reserved (held) embrace

Practice of penile insertion in the vagina followed by withdrawal before ejaculation. Since the man did not ejaculate in this practice, unlike *coitus interruptus* (*q.v.*), its morality was debated over the centuries among moral theologians, and several argued for its ethical acceptability. The Holy Office (institutional precursor to the Congregation for the Doctrine of the Faith) eventually issued a *monitum* (*q.v.*) in 1952 that warned theologians not to "describe, praise, and urge *amplexus reservatus*." See also *Copula dimidiata*.

Analogia entis
Analogy of being

Theological position which holds that there is a certain level of commonality in all reality and that God is the fullness of being. Human existence and experience have a capacity to be transparent to divine presence and action but can never fully comprehend or embrace the mystery of God who is always greater than that which humans can conceive (*Deus semper maior*, *q.v.*). This concept has been used traditionally in Roman Catholic systematic theology. See also *Res analogata*.

Analogia fidei
The analogy of faith

This expression comes from Romans 12:6 (ἀναλογιαν τῆς πίστεως), which is often translated as "in proportion to the faith" and which indicates that an individual biblical passage or text which deals with the Christian faith must be interpreted within the larger context of the whole faith which the church holds (cf. *DS* 3016, 3283). See also *Analogia Scripturae* and *Res analogata*.

Analogia Scripturae
The analogy of Scripture

This concept is related to the basic idea expressed in the term *Analogia fidei* (*q.v.*) and as applied to Scripture indicates that a particular biblical passage or text, especially if it seems ambiguous or unclear, should be interpreted in accord with the message and interpretation of other biblical texts which deal with the same issue or theme. Thus, the *Analogia Scripturae* would guard against "proof-texting" in an irresponsible manner, or taking some given biblical verse or passage out of the context of the rest of the Scripture. See also *Res analogata*.

Analysis fidei
Analysis of faith

Theological theme that describes the structure and process of faith and considers the reasons and motives that lead the individual to faith in God, as revealed in and through Jesus Christ.

Anathema/Anathemata (singular/plural)
(Something which has been pronounced to be) anathema or heretical

As a noun this refers to a proposition which is formally (or informally) held to be heretical or contrary to the faith or acceptable practice. See also *Anathema sit/Anathema sint*.

Anathema sit/Anathema sint
Let him/her be anathema (accursed)/Let them be anathema

Based on a Hebrew curse, this traditional formulaic phrase appended to formal doctrinal definitions: "But if anyone presumes to contradict this our definition—which God forbid—*anathema sit*." This particular example is taken from the definition of papal infallibility contained in **Pastor aeternus**, Dogmatic Constitution on the Church of Christ, Vatican I (*DS* 3074–75). Thus, such a defined doctrine must be accepted by all the faithful. For an explanation of **DS** see **Enchiridion Symbolorum Definitium Et Declarationem**. See also *Anathema/Anathemata* and *Latae sententiae*.

Angelus
The angel

Refers to the prayer in honor of the Blessed Virgin Mary that is traditionally recited at morning, midday, and evening (or sometimes just at midday). The opening lines are *Angelus Domini nuntiavit Mariae. Et concepti de Spiritu Sancto* (The Angel of the Lord declared unto Mary. And she conceived by the

Holy Spirit). A Hail Mary (*Ave Maria, q.v.*) would then be recited, after which the next verses of the prayer would be recited. During the Easter Season, instead of the *Angelus* the *Regina Coeli* (*q.v.*) is said.

Anima/animus
Soul

Latin has two very similar words for "soul," *anima* and *animus*. *Anima* (feminine noun) refers to the soul as the principle of life. Thus, the Latin Vulgate's translation of the opening words of Mary's song of praise uses this word to render "My soul praises the Lord": *Magnificat anima mea Dominum* (Luke 1:46). *Animus* (masculine noun) also refers to "soul" but connotes the soul more as the principle of intellect and/or feeling. Thus, one can speak of having a certain *animus*, or bad feelings, toward another person.

Anima Christi
Soul of Christ

Opening words of a medieval prayer to Jesus Christ, which was much loved by St. Ignatius of Loyola and is usually found in the beginning of his *Spiritual Exercises*.

Anima naturaliter Christiana
The soul is naturally (by its nature) Christian

Expression of Tertullian (d. circa AD 220) which holds that the human soul is endowed with a certain natural knowledge of God, which, though it can be obscured, can never be completely obliterated. Thus, the soul has a natural inclination toward God. See also *Potentia Obedientialis*.

Animarum zelus
Zeal for souls

Principle of pastoral ministry, namely the care for souls (referencing primarily the living and not the dead). See also *Cura animarum* and *Salus animarum suprema lex*.

Anno Domini
In the year of the Lord

Usually abbreviated AD and refers to the division of the centuries before (BC) and after the birth of Christ. Thus, "AD" refers to the common era after Christ's birth. Nowadays, instead of BC and AD, many people prefer to use "BCE" (before the common era) to designate BC and "CE" (common era) to refer to AD.

Annuario Pontificio
Pontifical Annual

The Roman Catholic official yearbook, published annually, which gives the names of all the official Vatican organizations along with their members, as well as the names of all the bishops and their dioceses in the world.

Ante
Before, prior

Common Latin adverb and preposition. Care should be taken that *ante* not be confused with *anti* (which denotes negation or contrariety).

Ante bellum
Before the war

In the United States this expression traditionally refers to the period before the

American Civil War (1861–65) and is usually used in reference to the American South or former slave states.

Apologia pro vita sua
   An apology (defense, explanation) for one's life

Though this expression can be used generically, in theology it often refers to Blessed John Henry Cardinal Newman's 1864 book of the same title in which he gave the reasons for his conversion from Anglicanism to Roman Catholicism. "Apologetics" was also a traditional theological course in which one studied how to defend or present the Christian faith to non-believers. Though the contemporary word "apology" comes from the same Latin root, the usual meaning of asking forgiveness for some offense is not at all related to these other uses of *apologia*.

Apostasia
   Apostasy

This term comes from the Greek (αποσ-τασία) and is usually understood to involve a complete rejection by an individual of his or her religion. In this sense apostasy is differentiated from heresy, which involves a denial or rejection of one or another tenet of the faith, but without encompassing a complete departure from the faith. For example, a Christian who became a Muslim would be called an "apostate" from Christianity, whereas another Christian who denied the virgin birth of Jesus but who accepted Jesus as God's Son and our Savior would be considered a "heretic" but not an "apostate." There is another general usage of *apostasia* in

canon law to refer to those who have either abandoned the clerical state (*apostasia ab ordine*—departure from Sacred Orders) or religious vows (*apostasia a religione*—departure from religious life [i.e., membership in a religious order]).

Apostolica signatura
   Apostolic signatura

The supreme tribunal of the Roman Catholic Church, located in Rome and similar to the Supreme Court in the sense of being the court of final appeal.

Apostolicam actuositatem
   Apostolic activity

Vatican II's Decree on the Apostolate of Lay People (1965), which emphasized the proper and essential role of the laity in the church and the world.

Apostolos Suos
   His Apostles

Pope John Paul II's *Motu Proprio (q.v.)*, "On the Theological and Juridical Nature of Episcopal Conferences," released by the Vatican on 23 July 1998. The document states that doctrinal declarations from episcopal conferences, in order to constitute an "authentic magisterium," must be unanimously approved by the individual bishops of the given conference or otherwise receive the *recognitio* (revision/confirmation) of the Apostolic See. "Authentic" magisterium is a term, though, that can be misleading, as in Latin the term *authenticus (q.v.)* means authoritative in a juridical sense and should *not* be misconstrued in the sense of holding a teaching that is not labeled "authentic magisterium" to be inherently suspect or spurious. An English translation is found in *Origins* 28 (30 July 1998): 152–58; and also found on the Vatican website: http://www.vatican.va/holy_father/john_paul_ii/motu_proprio /documents/hf_jp-ii_motu-proprio_ 22071998_apostolos-suos_en.html. See also *Authenticus,* **Christus Dominus***, Collegium, Collegialis affectus, Ecclesia docens, Munus docendi, Primus inter pares*, and *Recognitio*.

Appetitus rectus
Right (ordered) desire ("appetite")

Expression which refers to the correct moral orientation of the individual who acts out of his or her rightly-ordered desires to chose the correct moral action according to the natural moral law. See also *Inclinationes naturales.*

Arbitrio suo
On one's own authority

See also *ad arbitrium.*

Argumentum e silentio
Argument from (tacit, approving) silence

Expression which indicates that when someone "could" speak up on an issue but does not say anything explicitly in support, his or her silence (depending on the context) could be construed as tacit support for the cause, proposition, idea, etc. For example, Vatican curial cardinals normally retire at age seventy-five, but when Joseph Cardinal Ratzinger, the then head of the Congregation for the Doctrine of the Faith, reached

that age Pope John Paul II refused to accept his resignation, and some Vatican observers concluded that this was an *argumentum e silentio* that indicated Pope John Paul II was hoping Cardinal Ratzinger would be elected to succeed him when he died (which, of course, happened with the election of Ratzinger in 2005 as Pope Benedict XVI). See also *Ex Silentio* and *Qui tacit consentire censetur.*

Arma virumque cano
I sing of arms and the man

Opening lines of Virgil's epic poem, the *Aeneid*, which portrays the end of the Trojan War and the wanderings of the Trojan refugee Aeneas who eventually founds Rome. The phrase today also can convey a certain sense of national destiny.

Ars celebrandi
The art (or manner) of celebration

This term usually would refer to the manner in which the liturgies of the Church are conducted, or celebrated, by the appropriate ministers and following officially established liturgical norms—though recognizing the possibility of legitimate adaptation as expressed in the rubrical directive "in these or similar words." The *ars celebrandi* would recognize on one hand the particular role and gifts that the individual minister does bring the celebration of a given liturgical rite, while at the same time respecting the norms and rubrics laid down by the Church which govern the celebration of these rites. There will always be a certain creative tension between excessive adaptation on one hand and rigid formalism on the other. This tension was referenced in Pope John Paul II's 2003 encyclical, **Ecclesia de Eucharistia.**

Ars erotica
Erotic arts

A phrase used by French philosopher Michel Foucault in his 1978 *History of Sexuality* to denote what Foucault characterized as the Eastern approach to sex as primarily an art form, contrasted with the Western approach to the study of sex focusing on knowledge leading to power over sex as *Scientia sexualis (q.v.)*.

Ars gratia artis
Art for art's sake

Also used as the motto of the American film company Metro Goldwyn Mayer (MGM).

Ars moriendi
Art of dying

In Christian theology, the term refers to how Christians ought to face death (e.g., in light of a firm belief in salvation and the resurrection). See also *Articulum mortis, Beati mortui qui in Domino moriuntur*, and *Bona mors*.

Artes praedicandi
Preaching arts

Term used to refer to the technique of good preaching, as well as the name given to a type of handbook for preachers that was popular in the medieval church.

Articulum mortis
The point of death

Articulum indicates the moment of time; therefore *articulum mortis* refers

to the last moments of life before death. See also *Ars moriendi, In extremis*, and *In periculo mortis*.

Articulus stantis et cadentis ecclesiae
The article by which the church stands or falls

Refers to an article of faith which is considered to be absolutely essential for a proper understanding of the Christian faith. In classic Lutheran theology, for example, the principle of justification by faith (*sola fide, q.v.*) could be considered to be the *articulus stantis et cadentis ecclesiae*. In an earlier age of christological controversies, the divinity of Christ was considered to be such an article. Rhetorically, this phrase is sometimes employed for dramatic effect to issues that clearly would not likely involve the continued existence of the church, such as women's ordination. See also *Credenda, De fide definita, Norma normans non normata*, and *Norma normata*.

Aspergillum
Sprinkler

Name given to the handheld instrument that holds holy water and is used in liturgical functions to bless the people (for example, during the Penitential Rite of the Eucharist) and/or objects, such as the coffin which contains the deceased in the Mass of Christian Burial.

(Christus) auctor sacramentorum
(Christ is) author of the sacraments

Expression dating back to St. Ambrose (cf. *De Sacram* IV, 4.13) that holds that

Jesus Christ is the true originator ("author") of all of the sacraments of the Church.

Auctores probati
Approved authors

These would be theologians whose writings and opinions are usually considered to be trustworthy, even if not definitive, on matters of theological dispute. For an opposite sentiment see *Damnanda et proscribenda*, and see also *Nihil obstat* and *Videantur auctores probati*.

Auctoritas
Authority, advice, support

In Latin there are two principal terms for authority: *auctoritas* and *potestas* (*q.v.*). *Auctoritas* refers more to the authority of counsel, wisdom, learning, advice, influence, support, etc., while *potestas* carries nuances of "power" in the sense of jurisdictional authority or efficacious ability to perform a function, carry out an office, make a decision, etc. However, it is important to keep in mind that neither the authority of *auctoritas* nor the authority of *potestas* is absolute in the sense that it can function or exist without the complementary element of the other. Sometimes the term *auctoritas* is paired in *inquisitio* (*q.v.*) to express complementary roles in theological investigation and authoritative teaching. In this latter example, *inquisitio* refers to the role of theologians to "investigate" a theological position and allows them to advance certain opinions that may be considered but which do not carry with them the claim of the "authoritative" teaching of the pope and bishops who exercise the *magisterium*.

The magisterium, in this sense, then, exercises the charism of the *auctoritas* of authoritative teaching while the theologians exercise the charism of the *inquisitio*, or exploratory theological investigation. See also *Authenticus*, *Ecclesia discens*, *Ecclesia docens*, *Inquisitio*, *Magisterium*, *Magisterium docens*, *Peritus*, and *Potestas docendi*.

Audio Dei
I hear (of) God

A somewhat awkward Latin expression (*Auditio Dei* would be better Latin: "hearing [of] God") which seems to have been coined to contrast with *visio Dei* ("the vision of God," *q.v.*). In general, we move spiritually from an *audio Dei* to a *visio Dei*.

Auditio Dei
Hearing God

See *Audio Dei*.

Auditus fidei
Hearing of faith

See the fuller discussion under the term *Intellectus fidei,* as well as the terms *Fides qua/Fides quae*, *Fides quae creditur*, *Fides quarens intellectum*, *Indefectabiliter adhaeret*, and *Sensus fidelium*.

Auriga virtutum
Charioteer of the virtues

Expression which denotes prudence (*prudentia*) whose role is to guide the other virtues, e.g., to discern what would be courage as opposed to foolhardiness in a particular situation.

Aut satisfactio aut poena
Either satisfaction (of a debt) or
payment

Anselm's dichotomy used in his theology of justification which held that
justice, especially God's justice, required
either payment of a debt by the debtor or
some means of "satisfaction" of the debt.
Through sin, humans acquired a debt to
God which they themselves could not
pay, and therefore God accepted the
death of Jesus Christ as satisfaction of
that debt, and this satisfaction thereby
saved and redeemed humanity. See also
Cur Deus homo, *Aut venia aut poena*,
and *Processus iustificationis*.

Aut venia aut poena
Either pardon or punishment

Expression from Tertullian, which expresses a theology of reconciliation
somewhat at variance with St. Anselm's
theology of satisfaction expressed in the
latter's axiom, *aut satisfactio aut poena*
(*q.v.*). Tertullian's view allows for God
either to punish sins or simply to forgive
them, without maintaining that God's
justice would require the punishment or
satisfaction of Anselm's *aut satisfactio
aut poena*. See also *Processus iustificationis*.

Authenticus
Authentic, authoritative

In Latin, and in church tradition, this
term is used to indicate something that
should be held to be authoritative in a
formal or jurisdictional perspective.
Thus, when this term modifies a noun
such as "teaching," it usually refers to
the formal teaching of the magisterium

on a given topic. The term should not
be construed to set up a separation of
"non-authentic" teaching that would
then be held as being suspect at best, if
not downright spurious or corrupt.
Other aspects of "authority" are expressed in terms such as *Auctoritas*
(*q.v.*) and *Munus* (*q.v.*) and these added
concepts are helpful in coming to a
proper understanding of what *authenticus* actually means when it refers to
magisterial teaching. See also *Auctoritas*, **Christus Dominus**, *Ecclesia docens*, *Magisterium*, *Munus*, *Obsequium
religiosum*, *Officium*, *Potestas docendi*,
and *Sensus fidelium*.

Ave
Hail

Latin vocative form of greeting, similar
to English "hello," but often used in
religious circles as a shortened form for
the prayer the *Ave Maria* ("Hail Mary,"
q.v.).

Ave atque vale
Hail and farewell

Similar to the English expression,
"Hello and goodbye," which would be
said to greet someone briefly when one
is forced to leave almost immediately
upon rendering the initial greeting.

Ave Maria
Hail Mary

Beginning in Latin of the famous Marian prayer. The prayer itself ("Hail
Mary" in English) is often referred to
simply as the "Ave," and thus a common
penance might be "three Ave's and three
Pater Noster's (say three 'Hail Mary's'
and three 'Our Father's')."

Ave Maris Stella
Hail Star of the Sea

Medieval Marian hymn which begins *Ave maris stella, Dei mater alma atque Semper Virgo, felix caeli porta* (Hail Star of the Sea, gracious Mother of God and ever Virgin, happy gate of heaven).

Aversio a Deo
Aversion to God

Expression for sin, which involves a turning of the person away from God, the true end of the human person, and going off in a direction other than that willed by God for the human person's true happiness. This expression is re-peated in the discussion on sin in Pope John Paul's 1984 post-synodal apostolic exhortation *Reconciliatio et Paenitentia* (On Reconciliation and Penance in the Mission of the Church Today). See also *Conversio ad creaturam*.

Axis mundi
Axis of the world

In other words, something of great importance such that the world turns on it and/or which connects earth to heaven and is thus important in many religious narratives and mythologies to represent the connection between the divine and the human.

B

Baptismus in voto
   Baptism by desire (will)

Expression used to denote those who lacked ritual baptism but who through their lives and/or through an expressed desire for Christian baptism evidenced Christian character in their lives. See also *A cruce salus, Communio sanctorum, Extra ecclesia nulla salus, Extra ecclesia nulla conceditur gratia, Extra mundum nulla salus, Extra pauper nulla salus, Fides implicita,* and *Radix Mali.*

Beati
   The Blessed

Refers usually to the saints or "blessed" who are in heaven with God and who therefore enjoy the beatific vision, though it can also be used colloquially to designate those who seem more fortunate or better off than others. See also *Visio beatifica* and *Visio Dei.*

Beati mortui qui in Domino moriuntur
   Blessed are the dead who die in the Lord

Pious expression used to announce the passing of someone, often in a religious context. See also *Ars moriendi, Bona mors,* and *Nil nisi bonum.*

Bellum iustum
   Just war

Expression to denote the concept of Just War Theory. The traditional component parts for this theory were a careful consideration of the reasons for going to war as a last resort, the so-called *ius ad bellum (q.v.),* followed by the just conduct of the war itself involving proportionality in the use of force, immunity of non-combatants, humane treatment of prisoners, etc.—the so-called *ius in bello (q.v.),* and more recently many theologians speak of the necessity of restoration and repair of damages suffered during the war, the so-called *ius post bellum (q.v.).* See also *Si vis pacem, para bellum.*

Bene docet, qui bene distinguit
   The one who teaches well is the one who distinguishes well

Classical adage which refers to the fact that the truth of a certain position is found in attention to those important details which distinguish it, or set it off, from another position or issue. This adage emphasizes the critical importance of making the proper distinctions in any argument or search for the truth.

Benedicamus Domino
Let us bless the Lord

Common invocation used in a variety of liturgical prayers and religious uses. The response is *Deo gratias (q.v.)*. In religious houses, it was common that one member of the community would awaken each member in the morning by knocking on the door and intoning *Benedicamus Domino*. The response *Deo gratias* would then indicate that the individual was awake.

Benedicite
Bless

Title of the Canticle of the Three Young Men (Meshach, Shadrach, and Abednego) who were thrown into the fiery furnace by the Babylonian King Necuchadnezzar in Daniel 3:52-90. This hymn is still recited as part of the Liturgy of the Hours (or Breviary).

Benedictus
Blessed (be the Lord)

As a stand-alone noun, this term usually refers to the whole of the Canticle of Zechariah in Luke 1:68-79 and comes from the opening word in Latin of that hymn. It is said as part of the Morning Prayer of the Church found in the Breviary traditionally called *Lauds* (derived from *laudo* "to praise").

Bono et aequo
Good and just (equitable)

See *De bono et aequo*

Bona fide
In good faith

In this expression, "fide" is usually pronounced in English as if it were a single syllable word and refers to a genuine article (as opposed to a fake).

Bona mors
Good (happy) death

While this concept has a very long history in human history, in theology it refers primarily to the idea of dying in the friendship of God, i.e., the state of grace. From the late Renaissance onward there were a number of pious associations founded by the Jesuits called the *Bona mors* Confraternity or Happy Death Society that fostered good works and preparation for an eventual pious death. Since a good life was the essential requirement for a happy death, attainment of a *bona mors* would depend on living an upright existence, and in this sense the *bona mors* society would help its members in this end. See also *Ars moriendi, Beati mortui qui in Domino moriuntur*, and *Nil nisi bonum*.

Bonum
Good

As an adjective, this word will modify the accompanying noun, such as *bona fide (q.v.)*, "in good faith." As a plural noun, *bona* can refer to goods and property. As a singular noun in theological usage, the word *bonum* generally refers to the moral character of goodness and/or the ultimate end of humanity which is the "good" of eternal beatitude which comes from union with God. In theological usages, *bonum* is usually found linked together with one or another of a number of different words, such as *bonum commune (q.v.)* or *summum bonum* (*q.v.*), and whose meaning then depends on the second word with which *bonum* is used. See all the other entries under *Bonum*, and especially *Bonum est faciendum et prosequendum, et malum vitandum.*

Bonum apprehensum
The apprehended good

This term refers to what is known or perceived to be good or a good in itself. The human capacity for *recta ratio* (*q.v.*) and practical moral reason is closely linked to seeing something as good and working toward it. Inasmuch as humans can err or sin in pursuing a "false" good, the notion of the *bonum apprehensum* is helpful in making the distinction between an "apparent" good and what is truly the "real" good. In the case of sin or moral error, what is mistaken for the good is in fact only a false good, which nevertheless appears to the individual as an apparent good and thus can be termed a *bonum apprehensum*. See also *Ens rationis, Lex indita non scripta, Lex naturalis, Lumen naturale, Ordo rationis, Per modum cognitionis / Per modum inclinationis*, and *Recta ratio.*

Bonum commune
The common good

Important concept in social ethics, which holds that the good of an entire community or society is of grave importance and should be the concern and ordering principle of social institutions, such as laws. While this should not be understood as a form of utilitarianism, this principle does establish limits on individual rights, including the right to private property, by calling for a just distribution of economic goods for the use of all. See also *Epikeia; In extrema necessitate omnia, societati humanae destinata, sunt communia; Iustitiam subsidiariam; Lex iniusta non est lex; Lex lata in praesumptionne periculi communis; Necessitas est lex temporis et loci; Necessitas non habet legem; Ordinatio rationis ad bonum commune; Ordo publicus; Quod non licitum est in lege necessitas facit licitum*; and *Salus publica suprema lex.*

Bonum est faciendum et prosequendum, et malum vitandum
The good is to be done and fostered, and evil avoided

Thomas Aquinas defines the nature of the "good" as that which all things seek after and goes on to give this as his first principle in the practical of the natural law, which would be self-evident to all reasonable persons upon rational examination and need not (nor cannot) be further proved (cf. St. Thomas Aquinas' *Summa Theologiae* I–II, q. 94, a. 2). This principle grounds all other moral norms, and much of the contemporary discussion (pro and con) on proportionalism hinges upon how this first principle is interpreted and applied.

Bonum ex integra causa, malum ex quocumque defectu
The (moral) good of an act comes from its causal integrity (of act plus intention); moral evil comes from any defect (in either act or intention)

However, the *full* aphorism reads: *Verum et falsum sunt in mente, bonum et malum sunt in rebus; bonum ex integra causa, malum ex quocumque defectu* ("truth and error exist in the mind, good and evil in things; good demands fullness of being, evil is predicated of any defect").

This statement can be read also as a metaphysical principle and not just a moral principle. However, this statement presupposes a certain understanding of metaphysics and has been the focus of considerable debate among contemporary moral theologians as to its precise meaning and ethical significance.

Bonum ex nocentibus
Good [product or result] from something harmful [e.g., an "evil" source or cause]

Expression of the silver lining in a cloud, or that good in fact sometimes does come from evil. This aphorism, however, is not meant to suggest that evil means should be chosen so that a good end might result.

Bonum fidei
Good of fidelity

According to Augustine, one of the three principal goods (*bona*) of marriage, i.e., marital fidelity and stability. Society as a whole is served by this good, as well as its being one of the three principal ends along with *Bonum prolis (q.v.)* and *Bonum sacramenti (q.v.)*, which had to be willed or intended simultaneously for a valid sacramental marriage. See also *Humano modo*.

Bonum honestum
Honest good

Refers to that which is useful, proper, or "honest" for realizing a certain good ob-ject, choice, or end. The end may also be termed a *bonum honestum*, and that which would frustrate such a good would be an *inhonestum (q.v.)*. See also *Bonum utile*, *Summum bonum*, and *Uti et frui*.

Bonum particulare
Particular good

Refers to an individual good that is aimed at one particular value and is not considered to involve the highest overall good of life (which is the *summum bonum* ("highest good," *q.v.*), or the common good of the *bonum commune (q.v.)*. See also *Bonum utile* and *Uti et frui*.

Bonum prolis (or prolix)
The procreative good

Traditional understanding (especially in Augustine) of the principal end of marriage, i.e., for the procreation of offspring. However, *bonum prolis* should not be equated simply with *generatio prolis (q.v.)*, the mere biological production of offspring. Rather, *bonum prolis* refers to the integral aspect of marriage as a union of love out of which children are conceived, brought into the world, nurtured, loved and educated. Anything which would operate morally against this good (*contra bonum prolis*), such as artificial contraception, would be viewed as morally evil. See also *Bonum sacramenti, Bonum fidei, Concubitus propter solam procreationem, Humano modo, Potentia coeundi/Potentia generandi*, and *Sine prole*.

Bonum sacramenti
Good of the sacrament

According to Augustine, one of the three principal goods of marriage, i.e., indissolubility of a valid sacramental marriage, which came to be widely accepted as grounding the legitimate sexual activity within marriage. This is also the grounding of the theology which holds that the two spouses themselves confer the sacrament upon each other (with the priest or deacon merely serving as the ecclesial witness to the marriage). Besides helping each other grow in holiness, the sacrament also symbolizes the fidelity that Christ has for the church. See also *Bonum prolis*, *Bonum fidei*, *Humano modo*, *Propter solam procreationem*, and *Res analogata*.

Bonum suum
Our good (literally, "one's" good)

Refers to the aspect of the "good" which leads us to love it for itself once we recognize and accept it as truly our own good. This concept of the good can be contrasted with a *bonum utile*, which we recognize as having a positive function or usefulness but which we do not love in and of itself. Thomas Aquinas referenced this concept in his discussion of the interrelation between hope and love in the theological virtues in ST I–II, q. 62, a. 4, *resp*. See the other entries under *Bonum*, and especially *Bonum utile* and *Summum bonum*.

Bonum totius
Good of the whole

The good of the whole can be taken into account in evaluating an individual action, which by itself may seem harmful or immoral. Thus, it would not be an immoral mutilation to amputate a leg in a diabetic person that had become infected with gangrene, since this operation would save the person's life. See also *Pars propter totum*; *Si finis bonus est, totum bonum erit*; *Mala moralia* and *mala praemoralia*; and *Ratio Proportionata*.

Bonum utile
Useful good

Refers not to the *summum bonum* ("highest good," *q.v.*), or a *bonum honestum* (*q.v.*) but rather some object or desire based on a well-considered choice, such as a means to an end. A *bonum utile* can be further distinguished from the *summum bonum* or a *bonum honestum* as having more the character of a means by which the *summum bonum* or a *bonum honestum* is attained. See also *Bonum particulare*; *Bonum suum*; *Desiderium consiliabile*; *Dominium utile*; *Ius utendi, fruendi, abutendi*; *Res frutificat dominum*; and *Uti et frui*.

C

Caeteris paribus
See Ceteris paribus

Cantatorium
Collection of (liturgical) chants

See the entry under *Liber Gradualis* and *Schola cantorum.*

Cantus firmus
Steadfast chant (or theme)

This expression can refer to a recurring leitmotif (as in a musical chant) but more often metaphorically refers to a strong theme running through a certain document or position. Thus, the Federation of Asian Bishops Conferences (FABC) maintains as the *cantus firmus* of the church in Asia that it must always be a "church of the poor."

Capax Dei
Receptive of God

Expression of Irenaeus, which indicates that the human person, as a self-transcendent spiritual being, is said to be capable of receiving God through God's free gift of God's self made through grace and revelation. See also *Summum bonum.*

Cappa magna
Great cape

Name given to the vestment worn by bishops and cardinals which had a hood and a long train. Since Vatican II, the form of the *cappa magna* has been much simplified and is worn less often than in the past, though some more recently elevated prelates have taken to using it in certain solemn liturgical rites, usually associated with the Tridentine Rite. See also *Coram Cardinale/Coram Episcopo.*

Caput mundi
The head of the world

Expression used for Rome and, by extension, to any location that considers itself to be of greater importance than the rest of the world. See also *Ab urbe condita*; *Roma locuta, causa finita*; and *Ultra montes.*

Caritas
Charity, love

Latin translation of the Greek *agape* (ἀγάπη), which is also rendered as love.

Caritas Christi urget nos
The love of Christ compels (urges) us

Expression from 2 Cor 5:14 which indicates that, ultimately, it should not be a consideration of pragmatic gain, etc., but the love of Christ which moves us to action. This expression was used by Pope Benedict XVI in his apostolic letter **Porta Fidei** (*q.v.*) #7 to mark the calling of the Year of Faith in October 2011 commemorating the commencement of the Second Vatican Council. See also *Ad majorem Dei gloriam* (*A.M.D.G.*), the motto of the Society of Jesus, which uses a chief principle of discernment the consideration of that which is "For the greater glory of God."

Caritas generis humani
Love of the human race

Spoken of by Cicero in his *De finibus bonorum et malorum* 5.23, and which refers to the basic social nature of human beings, i.e., that they have a basic innate disposition to love humanity (even if this is imperfectly realized in the concrete).

Caritas in Veritate
Charity in truth

Title of Pope Benedict XVI's third encyclical issued on 29 June 2009, which dealt primarily with social and economic ethics, especially in the light of increasing globalization. See also *Caritas in veritate in re sociali*; **Deus caritas est**; *Ubi caritas*; *Deus ibi est*; and *Ubi societas, ibi ius*.

Caritas in veritate in re sociali
Charity in truth in social matters

Catholic social doctrine enunciated by Pope Benedict XVI in his third encyclical, **Caritas in Veritate**, issued on 29 June 2009. See also **Caritas in Veritate**; *Ubi caritas*; *Deus ibi est*; and *Ubi societas, ibi ius*.

Caritas non obligat cum gravi incommodo
Charity does not oblige in cases of grave inconvenience (or danger)

Scholastic axiom that indicates the boundary of prudence over charity. Where there is a proportionate or sufficient reason present one may elect *not* to come to the aid of another in distress or need (e.g., to risk one's life to attempt to rescue a drowning person in heavy seas). See also *Semper sed non pro semper*.

Caro cardo salutis
The flesh is the hinge on which salvation depends

Expression of Tertullian (*On the Resurrection of the Flesh*, ch. 8) which indicates that an authentic orthodox Christian anthropology holds that we are *embodied* spirits, not a separable dualistic combination of body and spirit.

Carpe diem
Seize the day

From Horace's *Odes*, the fuller expression being *carpe diem, quam minimum credula postero*, which is understood as "enjoy today, and don't pay much attention to what tomorrow may bring." This expression also can be abused as a rather hedonistic moral stance as in "eat, drink, and be merry, for tomorrow we may die."

Casti connubii
Of chaste wedlock

Pius XI's encyclical On Christian Marriage, condemning artificial contraception and written in response to the

Anglican Communion's Lambeth Conference resolution which gave guarded approval to the use of artificial birth control (1930). Paul VI's 1968 **Humanae vitae** (*q.v.*) reaffirmed the Catholic Church's prohibition of every use of artificial contraception (though it acknowledged the legitimate use of natural family planning for serious reasons). See also *Intrinsece inhonestum.*

Casus
Case

This is a rather general word in Latin as in English and could refer to a certain issue in a broader sense, as well as a specific legal case. In moral theology the *casus* was used to illustrate the application of moral principles to concrete situations. This was often termed casuistry (case-study moral analysis). If the morally relevant features of a case could be separated apart from the non-morally relevant features (e.g., the names of the individuals would generally not be considered morally relevant, but their marital state might be), then the application of the morally appropriate principles could be transferred to similar cases. See also *Casus conscientiae* and *Summa Casuum Conscientiae.*

Casus belli
Case (or cause) for war

A justification for waging war. In less extreme situations the expression may refer to making a mountain out of a molehill, thus, "don't make his cutting class a *casus belli*." See also *Ius ad bellum.*

Casus conscientiae
Case of conscience

Application of the method of casuistry (see *Casus* above) to the confessional forum. These confessional cases were often used to help train seminarians and young priests in their exercise of the Sacrament of Penance. See also *Casus conscientiae, Libri paenitentiales, Summa Casuum Conscientiae,* and *Summae confessariorum.*

Catechesi tradendae
Handing over the teaching (catechesis)

John Paul II's post-synodal apostolic exhortation On Catechesis in Our Time (1979). The document, which has special emphasis on the catechesis of children and young people, was begun by Paul VI after the conclusion of the triennial Synod of Bishops, which met on the theme of catechesis, and the apostolic exhortation was concluded by John Paul II.

Cathedra
Chair (in the official sense)

Term used to designate the "chair" or seat of office of a bishop or the pope as Bishop of Rome. The church in which the bishop's seat is located is called his cathedral. The *cathedra* is a symbol of the bishop's authority. One of the criteria of an exercise of the "extraordinary magisterium" of the pope, which carries with it the claim of infallibility, is that the papal pronouncement must be delivered officially, "*ex cathedra*" (*q.v.*).

Causa excusans
Excusing cause

In law, that which would render the observance of a particular law impossible or very difficult and therefore renders that particular law non-binding in that situation.

Causa finalis est prima inter omnes causas
The Final Cause is the first (most important) among all the other causes

Essentially the same notion as *Finis est causa causarum* (*q.v.*). See *Ea* (*eorum*) *quae sunt ad finem, Finis enim dat speciem in moralibus, Finis est nobilior iis quae sunt ad finem, Finis operis, Finis operantis,* and *Qui vult finem vult media.*

Cautela abundans non nocet
See *Abundans cautela non nocet*

Caveat emptor
Let the buyer beware

Roman maxim which supposedly "justifies" any sort of false advertising or misrepresentation since it puts the burden of judging the veracity of advertising claims on the buyer rather than the seller—presuming that most vendors will exaggerate the merits of their products and thus a prudent buyer should take these *cum grano salis* (*q.v.*), i.e., with a grain of salt.

C.C.E.O.
Latin abbreviation for ***Codex Canonum Ecclesiarum Orientalium***, (*q.v.*), the Code of Canon Law for the Oriental (Eastern uniate) Churches.

Celebret
He may celebrate

Official written attestation given to a priest by his legitimate superior or ordaining prelate that he may celebrate the Eucharist, i.e., that he is a priest in good standing. This document has become more important of late to indicate that not only is the individual a validly ordained priest, but he also has no pending charges or suspicions of clerical or sexual misconduct.

Censor deputatus
Deputed (appointed) censor

In ecclesiastical publications, the bishop or other appropriate ecclesiastical superior usually delegates examination of a potential publication for doctrinal orthodoxy to a theological specialist who makes a determination whether a *Nihil obstat* (*q.v.*) can be given, allowing for the granting of an *Imprimi potest* (*q.v.*) and the *Imprimatur* (*q.v.*), indicating the work carries with it ecclesiastical approval (*Cum approbatione ecclesiastica, q.v.*).

Centesimus annus
The hundredth year (anniversary)

John Paul II's 1991 social encyclical written to commemorate the hundredth anniversary of Leo XIII's ***Rerum novarum*** and which was published shortly after the fall of communism in Eastern Europe. The encyclical critiqued both communist ideology and the excesses of free-market capitalism.

Certa bonum certamen
> Fight the good fight

Common expression and used as the motto for Iona College, the Christian Brothers liberal arts school in New Rochelle, New York.

Certum est quia impossibile est
> It is certain because it is impossible

Expression of Tertullian in his *De Carne Christi*, in which he argues that in matters of faith, what seems to be impossible when judged according to human evidence indicates instead the truth of the supernatural reality. See also *Corde creditur, Credo quia absurdum, Ne fides rideatur*, and *Tantum valet quantum probat*.

Cessante causa cessat effectus
> The cause ceasing, so does the effect cease

See *Cessante fine cessat lex* (The end [goal, reason] ceasing, the law ceases) and also *Ubi cessat ratio legis, cessat ipsa lex*.

Cessante fine cessat lex
> The end (goal, reason) ceasing, the law ceases

Axiom of law, especially relevant in the interpretation of church law, that states that when the reason or goal of a law no longer holds, then the particular law which was oriented to that goal loses its legal force (cf. ST I–II, q. 96). Other similar versions of this maxim are *Cessante causa cessat effectus* (the cause ceasing, the effect ceases) and *Cessante ratione legis cessat ipsa lex* (the reason for the law ceasing, the law itself ceases). See also *Ad literam*; *Consuetudo optima legum interpres*; *Ex abusu non est argumentum ad desuetudinem*; *Exceptio firmat regulam*; *Odia restringi, et favores convenit ampliari*; *Sensum, non verba spectamus*; and *Ubi cessat ratio legis, cessat ipsa lex*.

Cessante ratione legis cessat ipsa lex
> The reason for the law ceasing, the law itself ceases

See *Cessante fine cessat lex* (The end [goal, reason] ceasing, the law ceases) and also *Ubi cessat ratio legis, cessat ipsa lex*.

Cessatio a divinis
> Suspension of divine service

Canonical penalty, which is a form of interdict, in which the holding of liturgical services (such as the Eucharist) is forbidden for a certain time in a certain church or chapel, usually due to a serious act to which the venue has been subjected, e.g., a murder that takes place in a church which requires its reconsecration by the local bishop. This penalty is contrasted with clerical suspension *a divinas* (*q.v.*) which would occur because of some serious lapse on the part of the priest penalized.

Ceteris paribus
> Other things being equal

E.g., "*ceteris paribus* the Vatican appoints native clergy as bishops of that region," meaning that when various candidates have similar qualifications the choice would go to the person who is a native of that place over the foreigner or missionary. An alternative spelling for *ceteris* is *caeteris*.

Cf.
Compare

Cf. is the Latin abbreviation for the Latin word *confer*, which means compare. *Cf.* is commonly used to indicate reference to another source, such as *cf. confer*.

Charisma veritatis
Charism (gift) of truth

In Roman Catholic theology, this notion is tied to the office of the magisterium, which enjoys the special assistance of the Holy Spirit given as a grace in episcopal ordination and exercised in communion by the pope and the college of bishops. This grace must still be exercised in a human way (cf. *Quidquid recipitur ad modum recipientis recipitur)* and should not be understood as a magical guarantee of total truth. As Cardinal Avery Dulles, SJ, has noted "the charism of the magisterium, like the grace of preaching, does not function *ex opere operato* [*q.v.*]. Thus in point of fact the power of an individual office-holder to express the faith of the Church in a correct and effective manner will depend on a number of imponderables" (Dulles, *A Church To Believe In*, 1982, p. 121). See also *Auctoritas, Authenticus, Ecclesia docens, Ex cathedra, Inquisitio,* **Lumen gentium**, *Magisterium, Magisterium attestans, Magisterium authenticam, Magisterium docens, Munus,* **Mysterium ecclesiae**, *Obsequium religiosum, Officium, Potestas docendi, Quaestio disputata, Quidquid recipitur ad modum recipientis recipitur, Sensus fidelium, Sententia probata, Status quaestionis,* and *Theologice certa.*

Chasuble
Little house

Name of the outer liturgical vestment worn by the presider over the alb at the Eucharist.

Christifideles
The Christian faithful

Refers to those who have been baptized and are therefore considered members of the church and part of the people of God. Since Vatican II more emphasis has been placed on the importance of the lay vocation in the world and the church.

Christifideles laici
Lay Christian faithful

Post-synodal apostolic exhortation of Pope John Paul II On the Vocation and the Mission of the Lay Faithful in the Church and in the World (1988).

Christus Dominus
Christ the Lord

Vatican II's Decree on the Pastoral Office of Bishops (1965), which emphasized the collegiality of the bishops with the Bishop of Rome, the pope. See also **Apostolos suos**, *Collegium, Collegialis affectus,* and *Recognitio.*

Christus Victor
Christ the Victor

Christological title that highlights Jesus' redemptive victory over sin and death and especially Satan and the powers of evil. This term was popular with many early church fathers, and Eusebius of Caesarea spoke of a great spiritual battle with the devil after Jesus' death but before his resurrection, when he "descended into hell" as the Apostles' Creed states. Jesus' victory in this battle saved humanity from Satan's dominion. See also *Risus Paschalis*.

C.I.C.
Code of Canon Law

Latin abbreviation for the 1983 **Codex Iuris Canonici** (*q.v.*). Prior to the 1917 Code, this abbreviation **C.I.C.** referred to the **Corpus Iuris Canonici** (Body of Canon Law), which was composed of various decrees, judgments, and the like—similar to the British tradition of constitutional law. See also *Codex*, **Corpus Iuris Canonici**, and the 2009 *Motu proprio* (*q.v.*) **Omnium in mentem**, by which Pope Benedict XVI amended some of the particular canons in the Code.

Cilicium
Hairshirt

A penitential garb made from goat's hair, obtained originally from the Roman province of Cilicia. Penitential hairshirts or sackcloth of whatever provenance were often designated by this term (cf. Ps 35:13).

Circuminsessio
Being together

In English this term is rendered as "circumincession" and refers usually to the trinitarian doctrine of the shared exis-

tence of the divine Persons in one God (Being), though it can be used also to refer to the Christological doctrine of the divine and human natures being present simultaneously in the person of Jesus.

Civitas
Citizenship, commonwealth, state

Refers to the body of citizens who together comprise a political entity such as a state.

Civitas Dei
City of God

Refers to Augustine's book of that name, as well as to his concept of Christians who are members of God's *civitas* but here on earth are still *in via*. See *In via* and *Viator*.

Clausura
Cloister

Refers to the limitations placed on free entry and/or exit from religious houses. A vowed religious who has an indult (i.e., canonical permission) to live outside of his or her religious community is said to be exclaustrated. Cloister more often refers to those areas of a religious house which nonmembers of the community are forbidden to enter. In this sense, *clausura* would be similar to the designation "Authorized Personnel Only."

Clavis David
Key of David

The fourth of the "O Antiphons" that mark the octave of anticipation or preparation for Christmas Eve, which in itself is the vigil of Christ's birth. See the fuller discussion under *O Adonai*.

Codex

A tree trunk, book, ledger

In theological usage, *codex* usually refers either to a code of laws, such as the *Codex Iuris Canonici* (*q.v.*), the church's Code of Canon Law (often abbreviated *C.I.C., q.v.*), or to a manuscript edition of some ancient text, such as the *Codex Vaticanus*, an early manuscript of the Greek New Testament.

Codex Canonum Ecclesiarum Orientalium

Code of Canon (Law) of the Oriental Churches

Promulgated in 1990, this is the Code of Canon Law for the Eastern-rite churches which are in union with Rome. *Codex Canonum Ecclesiarum Orientalium* is abbreviated as *C.C.E.O.*

Codex Iuris Canonici

Code of Canon Law

The church's official collection of laws. The Roman Catholic Church has two complete Codes (systematic collections) of canon law: the 1917 version (which contained 2414 canons) and the current 1983 Code (which has 1752 canons). Latin is the official language of the Code, and thus the technical meaning of the concepts and vocabulary terms in Latin is critical to a proper understanding and application of the Code. *Codex Iuris Canonici* is abbreviated as *C.I.C.* See also *Corpus Iuris Canonici*, as well as the 2009 *Motu proprio* (*q.v.*) *Omnium in mentem*, by which Pope Benedict XVI amended some of the particular canons in the Code.

Coena Domini

The Lord's Supper

Refers to the Last Supper Jesus had with his disciples and, by extension, to the celebration of the Eucharist.

Coetus

Meeting, assembly, committee

In ecclesial circles, this term is usually used to refer to some sort of committee that is charged with a certain task, e.g., to prepare a working text, agenda for a meeting, etc.

Coetus fidelium

Group of the faithful

This term was used by Pope Benedict XVI in his 2007 *Motu proprio* (*q.v.*) *Summorum Pontificum* to refer a group of the faithful who may legitimately request the celebration of the Tridentine Latin Mass as a *forma extraordinaria* in *Summorum Pontificum*. This term was clarified in *Universae Ecclesiae* (*q.v.*) as an indefinite number of the faithful who do not necessarily have to belong to the same parish but who are considered a "stable" group (*stabiliter existens*). See also *Ad orientem*, *Cappa magna*, *Forma extraordinaria*, *Missale Romanum*, *Novus Ordo*, *Summorum Pontificum*, *Universae Ecclesiae*, and *Versus populum*.

Coetus Internationalis Patrum

International Group of (Council) Fathers

Name given to a group of around two hundred conservative bishops from various parts of the world at Vatican II that called into question the legitimacy of the Council as a true Ecumenical Church Council after it concluded in 1965. See also *Sede vacante.*

Cogito ergo sum
I think therefore I am

Well-known adage of French philosopher René Descartes (1596–1650) in which he sought a certain and unassailable philosophical starting point for knowledge and method.

Cognitio aenigmatica
Enigmatic (obscure) knowledge

Expression which often refers to things known in the light of faith (*Lumen fidei, q.v.*) which will always remain opaque to a certain extent, not (according to Thomas Aquinas) due to our sin, but rather because of the limitations of the human intellect. Cf. ST II–II, q. 7, a. 2, reply to obj. 3. See also *Deus semper maior* as well as the entries under *Credo* and *Fides.*

Coitus interruptus
Interrupted coitus

A morally illicit (and rather ineffective!) form of contraception in which the sexual act is terminated by the withdrawal of the penis just prior to ejaculation in the vagina. As distinguished from *amplexus reservatus* (*q.v.*), ejaculation takes place, though not in the vagina. See also *Copula dimidiata.*

Coitus reservatus
Reserved coitus

Alternative expression for *amplexus reservatus* (*q.v.*). Since no ejaculation takes place in *coitus reservatus* it was traditionally distinguished from *coitus interruptus* (*q.v.*). See also *Copula dimidiata.*

Collegialis affectus
Collegial bonds, affective collegiality

This expression was used in **Lumen gentium** #23 and is somewhat clumsily translated there as "collegiate feeling," and again in **Ad gentes** #6 as "collegial spirit." However, the notion really refers to the common pastoral office of bishops who by their office should work together with one another and in communion with the Bishop of Rome, who is *Primus inter pares* (*q.v.*). See also **Apostolos suos,** **Christus Dominus***, Collegium,* and *Primus inter pares.*

Collegium
College, Group of associates

While "college" is the closest cognate in English, *collegium* does not really refer to an academic institution, but rather a group of associates, members, etc., of similar rank. Thus, we speak of the College of Bishops as being in communion with the Bishop of Rome, the pope, one of whose titles that speaks to this union is *Primus inter pares* (*q.v.*). This notion of episcopal collegial authority is well expressed in Vatican II's Decree on the Pastoral Office of Bishops, **Christus Dominus**. See also **Apostolos suos, Christus Dominus***, Collegialis affectus,* and *Primus inter pares.*

Communicatio idiomatum
Idiomatic communication; exchange of properties

This single expression has two rather distinct meanings. As a close cognate, "idiomatic communication" could mean an imprecision or technical error in the formulation of an expression, without necessarily intending a more serious lapse such as a heresy. However, in Christology the expression deals with the dual nature of Jesus Christ as true God and true human. While these natures are unified in Jesus this does not mean that his human nature shared fully in divine omnipotence or that his divine nature was extinguished on the cross. The Spanish Jesuit liberation theologian, Jon Sobrino, admitted a technical error of this sort in response to the 2006 Notification of the Congregation for the Doctrine of the Faith on his work but denied the implicit charge of heresy in his writings. See also *Homo assumptus*.

Communicatio in sacris
Participation in the sacred rites

Refers usually to the participation of non-Catholics in a Catholic religious service, e.g., the Eucharist, or the administration of the sacraments by a Catholic minister to non-Catholics or viceversa, in which Catholics participate in non-Catholic rituals (cf. *C.I.C.* #844). Colloquially, the phrase is often used to connote a negative attitude toward ecumenical worship services.

Communio
Communion

The primary theological meaning of the word *communio* is the notion of being together in a cohesive group and thus carries nuances of cooperation and collegiality. *Communio* can be used to describe a certain ecclesiological understanding of the church, sometimes in distinction from seeing the church as a *societas perfecta* (*q.v.,* "perfect" so-

ciety). *Communio* is also the name given to an international theological journal of a more conservative bent that provides a counterbalance to the more liberal *Concilium* (*q.v.*).

Communio episcoporum
Communion of bishops

Refers to the notion of collegiality of bishops which they enjoy with one another and with the Bishop of Rome. A violation of this *Communio episcoporum* is considered to be very serious and can lead to a number of penal sanctions, such as when Bishop Thomas Gumbleton, retired auxiliary of Detroit, was removed from his parish in 2006 after he spoke out in favor of extending the statute of limitations for sexual abuse crimes at the same time that the Ohio bishops were opposing that piece of legislation. In the letter from the Vatican informing him of his removal, this violation of the *Communio episcoporum* was given as a principal reason for this sanction.

Communio personarum
Communion of persons

Term popularized by Pope John Paul II (1978–2005) in his Theology of the Body to denote the union of the man and woman in marriage which is then expressed in a conjugal act in which the procreative dimension is inseparably linked to the unitive dimension. The family too constitutes a communion of persons (cf. *Familiaris consortio* #17–27). Historically, the expression had been originally used to describe the nature of the Blessed Trinity as a communion of three persons in one God, as well as the relation of the Trinity to the church and humankind since the human being made in the image of God (*imago Dei, q.v.*) likewise exists in this relation of communion with God.

Communio sanctorum
Communion of saints

Expression which is found, among other places, in the Apostle's Creed and refers to the Christian community as the Mystical Body of believers, both living and dead, including the souls in purgatory and those who enjoy the beatific vision of God in heaven. See also *Congregatio fidelium.*

Compos mentis
Of sound mind

Necessary condition for doing a moral action, as well as in canon law a requisite for entering into a contractual obligation (such as vows, marriage, etc.). See also *Non compos mentis* and *Non sui compos.*

Concilium
"Council"

Group of advisors and, depending on the particular usage, may also refer to the legal council whose consent or advice must be sought in certain matters as required by either canon law or the particular law of the given religious institute or congregation. **Concilium** is also the name for an international theological journal published since the Second Vatican Council that seeks to continue the conciliar mandate for the updating of theology in conversation with the modern world. **Communio** (*q.v.*) is another international theological journal founded in part to counter the more liberal perspective of **Concilium**.

Concubitus propter solam procreationem
Coitus (or cohabitation) only for the purpose of procreation

Position initially advanced in the Augustinian theology of marriage that justified conjugal relations because they were engaged in for the purpose of producing and raising offspring. The problem with this view is that it seemed to render morally suspect any other reasons for having conjugal relations, or conjugal relations which were not entered into with the explicit intention of trying to produce offspring. This position was later nuanced by the acceptance of having conjugal relations as a "remedy" for concupiscence or sexual desire. See also *Bonum prolis, Bonum fidei, Bonum sacramenti, Debitum, Potentia coeundi/Potentia generandi,* and *Remedium concupiscientiae.*

Condicio (or Conditio) sine qua non
Necessary condition or criterion (literally, "condition without which nothing [is possible]")

An indispensable condition, which can be understood contractually or philosophically. Thus, a *conditio sine qua non* of a treaty might be a specific provision that must be included if there is any hope for agreement. A *conditio sine qua non* of the moral life is individual freedom. The expression, though, has a wide variety of usages; for example, in traditional sexual ethics a *condicio sine qua non* for licit sexual relations would be the conditions of intercourse between a man and a woman that is open to the physical possibility of procreation. If this *condicio sine qua non* were not present then the act would be considered immoral. See also *Contra naturam, Secundum naturum, Secundum rationem*, and *Sequi naturam.*

Conditio humana
The human condition

Basic concept in theological anthropology that refers to the "human condition" as one marked by finitude and sin on the one hand but openness to grace and the potentiality for human flourishing and moral goodness on the other hand.

Confer
Compare

Usually abbreviated as *cf.* (*q.v.*).

Confessio
Confession (of faith of a martyr)

Term used for the tomb or reliquary of a martyr who died professing (i.e., confessing) the faith. As a proper noun, *Confessio* often designates the resting place of the bones of St. Peter enshrined in the crypt under the high altar of the basilica in Vatican City.

Confessio laudis
Confession (acknowledgment) of praise.

This term was used to express praise for God's mercy in pardoning sinners. Thus, a sinner not only confessed or acknowledged her sins, but at the same time would express praise for the great mercy of a loving God who had pardoned her.

Confiteor
I confess

First word in the act of contrition, which is found in the Penitential Rite of the Latin Eucharist. The word *confiteor* can also be used to refer to the entire prayer itself.

Congregatio fidelium
Congregation of the faithful

Early designation of the church as the gathering of believers in Jesus Christ. See also *Communio sanctorum* and *Sensus fidelium.*

Consensus fidelium
Consensus of the faithful

See *Orbis terrarum, Securus iudicat orbis terrarum, Sensus fidelium*, and *Solus consensus obligat.*

Consensus non facit veritatem
Consensus does not make truth.

Aphorism which indicates that the mere fact of widespread agreement is no guarantee that one has arrived at the truth. On the other hand, there are several similar aphorisms that argue to an opposite conclusion. See also *Consuetudo optima legum interpres, Ecclesia discens, Orbis terrarum, Quod ubique quod semper quod ab omnibus creditum est, Securus iudicat orbis terrarum*, and *Sensus fidelium.*

Consensus Patrum
Consensus of the fathers

Based on the belief that the writings of

the fathers (the patristic authors, such as Augustine, Jerome, etc.), as witnesses and authentic teachers, faithfully tell the faith of the church. Therefore, when the fathers expressed a unanimous opinion on teachings on faith and/or morals, these teachings were held to be a sound expression of the Christian faith. See also *Ecclesia docens* and *Magisterium*.

Consuetudinarius
A habitual (sinner)

Usually this term is found in the context of the sacrament of reconciliation and refers to someone who has a certain sin which has become habitual. Thus, extra pains must be taken to break the cycle of sin, and especially to avoid those occasions which lead the individual into this or that particular sin. See also *Occasionarii* and *Recidivus*.

Consuetudo optima legum interpres
Custom is the best interpreter of laws

Legal axiom, traditionally used in the application of church law, which states that custom—i.e., how people "follow" a given law—is the best guide to the meaning of the law itself. Thus, custom enjoys a certain force of law (which is stated explicitly in canon 26 of the 1983 Code of Canon Law. This axiom itself comprises the whole of canon 27 of the 1983 Code of Canon Law (*C.I.C.*). A slightly different version of this axiom, using different word order but with the same basic meaning is *Optima legum interpres consuetudo*. See also *Ad literam*; *Cessante fine cessat lex*; *Conventio est lex*; *Dura lex sed lex*; *Ex facto ius oritur*; *Exceptio firmat regulam*; *Iuxta legem*; *Nihil consuetudine maius*; *Odia restringi, et favores convenit ampliari*; *Optimus interpres rerum usus*; *Praeter legem*; *Quod omnes tangit ab omnibus approbetur*; *Sensus fidelium*; *Sensum, non verba spectamus*; and *Ubi cessat ratio legis, cessat ipsa lex*.

Consummatum est
It is consummated (finished, completed)

Jesus' last words on the cross in the Latin Vulgate translation of John 19:30, and the expression is widely used to refer to some deed which has been completed. See also *ratum et consummatum*.

Contra
Contrary to, against

Common Latin preposition; see below for some usages.

Contra bonos mores
Against good mores (customs, morals)

Legal phrase which indicates something considered harmful to society (such as a contract to poison the water supply) and therefore null and void from a legal standpoint. Thus, in law a party could not be held accountable for the non-completion of such a contract.

Contra caritatem
Against charity

According to St. Thomas and scholastic theology, mortal sin is by its nature against charity (*contra caritatem*), against the proper directionality or "end" of the human person (*contra finem*), and against the basic moral order established by God (*contra ordinem*).

Venial sin, by contrast, would not be directly opposed to these things but instead would be sin as standing "outside" of (or not in accord with) charity, the human end, and divine order. Thus, venial sins were described of as being of their nature *praeter caritatem, praeter finem,* and *praeter ordinem.*

Contra finem
Against the end (understood as goal)

Essentially the same concept as *Contra naturam (q.v.),* namely that if something is seen as operating against the natural end or goal of a creature or a faculty (such as speech), then that action would be *ipso facto* wrong or immoral, since it moved against the proper direction or end. In terms of the distinction between mortal and venial sin the former was seen as *contra finem* in the sense that it worked against the human's ultimate end or goal, which is union with God. Venial sin was considered less grave because it did not attack the ultimate end of the human person as such, but rather was seen to operate against one of the means to that end.

Contra legem
Against the law

Refers to something which is illegal according to a given code of laws. See also *Praeter legem.*

Contra mundum
Against the world

Expression which usually indicates a negative stance toward the world and especially the beliefs and mores of secular culture. While this attitude has had a long history in Christian theology, significant changes were seen at the Second Vatican Council, especially in **Gaudium et spes** (*q.v.,* the Pastoral Constitution on the Church in the Modern World) which outlined a more positive and hopeful stance of engagement with the world and the positive contributions even secular culture could make.

Contra naturam
Against nature

Term associated with teleological moral reason, and used especially in scholastic moral theology to denote any action which went against the perceived "natural order," understood as related to the human being's true moral nature. Such an action, since it countered or obstructed true human moral nature was *ipso facto* against the natural law as well, and therefore intrinsically evil. Furthermore, as expressed in the axiom *peccata contra naturam sunt gravissima* (sins against nature are grave) the presumption was that any sin against nature was nearly always very seriously sinful (i.e., a potential mortal sin). A difficulty with the term is that in traditional practice it was often identified with activities not thought to exist among other animals, and therefore bestiality and homosexual actions were two examples often cited as being *contra naturam.* More recent documents from the Roman Catholic magisterium (e.g., **Persona humana,** *q.v.*) tend to use the expression "disordered" to refer to behaviors which in the past had been labeled *contra naturam.* See also *Ex toto genere suo, Humano modo, Intrinsece malum, Ius naturae est immutabile, Lex spectat naturae ordi-*

nem, Natura nihil facit inane, and *Secundum naturam.*

Contra ordinem
Against (God's) prescribed order

A serious violation against God's design. *Contra naturam* is a similar concept, though focused more on a violation of the *Lex naturalis (q.v.).* See also *Contra caritatem* and *Praeter ordinem.*

Contra vim non valet ius
Against force the law is powerless

A Latin equivalent of "might makes right." See also *Consensus non facit veritatem; Conventio est lex;* and *Vox populi, vox Dei.*

Conventio est lex
Convention (custom) is law

A hermeneutical principle of legal interpretation very similar to *Consuetudo optima legum interpres* and *Nihil consuetudine maius.* However, for opposite sentiment see *Consensus non facit veritatem.*

Conversi
The converted ones

Term used from around the fifth century onward (especially in Spain and Gaul) to denote those who voluntarily became public penitents and also used as well as a term for those who entered monastic life. Thus, the term expresses a certain connection between becoming a monk and living a life of penance.

Conversio ad creaturam
Turning toward the creature [or "created thing"]

Expression for sin, which involves a turning of the person away from God, the true end of the human person, and substituting some created thing for God's rightful place in the human heart. This expression is repeated in the discussion on mortal sin in Pope John Paul's 1984 post-synodal apostolic exhortation **Reconciliatio et Paenitentia** (On Reconciliation and Penance in the Mission of the Church Today). See also *Aversio a Deo.*

Cooperatio in malum
Cooperation in evil

Traditional term which is distinguished into two major categories, formal and material cooperation, and a number of further specifications and distinctions. One can never cooperate "formally" in the sense of sharing the same evil intent of another, but in the actual world we all at some time or another find ourselves in situations of "material" cooperation, in which in fact our actions may aid and abet the commission of a morally bad action by another. Thus, a hostage might be forced to drive a get-away car in a bank robbery. This would be an example of "material" cooperation, but not "formal" cooperation. However, a member of the same gang of robbers who helps plan the heist is guilty of "formal" cooperation as well as "material" cooperation. "Formal" cooperation is always morally culpable. "Material" cooperation may or may not be morally culpable, and to a greater or lesser degree, depending on a wide variety of circumstances, motives, and other factors. See also *Finis operis/Finis operantis; Malum non est faciendum ut eveniat bonum*; *Minus malum*; *Ne cede malis*; *Non facias malum, ut inde fiat bonum*; and *Qui vult finem vult media*.

Copula dimidiata
Half-connected

Refers to partial penetration of the penis in the vagina. The acceptability of this practice in order to reduce the chances of procreation was debated by moralists. Some, e.g., John Ford, SJ, and Gerald Kelly, SJ, who were prominent moral theologians in the period immediately prior to Vatican II, argued that the practice would not be wrong if done for proportionate reasons. Connected to this issue was a discussion over how far the penis had to penetrate the vagina for the sexual act to be "completed." Ford and Kelly maintained that a one-third penile penetration "completed" the sexual act. See also *Amplexus reservatus*, *Coitus interruptus*, and *Coitus reservatus*.

Cor ad cor loquitur
Speaking heart to heart

Used by Augustine in his *Confessions*, this expression denotes a mode of prayer to God. It also is used in Medieval and Renaissance art to refer to a genre of religious paintings which portray (usually) the Blessed Virgin, the Infant Jesus, and other saints gathered together in silence, yet in seeming communication. This type of painting, also called in Italian a *Sacra Conversazione* (Sacred Conversation), stresses the understanding of deepest communication to lie on the spiritual plane of meditation and not on the worldly level of audible conversation. In reference to interreligious dialogue it might be noted that other religious traditions have a similar expression, such as the "heart-to-heart" communication found in Buddhism. The expression was also used by Blessed John Henry Newman (1801–90) as the motto in his coat of arms when he was raised to the cardinalate by Pope Leo XIII in 1879. The saying can also refer to either a frank and earnest or open conversation.

Cor Unum
One heart

Vatican relief services organization founded by Paul VI in 1971.

Coram
In the presence of, before

Latin preposition; see entries immediately below for some common examples.

Coram Cardinale/Coram Episcopo
In the presence of a cardinal or bishop

Expression used in the pre–Vatican II Tridentine Mass which was celebrated by another priest, though in the presence of a cardinal or bishop who would be attending vested in his ceremonial robes but not concelebrating. At the end of the Mass, the higher ranking prelate then would impart the Final Blessing instead of the presiding priest. See also *Ad orientem*, *Cappa magna*, *Coetus fidelium*, *Forma Antiquior*, *Missale Romanum*, *Novus Ordo*, *Nulla Veritas sine Traditione*, **Sacrosanctum concilium**, **Summorum Pontificum**, *Quidquid latine dictum sit altum videtur*, *Tu Es*

Petrus, **Universae Ecclesiae,** *Usus Antiquior,* and *Versus populum.*

Coram Deo
Before God

How we stand in relationship to God, before God's face, which posture should indicate a certain stance of humility. This expression is also used to represent the sanctuary of conscience, which is the privileged place where the individual meets God *solus cum solo (q.v.).* Cf. **Gaudium et spes** #16 and the *Catechism of the Catholic Church* #1776 for some magisterial exemplars of this concept.

Coram hominibus
Before, in front of, humanity

Refers to what will appear or be evident before or by other people. *Coram hominibus* can be distinguished from what is *coram Deo (q.v.),* as the human person stands before, and is known by, God.

Coram Sanctissimo
In the presence of the Most Sacred (i.e., the consecrated Host)

Expression used to denote the consecrated Host (the Body and Blood of Christ) which is displayed in a monstrance for the devotion of the faithful, e.g., in eucharistic adoration, Forty Hours Devotion, Benediction, etc. See also *Laus Perennis.*

Corde creditur
Let the heart believe

Expression often associated with a stress on the primacy of faith over reason, as found, for example, in the theology of

St. Athanasius (who was sometimes called Athanasius *contra mundum, q.v.*). See also the terms under *Credo* and especially *Credo quia absurdum.* A contrary strain would be found in expressions such as *Credo ut intelligam* and *Fides quarens intellectum (q.v.).*

Corpus
Body

This word has both a literal and a figurative meaning, as in English. For example, a *corpus iuris civili* would be a body or collection of laws. *Corpus* can also refer to a body of knowledge, as well as a body of persons, believers, etc. It should be noted, however, that the Latin word *corpus* is *not* the word for the English word "corpse."

Corpus Christi
Body of Christ

Usually refers, though, to the liturgical feast celebrated after Trinity Sunday to commemorate the Real Presence of Christ in the Eucharist. This feast also has a special sequence, the *Lauda Sion* *(q.v.),* and is one of only four medieval sequences that were preserved in the reform of the *Missale Romanum (q.v.)* published in 1570. The other three are the *Victimae Paschali (q.v.)* for Easter, the *Veni Sancte Spiritus (q.v.)* for Pentecost, and the *Dies Irae (q.v.)* for the Requiem Mass.

Corpus delicti
Body (evidence) of the crime

Legal term which refers to evidence that a crime has been committed. A dead cadaver with a knife stuck in its back would be a *corpus delicti* for the probable crime of murder. See also *Graviora delicta* and *In flagrante delicto*.

Corpus diaboli
The body of the Evil One

Expression usually used in relation to Luther's theology of the two kingdoms, in which all humanity is divided into a *corpus* (body or group) of believers and unbelievers. The *corpus* of believers acknowledges Jesus Christ as its head, but the *corpus diaboli* fall under the dominion of Satan.

Corpus in substantia et corpus in omnibus partibus
Body in substance and body in all parts

Philosophical expression of the part/whole relationship. E.g., while a "hand" arguably does not constitute the "whole" of the body, nevertheless it has no particular meaning that can be intelligibly addressed outside of its essential relationship to the body as a whole. In this context see *Pars propter totum*. This expression is also employed theologically to speak of the relationship of the particles of the consecrated host as belong to the "whole" of the body of Christ. While the host broken into many parts contains the "whole" of the consecrated body of Christ, the church has never held the problematic position that even microscopic particles of the consecrated host somehow contain the "body" of Christ.

Corpus Iuris Canonici
Body of Canon Law

Term used for the collection of canon law prior to its first systematic codification in the 1917 Code of Canon Law. This **Corpus Iuris Canonici** was composed of various decrees, judgments, and the like—similar to the British tradition of constitutional law. See also **Codex Iuris Canonici** and **Corpus Iuris Civilis**.

Corpus Iuris Civilis
Compendium of Civil Law

Sixth-century work which sought to bring together the various bodies of law with the view of trying to collect a sort of law of all nations (a *ius gentium*, *q.v.*). See also **Corpus Iuris Canonici** and *Ius gentium*.

Corrigenda
(Items) to be corrected

Scholarly term found in manuscripts, books, and journals to indicate items which are found to be in error (e.g. typographical or numerical mistakes) after the text has gone to print. Frequently, *corrigenda* are listed on a separate page and are sometimes called *errata* or *errata corrigenda*.

Corruptio optimi pessima
The corruption of the best is worst

Aphorism which indicates that when good people become corrupt, or fail in some virtue, the evil they can create is often worse than the evil produced by those who are not virtuous. See also *Summum ius, summa iniuria*.

Creatio continua
Ongoing (continuous) creation

Theological concept that is often used in conjunction with *creatio originalis* (original creation) and *creatio nova* (new creation). *Creatio continua* refers to God's ongoing presence and action in our world, as well as the ways in which humans are cocreators with God. See also *Creatio originalis*, *Creatio nova*, and *Creatio ex nihilo*.

Creatio ex nihilo
Creation out of nothing

Refers to the divine act of creation, since only God can bring something out of nothing. See also *Creatio originalis, Creatio continua, Creatio nova*, and *Ex nihilo*.

Creatio nova
New creation

This theological concept is often used together with *creatio originalis* and *creatio continua*, and in this context refers to the fulfillment of creation. However, it is also employed as a stand-alone concept which refers to St. Paul's proclamation that we are all a new creation in Jesus Christ (cf. Gal 2:19-20 and 6:15). See also *Creatio continua, Creatio originalis*, and *Creatio ex nihilo*.

Creatio originalis
Original creation

This concept refers to the creation of the universe by God *ex nihilo* (out of nothing), and thus is similar to the expression *Creatio ex nihilo*. However, *creatio originalis* is also used in conjunction with *creatio continua* and *creatio nova* to highlight different dimensions of the total work of God's creation, grace, presence and action in the world. See *Creatio continua, Creatio nova,* and *Creatio ex nihilo*.

Crede ut intelligas
Believe that you may understand

Augustinian principle which indicates that faith is the necessary grounding and inspiration for the task of theological understanding (cf. his *Sermon* 43, 7 and 9). See also *Credo ut intelligam* and *Fides quaerens intellectum*. For an opposite sentiment see *Corde creditur, Credo quia absurdum*, and *Credo quia impossibile*. See also *Credibilia, Lumen fidei*, and *Ne fides rideatur*.

Credenda
Things to be believed

Refers to a doctrine that must be believed by the Christian faithful as pertaining to the faith itself. There is, however, an important distinction between doctrines that are to be believed (*credenda*) from those which must be "held" (*tenenda, q.v.*) when proposed in an authoritative manner by the magisterium. See also *Articulus stantis et cadentis ecclesiae, De fide definita, De fide vel moribus, Depositum fidei, Ex Cathedra*, and *Tenenda*.

Credibilia
Things which are believable

While the expression could refer to anything in physical reality, in theology it usually refers to principles or propositions which seem worthy of belief in the life of faith. See also *Crede ut intelligas* and *Credo ut intelligam*.

Credo
I believe

Also used to denote a set of faith-beliefs or a doctrinal creed, such as the Nicene

Creed. Note that the Latin is in the first person *singular*, even though in liturgical celebrations *Credo* was rendered in the first person *plural* ("We believe") until the promulgation of the new English translation of the *Missale Romanum (q.v.)* on the First Sunday of Advent in 2011.

Credo quia absurdum
I believe because it is absurd

Principle which holds that belief held in faith (rather than because of logical persuasion) helps toward a deeper knowledge and understanding. Essentially, this is the same sentiment expressed in *Certum est quia impossibile est (q.v.)* and *Credo quia impossibile (q.v.)*. See also *Corde creditur, Tantum valet quantum probat.* For an opposite sentiment see *Crede ut intelligas* and *Ne fides rideatur.*

Credo quia impossibile
I believe because it is impossible

Essentially the same sentiment expressed in *Certum est quia impossibile est (q.v.)* and *Credo quia absurdum (q.v.)*. See also *Tantum valet quantum probat.* For an opposite sentiment see *Credo ut intelligam* and *Ne fides rideatur.*

Credo ut intelligam
I believe so that I can understand

Expression of Anselm, found in his *Proslogion*, 1, which echoes Augustine's principle of the relationship of faith to reason. See also *Crede ut intelligas, Fides quaerens intellectum, Ne fides rideatur,* and *Tantum valet quantum probat.* For an opposite sentiment see *Corde creditur, Credo quia absurdum,* and *Credo quia impossibile.* See also *Credibilia.*

Crimen
Crime

Besides the general notion of a misdeed, this term has a more specific meaning in canon law to distinguish the more serious misdeeds from other irregularities and illicit activities that all fall under adjudication in the ecclesial arena. See also *Crimen sollicitationis, Crimen pessimum, Corpus delicti, Delicta graviora,* **Epistula de delictis gravioribus,** *Graviora delicta, In flagrante delicto,* **Sacramentorum sanctitatis tutela,** *Secretum pontificium, Sub secreto pontificio,* and *Sub rosa.*

Crimen pessimum
Worst crime

Expression used in canon law and ecclesial documents to refer to the most serious misdeeds that can be punished by the church. This expression was used in **Crimen sollicitationis,** the 1962 document of the Holy Office (today the Congregation for the Doctrine of the Faith) instruction, to describe deviant sexual activity of "obscene behavior with preadolescent children of either sex or with brute animals." See also **Crimen sollicitationis,** *Corpus delicti, Delicta graviora,* **Epistula de delictis gravioribus,** *Graviora delicta, In flagrante delicto,* **Sacramentorum sanctitatis tutela,** *Secretum pontificium, Sub secreto pontificio,* and *Sub rosa.*

Crimen sollicitationis
Crime of solicitation to a crime

16 March 1962 instruction of the Supreme Sacred Congregation of the Holy Office (today the Congregation for the Doctrine of the Faith) addressed to all

patriarchs, archbishops, bishops, and other local ordinaries, "even of an Oriental Rite," which established a manner of proceeding in such cases involving the grave abuse of the Sacrament of Penance (Reconciliation) or the confessional to attempt to solicit someone for sexual purposes. This document was referenced by Pope John Paul II in his 2001 apostolic letter **Sacramentorum Sanctitatis Tutela** (*q.v.*, "Safeguarding of the Sanctity of the Sacraments") which established procedural norms for handling of the reporting and follow up of charges of sexual abuse by priests in the light of the scandal that broke in the 1990s. See also *Crimen pessimum*, *Corpus delicti*, *Graviora delicta*, *In flagrante delicto*, and **Sacramentorum Sanctitatis Tutela**.

Cui bono (fuerit)
(To) whose good (is served)?

Refers to a question which enquires as to the beneficiary of a certain action or object. Know for what or whom something is of benefit (i.e., "good") is often helpful for determining the inherent worth of the issue or object under discussion. *Cui bono* also can be used as a principle to help indicate probable responsibility for an act or event by looking to determine the one who would stand to gain most from this act or event.

Cui licet quod est plus, licet utique quod est minus
One for whom it is licet to do more, may also do less

Hermeneutical principle of legal interpretation similar to *Qui potest plus,*

potest minus. See also *Potentia iurisdictionis*; *Prima sedes a nemine iudicatur*; and *Summum ius, summa iniuria*.

Cuius regio, eius religio
Whose land, his religion

Principle accepted at the Peace of Augsburg in 1555, which put an end to the religious civil wars in the German-speaking lands. The principle held that the religion of the prince or ruler of a particular area would determine the religion for all the people of that same area. Note the absence of "freedom of religion" of the individual in his or her own conscience (articulated in Vatican II's Declaration on Religious Liberty, **Dignitatis humanae**).

Culpa
Fault

Perhaps this Latin word is most recognized from the *Confiteor (q.v.)* which had a line *mea culpa, mea culpa, mea maxima culpa* (through my fault, through my fault, through my most grievous [literally, "greatest"] fault). However, in canon law the term *culpa* refers to some violation, defect, or irregularity that is due to a lack of knowledge, oversight, or indiscretion on the part of the individual but is not considered to be a willful, premeditated act. Thus, a *culpa* is distinguished from a *dolus*, the latter being a deliberate act of deception (even if not "malicious" in the moral sense). See also *De defectibus*; *Dolus*; *Extra ecclesia nulla salus*; *Ignorantes*; *Ingnorantia invincibilis*; *Mens rea*; *Nemo dat quod non habet*; *Sanatio in radice*; *Sine culpa*; and *Ubi non est culpa, ibi non est delictum*.

Cum
With

Latin preposition, see below for some common examples.

Cum approbatione ecclesiastica
With ecclesiastical approval

Certification found in certain Catholic books and periodicals indicating that the material published has been vetted and approved by the competent magisterial authorities as containing nothing against orthodox Catholic teaching. It does *not* necessarily indicate that the magisterial authority particularly supports the opinions or positions expressed in the publication, merely that there is nothing therein contrary to the Catholic faith. See also *Censor deputatus*, *Imprimatur*, *Imprimi potest*, and *Nihil obstat*.

Cum grano salis
With a grain of salt

Sage advice to take many claims, especially if they seem exaggerated or hyperbolic, with a healthy dose of skepticism. See also *Caveat emptor*.

Cum gravamine poenitentis (paenitentis)
When it burdens (harms) the penitent

This expression refers to the context of the sacramental seal of confession. The confessor is absolutely forbidden by the seal to ever reveal the identity of the penitent and/or nature of the sin(s) confessed. Furthermore, the Code of Canon Law (canon 984 in the 1983 Code, canon 890 in the 1917 Code) expressly forbids even using knowledge acquired from confession "when it might harm the penitent" *cum gravamine paenitentis*. "Harming" the penitent is understood to be anything the penitent might find burdensome, displeasing or odious, whether of the spiritual or temporal order. For these reasons those in governance, e.g., novice directors, are forbidden by canon law to hear the confessions of their subjects, unless freely and spontaneously requested by an individual (cf. canon 985 of the 1983 Code). What such knowledge included, often referred to in a shorthand term as the *gravamen* (*q.v.*), was the focus of a considerable amount of casuistic discussion throughout the centuries but now is generally interpreted very broadly so as to protect the penitent her/himself as well as to maintain the highest degree of trust in the forum of sacramental confession. See also *Gravamen*, *Prodere peccatorem*, and *Proditio peccatoris*.

Cum iure successionis
With the right of succession

Term used for a coadjutor (auxiliary) bishop who is appointed to assist a local ordinary (bishop or archbishop) but who has right of succession to the diocesan see upon the resignation or death of the reigning ordinary. The right of succession distinguishes the auxiliary bishop from any other assistant bishops whose status in the diocese would not necessarily change upon the death or resignation of the reigning ordinary. See also *Sede impedita*, *Sede vacante*, and *Sede vacante nihil innovetur*.

Cum laude
With praise

Often used in academic honors, such as a diploma which is awarded *cum laude* (with honors), *magna cum laude* (with great honors), or *summa cum laude* (with highest honors).

Cum Petro et sub Petro
With Peter and under Peter

Can be taken as an expression of collegiality of bishops with the pope, as well as an indication that the pope stands above all (cf. Pope John Paul II's 1993 encyclical **Veritatis Splendor**, #116).

Cupiditas
Desire

This meaning of desire was usually seen as negative, i.e., a disordered will for something not properly ordered to authentic human existence, often connected with one or more of the capital sins (such as lust or gluttony). *Cupiditas* was viewed as one of the effects of original sin, that is, the weakness of the human condition arising from the sin of our first parents and communicated to all humans ever since.

Cur Deus Homo
Why God became human

Title of St. Anselm's great work which expresses God's salvific will in the decision of the Godhead that the Second Person of the Trinity become human in order to save humanity from its sins. See also *aut satisfactio aut poena, aut venia aut poena,* and *processus iustificationis.*

Cura animarum
Care of souls

In this phrase the "souls" is understood to refer to the living and not the dead. The phrase refers primarily to the pastoral obligation to care for the faithful through teaching, preaching, and celebration of the sacraments. Thus, the faithful have a right to such pastoral care and the pope, bishops, and clergy have a corresponding moral and canonical obligation to make that pastoral care readily available. This obligation has been raised by some as an argument for expanding priestly ordination beyond male celibates. See also *Alter Christus, Animarum zelus,* **Ordinatio sacerdotalis**, and *Viri probati.*

Cura apostolica
Apostolic care

Commonly refers to the "care," i.e., canonical jurisdiction a major superior (such as a Provincial of a religious order) has for the apostolic works under him/her. Thus, *cura apostolica* refers to the soundness and well-being of the institution in question (school, parish, etc.) as an apostolic work. See also *Cura personalis.*

Cura personalis
Care of personnel

Commonly refers to the "care" of individuals a superior (such as a Provincial of a religious order or a superior of a religious community) has for the individuals under him/her. *Cura personalis* focuses on the needs and well-being of the individual as an individual. See also *Cura apostolica.*

Curet primo Deum
   Attend to God first

Spiritual aphorism which indicates our highest duty and first concern always should focus on our relationship to God and the divine will. See also *Ad maiorem Dei gloriam (A.M.D.G.)* and *Soli Deo gloria.*

Curriculum vitae
   The course of (one's) life

Refers to a professional résumé. Often abbreviated as *C.V.*

Cursus extraordinarius rerum
   The extraordinary course of things

See *De potentia Dei absoluta.*

Cursus honorum
   Course of honors

Refers to the hierarchical principle of advancement through the ranks of the clerical state, moving through the minor orders (such as tonsure, porter, etc., which were abolished in the 1970s) and up to and through the major orders (deacon, priest, bishop). *Cursus honorum* reflects a certain hierarchical conception of ministry and the clerical state. It can also be used to indicate an itinerary of career advancement moving from lesser positions to promotion to greater ones, e.g., starting out as a department head and finally moving up to chief executive. See also *Fraternitas.*

Cursus ordinarius rerum
   The ordinary course of things

See *De potentia Dei absoluta.*

C.V.
   Abbreviation for *Curriculum vitae (q.v.).*

D

Da mihi factum, dabo tibi ius
Give me the facts and I will give
you justice

Basic principle of legal justice that
shows the intrinsic correlation between
discovery of the facts of the issue and a
just resolution of the same issue. However, "facts" need to be proved, as is
indicated by a related legal axiom *In
dubio factum non praesumitur sed probatur (q.v.)*. See also *Allegatio contra
factum non est admittenda.*

Damnanda et proscribenda
Condemned and forbidden
(proscribed)

Censure given to certain propositions
that ecclesiastical authorities felt to be
dangerous for the faithful to entertain
or consider. This disapproval does not
indicate the proposition to be necessarily heretical or untrue, but rather it
could lead to conclusions or activities,
etc., which would be injurious to the
faith or virtue of the community. The
Index of Forbidden Books and the Le-
gion of Decency's ratings for movies
would be examples of this principle put
into practice. For the opposite sentiment
see *Auctores probati.*

D.D.
Divinitatis Doctor (Doctor of
Divinity)

Latin abbreviation for an honorary degree
given to bishops. In this sense, "doctor"
connotes teacher and not physician.

De
About, concerning, from, for, according to

Common Latin preposition. In Latin,
certain treatises on principal theological
themes would often begin with *De*. E.g.,
De Auxiliis (on assistance) was the
name of the tract which dealt with actual (or "helping") grace (in distinction
to "sanctifying" grace).

De absentibus nil nisi bonum
Concerning the absent [speak]
nothing except good

Common moralist axiom found in a variety of contexts (such as inscriptions)
which counsels us not to speak ill of
those absent (or dead). Thus, if we are
to say anything about these people let
whatever we say be good or complimen-
tary. Another version of this saying is *nil
nisi bonum de mortuis dicere* and the
expression is often abbreviated to *nil
nisi bonum (q.v.)*. See also *Bona mors.*

De attritione fit contritio
From attrition comes contrition

Expression used first by William of Auvergne (1248) to note the movement from initial sorrow for one's sins (attrition), which could also include fear of punishment, to a deeper and more profound hatred for sin because it offends God (contrition). See also *Ex attrito fit contritus*.

De Auxiliis
On the helps (or aids)

Theological tract on actual grace, as well as reference to a sixteenth-century theological dispupte between the Jesuits (chiefly through the position of Luis de Molina [1535–1600]) and the Dominicans (chiefly through the position of Domingo Bañez [1528–1604]) on the relationship of grace and free will. See also *Scientia media.*

De bono et aequo
According to what is good and equal

Expression of the principle of equity which can be used in determining what is required according to some form of justice. For example, the "one person, one vote" principle would express "equity" in this sense, whereas another application drawn from distributive justice such as "to each according to their need" would also be a valid expression of this principle of equity, even if this would mean that some individuals got more and some less. The graduated income tax would be a good example of this latter application of the principle

De bono et aequo. See also the various entries under *Bonum, Ius, Lex,* and also *Reddere suum cuique.*

De Defectibus
Concerning defects

Expression found primarily in canon law which addresses certain "defects" which might render an action, such as a sacrament, illicit or invalid. For example, if white wine were to be used at Mass and the water and the wine cruets were mixed up at the offertory the priest would discover at his communion that he had not consecrated the wine, because in fact there was only water in the chalice. Remedying this "defect" (which if not treated would leave the consecration invalid), the *General Introduction to the Roman Missal* instructs the priest to pour the water into another container, pour wine with water into the chalice in the usual way, and then just say the part of the institution narrative that consecrates the wine (*GIRM* #286). See also *Dolus, Culpa,* and *Sanatio in radice.*

De duobus malis, minus est semper eligendum
Of two evils, the lesser is always to be chosen

See *Minus malum.*

De facto
For a fact; a matter of fact; concerning the fact

This expression occurs commonly in English and means "in reality." *De facto* often connotes a contrast between something that in fact is, or exists, but which is not entirely licit. For example, the *de facto* ruler of a country may be a dictator who has not been legally elected. In this sense, *de facto* is contrasted with *de iure* ("according to law," i.e., legal). See also *De iure*.

De fide
(A matter) of the faith

Essential to the faith and based in revelation. A doctrine proposed *de fide* in an *ex cathedra* (*q.v.*) fashion is said to possess the highest degree of certainty of truth and must be believed by the faithful. See also *De fide definita*, *De fide vel moribus*, and *Depositum fidei*.

De fide definita
(Matter) of the defined faith

Refers to a doctrine which is held to be formally defined by the Church's *magisterium* (*q.v.*), and therefore not open to denial, further speculation, or revision, and which is required to be held as an article of faith by all believers. See also *Articulus stantis et cadentis ecclesiae*, *Credenda*, *De fide*, *De fide vel moribus*, *Depositum fidei*, *Diffinimus*, *Ex cathedra*, *Pia opinio*, *Sensus fidelium*, *Sententia probata*, and *Theologice certa*.

De fide vel moribus
Concerning faith or morals

Common expression to indicate matters about which the magisterium maintains that it can give authoritative teaching. The Vatican I definition of papal infallibility in **Pastor Aeternus** uses this term to restrict the matters by which the pope could offer an *ex cathedra* statement that would have to be believed (*credenda,*

q.v.) or held (*tenenda, q.v.*) by the Christian faithful. However, there is some debate among scholars as to the proper translation and meaning for *moribus*. Some hold that the term refers to concrete precepts of the natural law, while others hold the term refers historically to the customs and practices of the church, such as liturgy. Another Latin version of this concept is *Res fidei et morum*. See also *Credenda*, *De fide definita*, *Depositum fidei*, *Ex cathedra*, and *Tenenda*.

De gustibus non disputandum (est)
Concerning matters of taste there should be no dispute

This expression is often shortened to *de gustibus* and refers to the traditional philosophical adage which indicates that matters of individual taste and preference are not governed by rules of logic or reason. Therefore, one person might prefer blue and another yellow. Since this is a matter of taste (*de gustibus*) any potential conflict about which color is "better" cannot be resolved by recourse to a logical or philosophical argument.

De iure (jure)
According to law

Refers to that which is legal or licit. However, there may be a distinction between something that exists *de iure* and that which exists *de facto*, for example, a legitimately elected government may exist *de iure*, but may have been overthrown by a coup and have its place taken by a military junta or dictator who is the *de facto* head of government, though not *de iure*. See also *De facto*.

De minimis non curat lex
The law does not treat small matters

Common legal aphorism that notes that the purpose of positive law, whether canon or civil, is not to deal with each and every possible situation, especially those that cover minor matters. Another variation on this adage is *Minima non curat praetor* (*q.v.*, "the magistrate does not treat small matters"). See also *Ad literam, Epikeia, Lex dubia non obligat, Libertas est inaestimabilis*, and *Quod raro fit non observant legislatores*.

De novo
Anew

Refers to something undertaken once more or done again, or possibly to make a new beginning or fresh start. See also *Ab initio, Ab ovo* and *Ex novo*.

De potentia Dei absoluta
See *De potentia Dei ordinata*.

De potentia Dei ordinata
Ordained (ordered) by the power of God

Theological axiom which explains why a certain thing is the way it is, namely, because God so willed it. This expression is related to another axiom, *de potentia Dei absoluta* (by the absolute power of God), which means that God could have arranged the matter in question in an entirely different way if God so chose. As one theological example these terms would be invoked to explain why the sacramental confession of mortal sins was necessary for divine forgiveness, namely in line with *de potentia Dei ordinata*. This was the manner in which God willed justification to take place, though in view of *de potentia Dei absoluta* God could have chosen some other means by which human beings would be absolved of their sins. See also *Voluntas Dei*.

De profundis
Out of the depths

Usually understood in the figurative sense of "out of the depths of despair." The Latin Vulgate translation of Psalm 130 begins with these words, and thus has become a shorthand expression for invoking the name of the Lord when one is in great trouble or despair. Psalm 130 was one of seven penitential psalms (Psalm 51 the *Miserere*, *q.v.*, being the best known of this set) and was used liturgically in services for the dead.

De rebus fidei et morum
Concerning matters of faith and morals (or *mores*)

Shorthand expression for matters which comprise the more important aspects of Christian faith, dogma, and practice, and often which are pronounced upon in an authoritative fashion by the *magisterium* (*q.v.*). See also *De fide vel moribus*.

Debitum
(Marital) debt

In sexual ethics, the *debitum* refers to the obligation each spouse has to the other to render conjugal relations upon request. This concept can be traced to the Latin Vulgate translation of 1 Corinthians 7:3 in which the Greek word *opheilen* (ὀφειλὴν) was rendered as *debitum*: "The husband should give to his wife her conjugal rights (ὀφειλὴν), and likewise the wife to her husband" (NRSV). This concept was then elaborated in both the theology and canon law of marriage as a contractual element "owed" by each "party" to the other. In feudal times, *servitium debitum* (debt of service, *q.v.*) referred to the military service that a vassal owed his lord, but this usage is not commonly found in theology. Physical inability to render the marital debt (to complete the sexual act) is a diriment impediment to marriage (cf. *C.I.C.* 1084 §3). See also *Concubitus propter solam procreationem, Ius in corpus (corpore)*, and *Remedium concupiscientiae*.

(Ex) Defectu obiecti; (Ex) Defectu iuris
Defect of an object; Defect of a right

Principle which holds that a certain action is immoral due to some "defect" in regards to either the "object" of the act or a "right" illicitly used in order to commit the act. Thus, lying is immoral *ex defectu obiecti* since its "object" (an untruth) is a defect in regards to what should be the genuine object of speech, i.e., communication of the truth. Suicide or or euthanasia is immoral *ex defectu iuris* since it presumes the taking or ending of life, which is a "right" reserved to God alone as the Creator and Lord of life. See also *Finis operis* and *Obiectum*.

Defensor Vinculi
Defender of the bond

In marriage annulment cases, the *Defensor Vinculi* was the individual who would argue (somewhat like a defense attorney) for the presumption of validity of the marriage that was being judged as to possible grounds for an annulment. See also *Ligamen, Non constat de nullitate*, and *Ratum et consummatum*.

Dei Verbum
Word of God

Name in Latin given to Vatican II's Dogmatic Constitution on Divine Revelation (1965) in which the council decided that revelation was the *norma normans non normata (q.v.)*, i.e., ultimate norm of Christian faith which stands above even tradition and all of the people of God, including the magisterium (cf. *DV* #10). See also *Optatam totius*, *Predicatio ecclesiastica*, *Traditio*, and *Verbum Dei*.

Delectatio morosa
Entertaining pleasure (literally, "morbid delight")

This expression usually referred to entertaining, i.e., dwelling on, "bad thoughts"—most commonly of a sexual nature. A prolonged dwelling on such thoughts could lead one to give into sin, and even the failure to turn one's mind quickly from such sins was considered sinful in itself. Two expressions also used in conjunction with this term are *gaudium* (joy, *q.v.*), which referred to the happy contemplation of sins already committed, and *desiderium* (desire, *q.v*), which referred to the desire for something sinful. This expression also is used when one uncharitably rejoices in the misfortunes of another, usually an enemy. See also *Male sonans* and *Piarum aurium offensiva*.

Delicta graviora (singular)/
Delictis gravioribus (plural)
Grave crime

See *Graviora delicta* for a fuller discussion. Usually this term is employed in the context of church penal law in the Code of Canon Law and covers actions considered to be particularly heinous, such as using the confessional forum for solicitation for sexual relations. The term also has appeared in connection with the scandal of the sexual abuse of minors by priests and led to some particular legislation promulgated by the pope and the Congregation for the Doctrine of the Faith on how these sorts of crimes should be handled juridically. More recently (July 2012), Cardinal Raymond Burke, Prefect of the *Apostolica Signatura (q.v.)*, included leaking Vatican correspondence among these crimes. See also *Crimen*, **Crimen sollicitationis**, *Corpus delicti, Delicta graviora*, **Epistula de delictis gravioribus**, *Graviora delicta, In flagrante delicto*, **Sacramentorum sanctitatis tutela**, *Secretum pontificium, Sub secreto pontificio*, and *Sub rosa*.

Deo gratias
Thanks be to God

Common expression found in prayers and also connotes thanksgiving and, at times, even a certain relief that something is finally over. In certain religious houses at mealtimes, there is/was either silence or reading at the table. When the superior said *Deo gratias* this was a signal that those present could then converse freely. See also *Benedicamus Domino* and *Ite Missa Est*.

Deo optimo maximo
To God, the best, the greatest

See *D.O.M.*

Deo volente
God willing

Often used in a certain pious mode of expression, such as "I'll return by next Monday, *Deo volente*" recognizing that ultimately it is God and not ourselves who governs the world in which we live.

Depositum fidei
The deposit of faith

Refers to the content of formal revelation (e.g., the Scriptures). The task of the church, especially in teaching *munus docendi (q.v.)* of its magisterium, is to safeguard from error and corruption this *depositum fidei*, and for this reason heresy, etc., is to be guarded against and rooted out. See also *Articulus stantis et cadentis ecclesiae, De fide, De fide definita, De fide vel moribus, Ecclesia docens*, and **Fidei depositum**.

Desiderium
Desire

By itself the term does not necessarily have a positive or negative meaning, and so much depends on the context in which it is used and/or the other terms which modify it. However, in the manualist moral tradition this single word was used to denote a desire for something that was sinful. In this latter context, see also *Delectatio morosa* and *Gaudium*. See also *Desiderium consiliabile* and *Desiderium naturale*.

Desiderium consiliabile
Well-considered desire

A choice made for a certain end or good, upon rational reflection. See also *Bonum utile* and *Uti et frui.* See also *Desiderium* and *Desiderium naturale.*

Desiderium naturale
Natural desire

There are many "natural desires," but when used theologically this term refers to the basic orientation of the finite human spirit for the infinite absolute, which is God, and the corresponding orientation of the human will to the good and its realization. The *desiderum naturale* is an important counter-concept to the notion of sinful human tendencies. Though these destructive tendencies exist in human nature they need not play the determining role in a person's moral makeup. The idea of the *desiderum naturale* is also important to an understanding of the so-called fundamental option theory in moral theology. See also *Desiderium* and *Desiderium consiliabile.*

Deus
God

Since Latin is a language in which the noun forms change according to the grammatical case used, *Deus* is the form for the nominative singular. Common grammatical forms for "God" in the other cases are *Dei* (genitive, used in the possessive sense), *Deo* (dative or ablative, used as indirect objects and/or with certain prepositions), and *Deum* (accusative, used as a direct object).

Deus absconditus/Deus revelatus
The hidden God/the revealed God

Theological pair of terms used by Martin Luther to express aspects of God as both "knowable" and "revealed" and at the same time "hidden" or beyond human knowledge. See also *Deus semper maior*; *Non ut explicetur, sed ne taceretur*; and *Si comprehendis, non est Deus.*

Deus caritas est
God is love

Title of Pope Benedict XVI's first encyclical, issued on 25 December 2005. See also **Caritas in Veritate**; *Caritas in veritate in re sociali*; **Spe salvi**; *Ubi caritas*; *Deus ibi est*; and *Ubi societas, ibi ius.*

Deus impossibilia non iubet
God does not command things which are impossible

Thus, no command of God, whether in divine or natural law, would be impossible for humans to fulfill, since God's grace is always available. This principle has been used often in ethics, especially sexual ethics, to answer the charge that the teaching of the church might be impossible to fulfill (e.g., as used by Pius XI in **Casti connubii** #61 [*q.v.*], his 1930 encyclical on artificial contraception). See also *Agere sequitur esse, Gloria Dei vivens homo, Humano modo, Lex iniusta non est lex, Lex non intendit impossibile, Lex sequitur esse, Lex spectat naturae ordinem, Nemo tenetur ad impossibile, Operari sequitur esse, Qui tenetur ad finem tenetur ad media, Quidquid percipitur ad modum percipientis percipitur, Quidquid recipitur* *ad modum recipientis recipitur*, and *Ultra posse* (or *vires*) *nemo obligatur*.

Deus nihil facit inane
God does nothing in vain

Axiom associated with a certain understanding of the natural law. Whatever is found in nature is considered to be part of God's plan and God's will. Therefore, any activity which would frustrate this perceived creative design would be considered intrinsically evil.

Deus semper maior
God is always greater (than
human attempts at understanding)

Refers to the inexhaustible mystery of God's presence, which can never be completely and fully grasped by humans whose knowledge will always be partial and limited. See also *Deus absconditus/Deus revelatus*; *Quis ut Deus*; *Non ut explicetur, sed ne taceretur*; and *Si comprehendis, non est Deus*.

Devotio moderna
Modern devotion

Refers primarily to a spirituality developed in the fifteenth century (Gerard Groote and Thomas à Kempis) which stressed a simple piety, asceticism, and imitation of Christ (*imitatio Christi* [*q.v.*]), as opposed to a more speculative approach to meditation and contemplation.

Dicta probantia
Statements proving

Refers to texts which are cited individually as "proof" of a certain position or doctrine, and taken as a collective concept refers to the practice of "prooftexting," usually through quotation of biblical texts (often taken out of context, and therefore can be suspect as offering real "proof" of the position in question). See also *Locus classicus* and *Unicum*.

Dictatus papae
Papal sayings

Papal document of twenty-seven propositions promulgated by Pope Gregory VII (Hildebrand) in 1075 which outlined presumed papal powers such as the assertion of supreme papal authority over civil as well as religious matters, and including the proposition that "the Roman Church has never erred, nor ever, by the witness of Scripture, shall err to all eternity."

Dies Christi
Day of Christ

The day of Christ's resurrection, and therefore holy to his church. This expression was also used in one of the chapter headings of Pope John Paul II's 1998 apostolic letter on Sunday worship, *Dies Domini* (*q.v.*).

Dies Dierum
Day of days

Refers to Sunday as the "primordial" day, the day of the Lord's resurrection and his final coming in glory at the end of time, and therefore truly the "Lord's Day." This expression was also used in one of the chapter headings of Pope John Paul II's 1998 apostolic letter on Sunday worship, *Dies Domini* (*q.v.*).

Dies Domini

The Day of the Lord; The Lord's Day (i.e., Sunday)

The 31 May 1998 apostolic letter of Pope John Paul II (released though on 7 July 1998) on the theme of keeping the Lord's day holy, and addressed to bishops, clergy and the faithful. The aspect of **Dies Domini** highlights the work of God as Creator, who rested after all the work of creation on the seventh day, and thus made that day "Holy" for it is truly the Lord's own day. This expression also looks forward to Jesus' promised Second Coming. An English translation of the papal document is found in *Origins* 28 (30 July 1998): 133, 135–51. See also *Dies Christi, Dies Dierum, Dies Ecclesiae, Dies Hominis*, and **Dominicae cenae**.

Dies Ecclesiae

Day of the Church

Refers to Sunday, the day that the Christian community gathers together in worship. This expression was also used in one of the chapter headings of Pope John Paul II's 1998 apostolic letter on Sunday worship, **Dies Domini** *(q.v.)*.

Dies Hominis

Day for Humans

Refers to Sunday, the day that is also set aside for rest and relaxation, and thus is one element which makes the day "sacred." This expression was also used in one of the chapter headings of Pope John Paul II's 1998 apostolic letter on Sunday worship, **Dies Domini** *(q.v.)*.

Dies Irae

Day of Wrath

Refers to the Day of Judgment and is the name given to a Gregorian chant that was traditionally sung at funerals. The opening lines are *Dies irae, dies illa, Solvet saeclum in favilla: Teste David cum Sibylla* (Day of wrath, that day will melt the world in ashes, on the testimony of David and Sibyl). The prayer itself is called a sequence and is one of only four medieval sequences that were preserved in the reform of the *Missale Romanum (q.v.)* published in 1570. The other three are the *Victimae Paschali (q.v.)* for Easter, the *Veni Sancte Spiritus (q.v.)* for Pentecost, and the *Lauda Sion (q.v.)* for Corpus Christi *(q.v.)*. See also *Lux Aeterna* and *Paridisium*.

Dies natalis

Day of birth

While "birthday" might seem to be the logical English equivalent of this term, the expression is used to denote the anniversary of the death of a saint—i.e., the day in which that holy person entered into the fullness of life with God. Saints feast days are usually assigned, if possible, to the day of the person's death (such as July 31 marking the feast day of St. Ignatius of Loyola, who died on that day in 1556).

Diffinimus

We define

Formula used in some early official church dogmatic formulations to indicate a doctrine that was being defined. See also *Ex cathedra* and *De fide definita*.

Digitus Dei est hic
The finger of God is here

Common expression to indicate that the clear imprint of the presence or will of God can be found in the situation under discussion.

Dignitas personae
Dignity of the person

2008 instruction of the Congregation of the Doctrine for the Faith which gives an update on the 1987 *Donum vitae* (*q.v.*) treating bioethical questions, mostly in the area of assisted reproductive technologies. While technology per se is not condemned, the instruction does find morally problematic any technology which separates the unitive and procreative dimensions of the conjugal act, or which would use embryos for research or experimentation.

Dignitatis humanae
Dignity of humans

Vatican II's Declaration on Religious Liberty (1965), which held that freedom of religion is a fundamental human right—reversing the long-standing semi-official position that "Error has no rights." This former position can be detected in Pope Gregory XVI's encyclical *Mirari vos* condemning indifferentism in religion and the supposed individual's freedom of conscience in choice of religion (1832). Gregory XVI's position was echoed in Pius IX's *Quanta cura* (1864) and the accompanying **Syllabus of Errors**. Nevertheless, there is some tension with this position dating from Roman times through Thomas Aquinas, which held contrary views. *Dignitatis huma-nae* reversed this position and ultimately enshrined the position of Thomas Aquinas, who held that no one should ever be forced to act against his or her conscience, and even if this is done the person should resist: "anyone upon whom the ecclesiastical authorities, in ignorance of the true facts, impose a demand that offends against his clear conscience, should perish in excommunication rather than violate his conscience" (Thomas Aquinas, 4 Sent. 38, q. 2, a. 4, Expos. Text). See also *Mirari vos*; *Nisi enim sponte et ex animo fiat, execratio est*; *Quanta cura*; and *Quod aliquantum*.

Dilige et quod vis fac
Love and do what you will

Patristic expression, sometimes also rendered as *Ama et quod vis fac* (*q.v.*). This phrase should not be interpreted that if one is loving whatever one does will be good. Rather, if one truly loves, then that which one "wills" or desires will be the good, and thus should be done.

Disciplina arcani
Discipline of the arcane (secret)

Referred to the practice of keeping religious rites and doctrines secret from nonbelievers. Thus, only baptized Christians would be allowed to be present for the liturgy of the Eucharist, and all others (including catechumens) would have to depart after the Liturgy of the Word.

Dives in Misericordia
Rich in mercy

Encyclical of Pope John Paul II, On the Mercy of God (1980).

Divino Afflante Spiritu
With the Divine Spirit blowing

Pius XII's encyclical on biblical interpretation, which allowed Catholic scholars to use the modern methods of exegesis and historical criticism (1943), issued on the fiftieth anniversary of Leo XIII's *Providentissimus Deus*. This encyclical reversed a long-standing position that emphasized biblical literalism and inerrancy and helped usher in a major period of flourishing in Catholic biblical studies.

Divortium a thoro
Separation (divorce) from the marriage bed

Juridical act of an ecclesiastical court in which a validly married couple obtains an ecclesiastically recognized separation, which is not an annulment, and thus which does not leave the parties free to marry again. This practice was canonically sanctioned by its inclusion in Gratian's *Decretum* 2.32.5 and in the *Decretals* 4.19. This term is sometimes also called *divortium imperfectum* (literally, "imperfect" divorce, as in the sense of being incomplete). See also *Divortium plenum/perfectum.*

Divortium plenum/perfectum
Absolute (full) divorce

This expression is contrasted with *Divortium a thoro (q.v.)*, sometimes also termed *divortium imperfectum* (as in the sense of incomplete or not absolute—like a temporary separation of the spouses). *Divortium plenum* (or *pefectum*) is the civil juridical dissolution of the marriage bond, though the Roman Catholic Church does not recognize the dissolution of a validly contracted sacramental marriage that has been duly *ratum et consummatum (q.v.)*. An annulment is a finding by the church marriage tribunal that one or more of the requisites for a valid sacramental marriage was in fact lacking at the time the marriage was celebrated and so therefore no sacramental marriage in fact took place (appearances to the contrary). See also *sanatio in radice.*

Do ut des
I give so that you may give

Positively, a *quid-pro-quo (q.v.)* in which one does something in order to receive something from another; negatively, a sort of *lex talionis (q.v.)*, a getting-even or taking revenge. See also *Ex iustitia.*

Doctor Angelicus, Doctor Communis, Doctor Universalis
Angelic, Common (of all), Universal Doctor (teacher)

Three appellations given to Thomas Aquinas (1225–75), with the "Angelic Doctor" being the most common.

Dolorosa
The sorrowful one

See *Mater Dolorosa* and *Stabat Mater Dolorosa.*

Dolus
Maliciousness, trick, deceit

A fraud or deceit deliberately perpetrated by an individual, such as a non-ordained person masquerading as a priest in order to gain something. Presence of *dolus* is important in judging certain actions and may involve a canonical impediment. E.g., the crime (*dolus*) of masquerading as a priest incurs an impediment against subsequent priestly ordination. A *dolus* is a deliberate act of deception (even if not "malicious" in the moral sense) and in canon law is distinguished from a *culpa* (*q.v.*), which also may involve a violation of canon law or some liturgical rubric, but a *culpa* is due rather to an oversight or a failure of due discretion, rather than through a knowing violation. See also *De defectibus*; *Mens rea*; *Nemo dat quod non habet*; *Sanatio in radice*; and *Ubi non est culpa, ibi non est delictum*.

D.O.M.
To God, the best, the greatest

Latin abbreviation for *Deo optimo maximo* and a common dedication found in works of art, especially architecture, in which the artist or benefactor dedicates the work to God.

Domine
O Lord

This is the vocative form of *Dominus* (*q.v.*) and thus is often found in prayers and intercessions in which the name of God is invoked.

Domine non sum dignus
Lord I am not worthy

The words of the centurion to Jesus in Mt 8:8 which are also now used (again) in the revised English translation of the *Missale Romanum* (*q.v.*) to be uttered by the faithful prior to receiving Holy Communion. It can also be used as an expression of humility upon receiving some sort of honor or promotion (e.g., priests have been known to utter this upon re-

ceiving the happy news they have been chosen to be a bishop).

Dominica in Albis
Sunday in White (garments)

The traditional name given to the first Sunday after Easter, since this was the day in which those converts who had been baptized at the Easter vigil took off their white garments which they received at the time of the baptism. This Sunday is also called Low Sunday (since it is more "low-key" than the high holy days of the Easter triduum), and also *Quasimodo* (*q.v.*). Since 2002 in the pontificate of Blessed Pope John Paul II this first Sunday after Easter is celebrated as Divine Mercy Sunday in commemoration of the visions of Jesus received by the Polish nun Sr. Faustina Kowalska, whom Blessed Pope John Paul II first beatified in 1993 and then subsequently canonized in April 2000. See also *Quasimodo*.

Dominicae cenae
The Lord's Supper

1980 letter of John Paul II to the bishops On the Mystery and Worship of the Eucharist. See also *Dies Christi*, *Dies Dierum*, **Dies Domini**, *Dies Ecclesiae*, and *Dies Hominis*.

Dominium
Dominion

Implies control and ownership, e.g., sovereignty. This concept was contrasted in classical Roman law with *possessio* (*q.v.*), which indicated usage and occupation, but without the attendant private property rights which would come with dominion. See also *Dominus/servus.*

Dominium utile
Control of Use (Usufruct)

Legitimate use of an object, e.g., the fruit or property of another, in a way that does not negatively impair its substance is termed usufruct in law. A tenant farmer who can claim most of the harvest, but not ownership of the estate, might be an agricultural example of this concept. See also *Bonum utile*; *Ius utendi, fruendi, abutendi*; *Res frutificat dominum*; and *Uti et frui.*

Dominum et Vivicantem
The Lord, the Giver of life

Encyclical of John Paul II on the Holy Spirit (1986).

Dominus
Lord, master

In Latin the nuance for *dominus* is lord or master in the sense of being a ruler, owner, or overlord. *Magister (q.v.)* is the Latin word which connotes "mastery" in the sense of being an expert, teacher, or director. *Dominus* is the Latin term often used as a title for God. See also *Domine.*

Dominus ac redemptor
Lord and Redeemer

Papal brief of Pope Clement XIV issued July 21, 1773, which suppressed the Society of Jesus (Jesuits). The brief was never promulgated in the Russian empire, so the Society continued to exist legally there. Pope Pius VII restored the Society on August 7, 1814, with his bull **Sollicitudo omnium Ecclesiarum** *(q.v.).*

Dominus Iesus
Jesus the Lord

Declaration of the Congregation for the Doctrine of the Faith dated August 6, 2000 (but not issued until September 5, 2000) and subtitled "On the Unicity and Salvific Universality of Jesus Christ and the Church." See also *Elementa ecclesiae*, *Extra ecclesia nulla salus*, *Plantatio ecclesiae*, and *Subsistit in.*

Dominus vobiscum
The Lord be with you

Greeting and formula used by the presider several times throughout the Latin celebration of the Eucharist. The response of the congregation is *Et cum spiritu tuo*: literally, "And with your spirit," though in the pre-2012 English translation of the *Missale Romanum* *(q.v.)* the congregational response had been rendered "And also with you." See also *Dominus* and *Pax tecum/vobiscum.*

Donec aliter provideatur
For the time being; until other arrangements are provided

Expression used, for example, by Pope Benedict XVI upon his election as pope in which he "confirmed" or retained in office the major figures of the Roman Curia—not indefinitely, but rather until such time as further arrangements might be made for either their longer-term confirmation in office or replacement. See also *Hucusque vigens*, *Ius vigens*, *Lex non obligat nisi promulgata*, and *Vacatio legis.*

Donum veritatis
Gift of truth

Instruction of the Congregation for the Doctrine of the Faith On The Ecclesial Vocation of the Theologian (1990). The instruction gives directives to theologians on how to be loyal and defend the magisterium. In the rare case in which a theologian might have genuine doubts about the truth or aptness of a magisterial document, the theologian is instructed to take the matter to prayer, and if still necessary after that to report his or her concerns privately to the proper magisterial office, but under no circumstances to make these concerns public. The text can be found on the website of the Holy See. See also *Authenticus, Ecclesia discens, Ecclesia docens, Ecclesia militans, Fides implicita,* **Lumen gentium***, Magister, Magisterium authenticam, Munus docendi, Obsequium religiosum, Officium, Potestas docendi,* and *Sensus fidelium.*

Donum vitae
Gift of life

Congregation for the Doctrine of the Faith's instruction On Respect for Human Life in Its Origin and on the Dignity of Procreation, which called for the banning of in vitro fertilization techniques (1987). See also **Dignitas personae**, the updated 2008 instruction on bioethical questions.

DS
Denzinger-Schönmetzer

See **Enchiridion Symbolorum Definitium Et Declarationem.**

Dubium
Doubt

This may be posed as a "doubt" or a formal question calling for clarification or a definitive interpretation. In 1995, for example, the Congregation for the Doctrine of the Faith issued a *Responsum ad dubium* giving its interpretation on the question of the level of authority to be attached to John Paul II's **Ordinatio Sacerdotalis**, which held that women could never be ordained priests. See also *Responsum ad dubium.*

Dubium facti
Doubt of fact

A legal term which refers to the lack of sufficient information concerning the facts of a given case or situation, and which therefore renders a decision difficult or impossible. See also *Da mihi factum, dabo tibi ius*; *Dubium juris*; *In dubio factum non praesumitur sed probatur*; *In dubio pars tutior sequenda*; *Lex dubia non obligat*; *Melior est conditio possidentis*; *Praesumptio hominis*; and *Praesumitur ignorantia ubi scientia non probatur.*

Dubium iuris
Doubt of law

Refers to a doubt about the text or meaning of a law, so that its binding force on a given point or in a given situation cannot be determined. See also *Da mihi factum, dabo tibi ius*; *Dubium facti*; *In dubio factum non praesumitur sed probatur*; *In dubio pars tutior sequenda*; *Lex dubia non obligat*; *Melior est conditio possidentis*; *Praesumitur ignorantia ubi scientia non probatur*;

Praesumptio iuris; and *Sententia incerta non valet.*

Dubium iuris vel facti
Doubt of law or fact

In cases about the doubt of either the facts of a given situation or whether a given law applies in this case the moral principle of probabilism could be invoked, or in instances of proper canonical jurisdiction the ecclesiastical principle of *ecclesia supplet* (*q.v.* "the church supplies [the lacking jurisdiction]") would apply. In confessional cases involving such a "doubt," the confessor is instructed to give absolution. See also *Da mihi factum, dabo tibi ius*; *Dubium facti*; *Dubium juris*; *In dubio factum non praesumitur sed probatur*; *In dubio pars tutior sequenda*; *Iuris et/vel facti*; *Lex dubia non obligat*; *Melior est conditio possidentis*; *Praesumptio hominis/Praesumptio iuris*; *Praesumitur ignorantia ubi scientia non probatur*; and *Sententia incerta non valet.*

Dum
While, during

Common Latin conjunction; see below for some common examples.

Dum tempus habemus operemur bonum
Let us do good while we have time

Attributed to St. Francis, and implies that we should do good deeds today since we do not know what tomorrow will bring. See also *Tempus fugit.*

Dum vita est, spes est
Where there's life, there's hope

Common expression, and especially in bioethics this adage connotes that even in serious illness physical life in general should be protected and prolonged. However, this maxim is *not* absolute and is conditioned by the application of the principle of "ordinary" and "extraordinary" means. "Means" in this sense refers to medical care, surgical interventions, drugs and therapies, etc., taken to minister to a sick, injured, or dying person.

Dura lex sed lex
A hard law is still law

This axiom calls for respect and obedience even to difficult laws. However, there are many other axioms that suggest a more moderate view. See, for examples, *Cessante fine cessat lex*; *Consuetudo optima legum interpres*; *Gravis neccessitas*; *Lex iniusta non est lex*; *Lex valet ut in pluribus*; *Odia restringi, et favores convenit ampliari*; *Salus publica suprema lex*; and *Sententia facit ius.*

E

Ea (eorum) quae sunt ad finem
   Those things which are for the end

This expression is just part of a longer phrase, and a more idiomatic English translation would be "means" to an "end" (*ad finem*). This is an important distinction in Thomistic moral theology since it is primarily the end of an action that determines the moral meaning of the act. Thus, the moral meaning of the action of a knife being driven in the chest would depend not on the choice of the knife per se, but rather the end (*finis operis, q.v.*) that motivated the end. This motivating end is the *finis operantis* (*q.v.*, the intention of the agent). If that end were murder then the action would clearly be morally evil; if, on the other hand, the knife thrust were part of an emergency operation in a situation in which other surgical tools were lacking then the end in this case would legitimate the choice and use of the knife. On this point, see Thomas Aquinas' treatment of human acts *(actus humanus, q.v.)* in his ST I–II, q. 6–17. See also *Finis enim dat speciem in moralibus, Finis est causa causarum, Finis est nobilior iis quae sunt ad finem,* and *Qui vult finem vult media.*

Ecce homo
   Behold the man!

In the Latin Vulgate translation of the Bible (John 19:5), these words were spoken by Pontius Pilate as he presented the scourged Jesus to the crowds on Good Friday in an attempt to win the crowd's pity for Jesus.

Ecclesia de Eucharistia
   Church of the Eucharist

Encyclical letter of Pope John Paul II on the relation of the church to the Eucharist issued on 17 April 2003. While acknowledging the life of the Eucharist throughout the church, the pope also laments the decline of eucharistic adoration and various departures from a strict adherence to liturgical norms. See also *Ars celebrandi.*

Ecclesia discens
   The learning church

The aspect of the church's nature which stresses its ability and obligation to learn more about the nature and meaning of its faith. Often the *Ecclesia discens* was understood to be those who were not part of the magisterium, which constituted the *Ecclesia docens*, though as many experts have observed, it is impossible to teach without first having learned, and the best teachers usually are those who are life-long learners, too. See also the fuller discussion of *Ecclesia docens* below, as well as the terms *Ecclesia militans, Errare humanum est, Fides implicita, Quidquid recipitur ad modum recipientis recipitur, Securus iudicat orbis terrarum*, and *Sensus fidelium*.

Ecclesia docens
The teaching church

The aspect of the church's nature which stresses its ability and obligation to teach concerning nature and meaning of the Christian faith. This division of the church into the "teaching church" (*Ecclesia docens*) and the "learning church" (*Ecclesia discens*) developed in the Post-Tridentine period beginning with Thomas Stapleton (died 1598). The "teaching church" was identified with the hierarchy and the "learning church" primarily with the laity, whose duty was seen to accept what the hierarchy would tell them. This construction, according to Cardinal Avery Dulles, SJ, in his *A Church to Believe In* (New York: Crossroad, 1982, p. 112), led to the earlier concept of *sensus fidelium* ceasing "to function as a distinct theological source." See also *Authenticus*, **Christus Dominus**, *Depositum fidei, Ecclesia discens, Ecclesia militans, Errare humanum est, Fides implicita,* **Lumen gentium,** *Magisterium, Magisterium cathedrae pastoralis & Magisterium cathedrae magistralis, Munus, Munus docendi, Obsequium religiosum, Officium, Potestas docendi,* *Quidquid recipitur ad modum recipientis recipitur*, and *Sensus fidelium*.

Ecclesia in America
The church in America [North and South]

Post-synodal apostolic exhortation of John Paul II given in Mexico City on January 22, 1999, following the synod on the Americas held earlier in Rome at the end of 1997.

Ecclesia militans
The church militant

Expression for the church in the contemporary world, which is expected to be vigilant and fight against the power of evil in the world. This ecclesiology was usually supplemented with the expression of the "Church Triumphant" for those souls in heaven with God, and the "Church Suffering," which referred to the souls in purgatory. See also *Ecclesia discens, Ecclesia docens, Ecclesia semper reformanda, Extra ecclesia nulla conceditur gratia, Extra ecclesia nulla salus, Extra mundum nulla salus, Extra pauper nulla salus, Per modum suffragii,* and *Plantatio ecclesiae*.

Ecclesia non moritur
The church will never die

Expression for the indefectibility of the church which has been guaranteed by Jesus Christ. See also *Tu Es Petrus* and *Ubi Petrus, ibi ecclesia, ibi Deus*.

Ecclesia semper reformanda
The church must always be reformed

Traditional maxim pointing out the necessity of the ongoing reform and conversion of the church. Whatever in the church distorts or does not correspond fully and completely to Christ and His will (*forma Christi*) must be reformed. Inasmuch as the church is sinful due to her human members and institutions, it is also part of the church's essential nature to be engaged in a continual process of self-reformation.

Ecclesia supplet
The church supplies

Theological and canonical principle that holds that even if there is some common error, such as in jurisdiction or the performance of a sacrament, as long as the minister, etc., intends to do what the church intends in that action the nature of the church "makes up" for any insufficiency or error on the priest's part. This can be a helpful pastoral principle to guard against scrupulosity.

Ecclesiam Suam
His church

Paul VI's encyclical on the church and its dialogue with the world (1964).

Editio typica
Typical (official) edition

An *editio typica* refers to the official edition of a document, such as a liturgical text, which often in the Roman Catholic Church would be the Latin version. Any other translation of this document should be based on the official translation, and the *editio typica* can help resolve disputes over the proper translation or interpretation of an official text.

E.g.
For the sake of an example

Abbreviation of *exempli gratia*. Used in English to indicate an example which may illustrate a point: "there was a lot of fruit for dessert, e.g., watermelon, cherries, oranges, etc." Care should be taken not to confuse the usage of *e.g.* with that of *i.e.* (*id est,* "that is," *q.v.*).

Ego te absolvo
I absolve you (of your sins)

Latin "core" formula considered necessary for the valid remission of sins in the forum of the sacrament of reconciliation (penance, confession). Manuals of moral theology would debate just how much of this formula had to be said for "validity" and a minimalist opinion held that "Te absolvo" ("I absolve you") would suffice. The concept of validity was foundational since it established the grounds for the efficacious celebration of the sacrament itself. See also *Ad validitatem, Ecclesia supplet,* and *Res et sacramentum*.

Elementa ecclesiae
Elements of the Church

Expression which refers, primarily, to those "separated" Christian Churches which are not in full union with the Roman Catholic Church, but which still contain elements of the true Church of Jesus Christ. See also **Dominus Iesus Lumen gentium**, *Extra ecclesia nulla salus*, **Mystici Corporis**, and *Subsistit in.*

Emmanuel
God with us

The seventh and last of the "O Antiphons" that mark the octave of anticipation or preparation for Christmas Eve, which in itself is the vigil of Christ's birth. See the fuller discussion under *O Adonai*.

Enchiridion
Manual, handbook

Usually used in theological circles to refer to a collection of various theological documents, the most well-known being the **Enchiridion Symbolorum Definitionum Et Declarationum** (*q.v.*).

Enchiridion Symbolorum Definitionum Et Declarationum
Handbook of creeds, definitions, and declarations

Collection of excerpts of church documents, especially of a dogmatic nature. The full title adds the words *De rebus fidei et morum* and is commonly called **Denzinger-Schönmetzer**, or more briefly **Denzinger**, and abbreviated as **DS** followed by the relevant number, e.g., **DS** 3074–75 the definition of papal infallibility taken from **Pastor aeternus** (*q.v.*). An English translation similar to and cross-referenced with the **Denzinger-Schönmetzer** is *The Christian Faith in the Doctrinal Documents of the Catholic Church*, edited by J. Neuner and J. Dupuis, and also commonly referred to as **Neuner-Dupuis**.

Ens
Being

Anything which can or does exist, i.e., that whose actuality is to be. See also *Esse*, *Essentia*, and *Suppositum*.

Ens rationis
Being of reason

Being of reason, as distinguished from real being. Human beings by virtue of their capacity as *rational* beings have an essential quality which distinguishes them from all other living beings. Rationality is the key ability which not only sets humans apart from others and gives them their special dignity and moral possibility. See also *Ens*.

Ens ut ens
Being inasmuch as it is (a) being

Metaphysical principle which refers to the existence of a being as such. See *Ens* and the related terms.

Ens ut sic
Underlying reality of being.

Expression similar to *ens ut ens* (*q.v.*) which refers to the underlying essence of a being. This could be distinguished from that which is merely "accidental" (like hair color for a human person) and not constitutive of the person's being as such (e.g., mortality is a constitutive factor of the being or *ens ut sic* of the human person). See also *Accidens*.

Epikeia
Fitting, suitable.

This is *not* a Latin term, but since so many readers of past editions have looked in vain for this important term, mistakenly thinking it to be Latin, it has been included here. The word comes from the Greek (επικεια) and refers to the long-standing moral tradition that allows for a law to be dispensed or modified under certain conditions, such as the impossibility or inhumanity of the law, or if the mind of the legislator could reasonably be interpreted such that the dispensation or modification in question would likely be granted. This applies especially to human laws (*Ius positum*, *q.v.*). A classic example of *epikeia* would be exceeding the posted speed limit on a deserted highway in order to bring a medical emergency more quickly to the hospital. Thomas Aquinas held that *epikeia* was a virtue since it sought refinement or perfection of the law and thus should be practiced as any virtue. See also *Ad literam*; *De minimis non curat lex*; *Mens legislatoris*; *Necessitas non habet legem*; *Necessitas non habet legem*; *Quod non licitum est in lege necessitas facit licitum*; *Quod raro fit non observant legislatores*; *Sensum, non verba spectamus*; *Singularia non sunt extendenda*; and *Statuta sunt stricte interpretanda*.

Epistula de delictis gravioribus
Letter on grave crimes

Letter of the then Cardinal Prefect of the Congregation for the Doctrine of the Faith, Joseph Ratzinger (later Pope Benedict XVI), sent on May 18, 2001, to the bishops of the world, outlining procedures for dealing with the serious crimes (*delictis gravioribus* in the plural; *delicta graviora* in the singular) of priestly sexual abuse and/or violation of the confessional. The procedures called for forwarding such cases to the Congregation for the Doctrine of the Faith but sealed under the strict confidentiality of the *secretum pontificium* (or *sub secreto pontificio*). See also *Corpus delicti*, **Crimen sollicitationis**, *Delicta graviora*, **Epistula de delictis gravioribus**, *Graviora delicta*, *In flagrante delicto*, **Sacramentorum sanctitatis tutela**, *Secretum pontificium*, *Sub secreto pontificio*, and *Sub rosa*.

Ergo
Therefore

Often used as a transition word to indicate a logical conclusion one can draw from an argument, or list of facts, etc., already enunciated. See also *Q.E.D.*

Ero Cras
Tomorrow I come

See the fuller discussion under *O Adonai*.

Errare humanum est
To err is human

This adage indicates the fallible and limited nature of humans and all human knowledge. See also *Ecclesia discens*, *Ecclesia docens*, and *Quidquid recipitur ad modum recipientis recipitur*.

Erratum/errata
Error/errors

Usually used in reference to printing mistakes. See also *corrigenda*.

Esse
To be

The Latin infinitive form of the verb "to be," this term also refers to the act or fact of being, as in *actus essendi* (*q.v.*). See also *Essentia*.

Essentia
Essence

Refers to the inner principle by reason of which a thing is what it is. Thus, the essence common to Peter, Paul, and Mary is the essence each has as a human being despite individual differences in terms of gender, body type, hair color, and so on. Thus, "what" one is is one's *essentia*; "that" one is (or exists) refers to *esse* (*q.v.*). See also *Accidens*, *Per accidens*, *Per se*, and *Suppositum*.

Et cum spiritu tuo
And with your spirit

Congregational response in the Latin celebration of the Eucharist to the presider's invocation *Dominus vobiscum* (*q.v.*) ("The Lord be with you"). Prior to the 2011 English translation of the *Missale Romanum* (*q.v.*), the English response was "And also with you."

Et et
Both/and

Though by itself *et* means "and" in Latin, when doubled it means "both/and."

Evangelii Nuntiandi
Announcing the Good News (Gospel)

Paul VI's post-synodal apostolic exhortation on evangelization (1975), which stressed that serious efforts had to be made in inculturation using the language and culture of the various peoples being evangelized if the church could hope to be successful with its missionary efforts.

Evangelium
Gospel

Literally, "good news" and can refer to the Gospel as a general concept referring to the message of Jesus Christ, or as a particular text, such as the Gospel of Luke (*Evangelium secundum Lucam* [The Gospel according to Luke]).

Evangelium vitae
Gospel of life

John Paul II's encyclical on certain issues concerning life, especially abortion, capital punishment, and euthanasia (1995). This encyclical (in #57) declared that a state's use of capital punishment was probably unjustified in most contemporary cases since other effective means to protect the citizenry now existed to render recourse to execution of criminals unnecessary.

Ex
Out of, from, of

Common Latin preposition, however, it should be noted that in Latin *ex* does *not* mean "former" as in the sense of an "ex-ballplayer."

Ex abusu non est argumentum ad desuetudinem
Abuse (of a law) does not argue for (the law) falling into desuetude (disuse or nonobservance)

This legal axiom expresses the same principle articulated in *Abusus non tollit usum* (*q.v.*). However, see also *Cessante fine cessat lex*, *Cessante ratione legis cessat ipsa lex*, and *Optimus interpres rerum usus*.

Ex attrito fit contritus
From an attrite person to a contrite person

Common teaching of the church regarding the way grace builds on the disposition of the penitent in the sacrament of reconciliation, moving him or her to deeper and true contrition. Attrition is sorrow for one's sins but was seen as less profound than true contrition. Thus, sacramental confession and absolution was seen as helping to bring about the transition from attrition to contrition, and this thinking lies behind the church's teaching that while perfect contrition is sufficient for the forgiveness of sins (even without sacramental confession), a sinner is bound to confess all mortal sins so as to be certain of forgiveness and restoration to the state of grace. For a fuller discussion of this point see the Council of Trent (**DS** 1678) and Pope John Paul II's 1984 post-synodal apostolic exhortation **Reconciliatio et Paenitentia** (On Reconciliation and Penance in the Mission of the Church Today) #31, note 185. Another slight variation of this same axiom is *de attritione fit contritio* (*q.v.*, "from attrition comes contrition"), used first by William of Auvergne (1248). See also *Processus iustificationis*.

Ex cathedra
From the chair (of office)

Usually referred to in relation to the highest exercise of authority of the papal magisterium. Thus, when the pope "acting in the office of shepherd and teacher of all Christians" declares *ex cathedra* "a doctrine concerning faith or morals to be held by the universal Church," such declared doctrines are considered "infallible" and "irreformable" of themselves (*ex sese*), and "not because of the consent of the Church (*non autem ex consensu ecclesiae*)." (Quoted phrases from the definition of infallibility given in **Pastor Aeternus**, "Dogmatic Constitution on the Church of Christ," of Vatican I [**DS** 3074–3075]). For an explanation of **DS** see *Enchiridion Symbolorum Definitionum Et Declarationum*. See also *Cathedra*, *De fide definita*, *Diffinimus*, *Depositum fidei*, and *Ecclesia docens*.

Ex convenientia
From fittingness (literally, convenience)

Expression used to refer to arguments advanced that may be "convenient" to the position that is being supported but which on their own merits neither prove (nor disprove) the position being advanced. Archbishop Rembert Weakland used this expression in his memoirs *A Pilgrim in a Pilgrim Church* (Eerdmans, 2009) to discuss the claim advanced in **Inter insigniores** (*q.v.*), which held that women could not be ordained priests since this action was not willed by Jesus Christ himself.

Ex corde ecclesiae
From the heart of the church

Pope John Paul II's apostolic constitution on Catholic Universities detailing the Catholic university's identity and mission, as well as a set of general norms which are meant to govern the functioning of universities (1990). See also *Ordinationes*, which in this case called for Catholic professors teaching philosophy and theology to seek a *Mandatum* (*q.v.*) from their local bishop to certify them as being faithful teachers in accordance with Catholic doctrine.

Ex Defectu iuris
> See *Defectu obiecti; Defectu iuris*

Ex Defectu obiecti
> See *Defectu obiecti; Defectu iuris*

Ex facto ius oritur
> Law is born from fact

The maxim recognizes the importance of experience and custom in the development of the notion of what constitutes a law. Therefore, if something is done and done repeatedly and not censured by the legitimate authority, one may infer that this deed then enjoys legal approbation. By extension, this principle can help us see how moral doctrine develops when practices that at one time might have been condemned (such as the taking of interest) are allowed to exist and then become accepted as part of moral practice. See also *Consuetudo optima legum interpres.*

Ex falso sequitur quidlibet
> From that which is false anything can follow

Aphorism that indicates that a false premise can lead to any number of possible conclusions, many of which likewise would be false. See also *Parvus error in initio magnus erit in fine* and *Parvus error in principiis, magnus error in conclusionibus.*

Ex imperfectione actus
> From an imperfection of the act

One of the ways in which a sin, which otherwise might be mortal due to its grave matter, remains "venial" due to some "imperfection" in the sense of lack of completion on the part of the agent who does the act. Usually, this would be understood as a lack of sufficient awareness and/or consent on the part of the agent committing the act, so that the act was not perfectly "deliberate."

Ex infirmitate
> From weakness

Thomas Aquinas in his treatise on sin in the *Summa theologiae* I–II, q. 77, a. 3, speaks of sins committed out of weakness (*ex infirmitate*) when a concupiscible or irascible power (e.g., a passion) contrary to the order of reason obscures the rational power of the soul to choose the good.

Ex iustitia
> From justice

Since technically there is no "j" in classical Latin, this expression might be found rendered as *ex justitia*, especially in later usages. It refers to the basic principle of something done out of respect for, or in view of, the fundamental requirements of justice. Thus, a parent may expect (and charge) *ex iustitia* an adult child who remains at home a sum to cover room and board. See also *Ex pietate.*

Ex nihilo (nihil)
> From nothing (nothing)

No thing can come out of nothing; everything must have a cause. Only God can create something "from nothing." The aphorism *nihil ex nihilo fit* (nothing from nothing comes) expresses this thought. See also *Creatio ex nihilo, Creatio continua, Creatio nova,* and *Creatio originalis.*

Ex novo
From anew

E.g., when a call is made for a radical restart, such as asserting that the church must return to its primitive roots of the first disciples and re-found itself *ex novo*. Similar in meaning to *de novo* (*q.v.*).

Ex obiecto (objecto)
From the object (of the act)

While this concept can be used in a variety of theological and/or philosophical contexts, in particular reference to moral theology it refers to an action whose very nature determines its morality (or immorality), regardless of further consideration of circumstances and/or intentions. In other words, the object of an act such as "murder" is *ex obiecto* morally evil, since the "object" of the act is immoral in itself. See also *(Ex) Defectu obiecti.*

Ex officio
By virtue of the office (itself)

Usually refers to some right an individual has because of the office she or he occupies. For example, the dean of a college may be *ex officio* a member of the Academic Senate (whereas other members may have to be elected).

Ex opere operantis
By the work (effect) of the worker (performer of the work)

This expression in the Catholic tradition refers to the efficacy of an action, such as the use of *Sacramentalia* (*q.v.*) called sacramentals such as holy water, medals, crucifix, etc. If such objects and actions are used with the proper disposition of an individual, then these will be of spiritual benefit by helping to increase piety and devotion and also remitting venial sin. Like other good works, the result comes not just from the mechanical completion of the action but from the interior disposition of the person performing the action. Thus, giving alms for vainglory does not produce a good effect (*opus operantis*) but must be performed with a right intention. See also *Ex opere operato, Sacramentalia,* and *Sacramentum.*

Ex opere operato
By the work performed

Principle of sacramental theology officially adopted at the Council of Trent indicating that the efficacy of a sacrament depends upon the valid performance of the sacrament itself and does not depend upon the personal holiness (or lack thereof) of the minister performing the sacrament (which would be *ex opere operantis*, i.e., the effect of the work depends on the operator of the work). Thus, according to the principle of *ex opere operato*, the graces to be obtained by participation in the Eucharist would not depend on the personal holiness (or lack thereof) of the priest who acts as the presider. See also *Ex opere operantis, Sacramentalia,* and *Sacramentum.*

Ex pacto divino
From/by God's pact (promise)

This expression refers to God's covenant with humankind, the saving will that grounds the whole economy of salvation.

Ex parvitate materiae
From the paucity of matter

One of the criteria that was used to describe venial sin, in this case a sin (even though fully deliberate) remained "venial" because of the lack of grave matter. See also *Ex toto genere suo* and *Parvitas Materiae in Sexto*.

Ex pietate
Out of devotion (literally, filial piety)

Contrasted with an obligation done *ex iustitia (q.v.)*, this principle refers to an obligation that arises out of a special relationship, such as that between parents and children such that adult children should feel obligated to arrange for their elderly parents' care *ex pietate* (rather than out of a strict sense of justice). See *Ex iustitia* and also *Do ut des* and *quid pro quo*.

Ex post facto
From after the fact

An *ex post facto* discussion of what should have been done instead of what was actually done may be interesting but rarely can reverse the situation. See also *Post factum*.

Ex scientia praesumitur consensus
(From) knowledge builds (presumes) consensus

Knowledge will lead (presumably) to consensus. It is important here *not* to translate *scientia* as "science," since the Latin word means knowledge in general and not just "scientific" knowledge. For related terms see *Facta non praesumuntur sed probantur* and *Praesumptio cedit veritati*.

Ex Silentio
From silence

Related to the aphorism "Silence gives consent" (*Qui tacit consentire censetur, q.v.*). See also *Argumentum e silentio*.

Ex toto genere suo (grave)
From the totality of its nature (intrinsically grave)

Traditional moral manualist expression concerning judgment of certain types of sins. For example, certain mortal sins were considered, *ex toto genere suo grave*, i.e., in themselves so evil that there would be no conceivable case in which the gravity of their evil could be diminished from an "objective" point of view. Traditionally, sins of a sexual nature were placed in this category. From the subjective point of view a number of other factors, such as an individual's ignorance, lack of freedom due to compulsion, etc., could diminish or remove the seriousness of the "objective" sin in a concrete instance. See also *Parvitas Materiae in Sexto* and *(In) re venerea*. Contrasted with sins which would be *ex toto genere suo grave* (of themselves involving intrinsical matter) would be sins *ex toto genere suo leve*, i.e., sins whose matter of itself would be "light" (*leve*) and therefore not easily made into matter for mortal sin. See also *Graviter et dolose* and *Intrinsece malum*.

Ex voto
From (under) a vow

Term often seen in churches which indicates that the donor of some chapel, statue, etc., has been the donation in response to a favor or grace received. I.e., the donor promised (*ex voto*) that if a certain favor were granted by God, then she or he would give testimony to this fact by making the donation to the church (or monastery, etc.).

Exceptio firmat regulam
The exception confirms the rule

Virtually the same as the English expression "the exception proves the rule" and is balanced by another legal aphorism, *Singularia non sunt extendenda* (*q.v.*). See also *Ad literam*; *Cessante fine cessat lex*; *Consuetudo optima legum interpres*; *Conventio est lex*; *Epikeia*; *Ex abusu non est argumentum ad desuetudinem*; *Dura lex sed lex*; *Lex valet ut in pluribus*; *Odia restringi, et favores convenit ampliari*; and *Sensum, non verba spectamus*.

Exempli gratia
For the sake of an example

See *E.g.*

Exitus acta probat
The result (exitus) validates the acts

The end justifies the means.

Exitus et reditus
Exit and return

Everything in creation comes from God and returns to God and thus is a basic principle of a theological understanding of the moral life, the natural law, and of all creation. The *reditus* should not be understood as decay in terms of dead material that is reabsorbed into the soil, but rather as the coming of all creation to completion and perfection in God. Cf. St. Thomas Aquinas' *Summa Theologiae* I–II, q. 92. See also *Finis ultimus*, *Gratia supponit naturam et perficit eam*, and *Summum bonum*.

Exsurge Domine
Rise up, Lord

Papal bull of Leo X condemning the errors of Martin Luther (1520) which was handed down only after Luther had been censured by the theological faculties of Mainz, Cologne, Louvain, and Paris. See also *Anathema/Anathemata* and *Magisterium*.

Extra
Outside of

Common Latin preposition; however, the Latin *extra* does *not* mean "left over" or "super-abundant" as in the sense of an "extra helping of potatoes."

Extra ecclesia nulla conceditur gratia
Outside of the church there is no grace

Extremist Jansenist proposition, based on the traditional axiom *extra ecclesia nulla salus* (*q.v.*), which was condemned by Pope Clement XI in 1713 (cf. **DS** 2429). See also *A cruce salus*, *Communio sanctorum*, *Extra ecclesia nulla salus*, *Extra mundum nulla salus*, *Extra pauper nulla salus*, *Fides implicita*, *Limbus*, and *Plantatio ecclesiae*.

Extra ecclesia nulla salus
Outside of the church there is no salvation

Traditional theological maxim, dating from Cyprian (*Epistles* 73, 21), which holds that the church is the place of salvation for all. However, over the centuries this term was much debated as to its precise meaning, and one position held that some sort of "membership" in the church is required of all people if they are to be saved. The understanding of what "membership" and "church" mean have been major issues in ecclesiology and ecumenism over the centuries. See also *A cruce salus, Baptismus in voto, Communio sanctorum,* **Dominus Iesus**, *Elementa ecclesiae, Extra ecclesia nulla conceditur gratia, Extra mundum nulla salus, Extra pauper nulla salus, Fides implicita, Limbus,* **Lumen gentium**, *Ignorantes, Ingnorantia invincibilis, Plantatio ecclesiae, Radix Mali, Sine culpa, Subsistit in,* and **Unam Sanctam.**

Extra mundum nulla salus
Outside of the world there is no salvation

Position of Edward Schhillebeeckx, OP, which has an obvious resonance to the theological maxim of *extra ecclesia nulla salus* (*q.v.*). Stresses the idea that human salvation has to be worked out in the world, and therefore a position would be suspect which calls for a flight from the world or suggests *solely* a "spiritual" and "otherworldly" dimension. See also *Ecclesia militans, Extra pauper nulla salus,* and *Fuga mundi.*

Extra nos
Outside of ourselves

Generally, this expression is used to refer to some sort of norm that is external to the human person. The word of God as contained in Scripture would be one of the most common examples of such a usage.

Extra pauper nulla salus
No salvation outside of the poor

Intentional reinterpretation of the classical axiom of *Extra ecclesia nulla salus* (*q.v.*) used in liberation theology and attributed to Jon Sobrino, SJ. This expression emphasizes the notion of God's preferential option for the poor which must be lived out in solidarity with the poor by the rest of humanity that hopes for eternal salvation. See also *Extra ecclesia nulla conceditur gratia* and *Extra mundum nulla salus.*

F

Facienda
> Things being done

In theology, this term usually refers to the acts or works of the Christian life.

Facta non praesumuntur sed probantur
> Facts are not presumed but must be proved

Basic tenet of legal justice and any knowledge-based inquiry. For a related term see *Ex scientia praesumitur consensus* and see also *Absolutus sententia judicis praseumitur innocens*; *Actori incumbit onus probandi*; *Allegatio contra factum non est admittenda*; *Da mihi factum, dabo tibi ius*; *Onus probandi*; *Praesumptio cedit veritati*; *Res ipsa loquitur*; *Si iudicas, cognossce; si regnas, iube*; and *Testis in uno falsus in nullo fidem meretur.*

Falsus in uno falsus in omnibus
> False in one, false in all

In terms of an argument based on certain premises or facts, if it can be demonstrated that one of these facts or premises are wrong then this means (likely) that the conclusion also will be erroneous. See also *Parvus error in initio magnus erit in fine* (small error in the beginning; large error will be in the end) and *Parvus error in principiis, magnus error in conclusionibus* (small error in the beginning leads to great error in the conclusion).

Fama habet/Fama est
> Rumor has it

Expression indicating something rumored to be true, or as being of common opinion or gossip.

Familiaris consortio
> The partnership of the household (the family)

John Paul II's post-synodal apostolic exhortation on the Christian family (1981).

Favores ampliandi, odia restringenda
> Favors being amplified and burdens being restricted

A shortened form of *Odia restringi, et favores convenit ampliari* (*q.v.*).

Felix culpa
> Happy fault

Phrase which is found in the Easter *Exsultet* sung at the Easter Vigil liturgy and which refers to the sin of Adam which led ultimately to the coming as a man of the Second Person of the Trinity. *Felix culpa* is often used more colloquially to refer to any apparent mistake which turns out to have a good effect or happy ending. See also *Radix Mali*.

Ferendae sententiae
A sentence which must be imposed

Refers to a penalty in canon law which must be formally imposed by the competent authority such as a local bishop. Most penalties in the 1983 Code of Canon Law are *ferendae sententiae* rather than *latae sententiae* (*q.v.*), the latter being a penalty which is incurred automatically upon commission of a particular offense. See also *Sub poena*.

Festina lente
Make haste slowly

Means to behave with care and caution.

Fiat
Let it be done

In English this word expresses a command or order that is to be performed.

Fiat iustitia, ruant coeli (or pereat mundus)
Let justice be done, though the heavens fall (or the world perish)

Occasionally rendered in the singular as *Ruat coelum*, this slogan indicates that "consequences" should never keep strict "justice" from being done, even if this should be burdensome or occasions negative consequences. "Come what may" might be an equivalent English expression. Nevertheless, this principle must be tempered by reason and does not trump the church's long-standing position that no one is called to do that which is considered to be morally impossible. The eighteenth-century German Enlightenment philosopher Immanuel Kant offered a slight variation on this aphorism: *Fiat iustitia, pereat mundus* (Let justice be done, though the world perish), which he translated more loosely as "Let justice reign even if all the rascals in the world should perish from it." See also *Deus impossibilia non iubet, Impossibilium nulla obligatio, Nemo tenetur ad impossibile, Qui tenetur ad finem tenetur ad media*, and *Ultra posse* (or *vires*) *nemo obligatur*.

Fiat lux
Let there be light

Translation from the Latin Vulgate of Genesis 1:3, but also more colloquially a prayer or wish for enlightenment on a certain matter.

Fiat voluntas Tua
Thy will be done

From the Latin Vulgate of the Lord's Prayer, expressing the desire that God's will always be done, even if the divine will does not correspond with our personal desires in a given instance. See also *Pater Noster*.

Fidei depositum
Deposit of faith

While the term means the same as *depositum fidei* (*q.v.*), in this instance it refers to the apostolic constitution by which Pope John Paul II formally promulgated on the thirtieth anniversary of the opening of Vatican II (11 October

1992), the *Catechism of the Catholic Church* calling it "a sure norm for teaching the faith . . . a sure and authentic reference text for teaching catholic doctrine and particularly for preparing local catechisms."

Fides et Ratio
Faith and Reason

Title of Pope John Paul II's encyclical, issued on 14 September 1998, on the relation between faith and reason as it is treated in philosophy and theology in the context of Christian faith. For some of the key concepts treated in this encyclical see also *Auditus fidei, Fides qua/Fides quae, Fides quae creditur, Fides quarens intellectum, Indefectabiliter adhaeret, Intellectus fidei,* and *Sensus fidelium.*

Fides ex auditu
Faith from hearing

Faith is born from hearing the word of God (refers to Romans 10:17 in the Latin Vulgate).

Fides fiducialis
Fiduciary (trusting) faith

Lutheran axiom which stresses that the individual's trust or will is more imporant than the intellect. See also *Sola fide.*

Fides implicita
Implied faith

Expression used similar to *Baptismus in voto (q.v.),* which referred to individuals who were not formally baptized but whose lives seemed to manifest a Christian character and thus the presence of the gift of faith—at least by analogy.

Blessed John Henry Cardinal Newman critiqued a certain problematic understanding of this term in his famous essay "On Consulting the Faithful in Matters of Doctrine," where he observed that the magisterium of the church at times exhibits a regrettable tendency to focus excessively on its role as the *Ecclesia docens (q.v.)* such that "she cuts off the faithful from the study of her divine doctrines and the sympathy of her divine contemplations, and requires from them a *fides implicita* in her word, which in the educated classes will terminate in indifference, and in the poorer in superstition" (John Henry Cardinal Newman, *On Consulting the Faithful in the Matters of Doctrine,* edited with an introduction by John Coulson [New York: Sheed & Ward, 1961], 106). See also *A cruce salus, Communio sanctorum, Ecclesia docens, Extra ecclesia nulla salus, Extra ecclesia nulla conceditur gratia, Extra mundum nulla salus, Extra pauper nulla salus,* and *Fides informis.*

Fides informis
Unformed faith

Faith which is possible even for sinners and which does not necessarily suppose obedience to the demands of morality. This faith is called "unformed" since it lacks the virtue of charity, which is understood to be the "form" of all the other virtues.

Fides qua/Fides quae
Faith through which/Faith that which

Fides qua refers to the *act* of faith, i.e., the personal commitment, by which or through which an individual and/or community believes, while *Fides quae* refers to the actual *content* of the faith, i.e., that which is actually believed. See also *Congregatio fidelium*, *Fides quarens intellectum*, *In credendo falli nequit*, *Indefectabiliter adhaeret*, *Intellectus fidei*, *Regula fidei*, *Sensus fidelium*, and *Sentire cum ecclesia*.

Fides quae creditur
The faith which is believed

See also *Congregatio fidelium*, *Fides qua/Fides quae*, *Fides quarens intellectum*, *In credendo falli nequit*, *Indefectabiliter adhaeret*, *Intellectus fidei*, *Regula fidei*, *Sensus fidelium*, and *Sentire cum ecclesia*.

Fides quaerens actionem
Faith seeking action

Principle for grounding canon law in the church, i.e., that the faith must be expressed in appropriate action. This concept of course is grounded first in the notion of faith which seeks understanding (*fides quaerens intellectum*, *q.v.*), which then guides the application in action.

Fides quaerens intellectum
Faith seeking understanding

Traditional maxim which comes from the title of a work by St. Anselm (c. 1033–1109) that expresses the view that the task of theology is grounded in faith and then building on that faith, seeks for greater understanding. See also *Corde creditur*, *Credo ut intelligam*, *Fides qua/quae*, *Fides quaerens actionem*, *Intellectus fidei*, and *Ne fides rideatur.*

Fides ratione illuminata
Faith illuminated by reason

The classic Protestant position is that our ethical understanding is based essentially on faith, which in turn is aided by human reason. This contrasts with the traditional Roman Catholic position that human reason is basically sound and trustworthy but that it needs to be illuminated by faith in order to counter the effects of the Fall and other sins. See also *Lumen fidei*, *Ratio fide illuminata*, and *Status antelapsarius*.

Fides supponit rationem et transcendit eam
Faith supposes reason and goes beyond it

Faith is not independent of reason but is built on a foundation of reason. However, faith goes beyond what can be known entirely from reason alone, especially in view of faith's relationship with divine revelation.

Filioque
And (from) the Son

Insertion of this term into the Nicene Creed to denote the procession of the Holy Spirit from both the Father and the Son. While this theology was accepted in the West it was rejected by the Eastern churches and became one of the disputed points which led to the separation of these two churches.

Finis
Boundary, limit, summit, end, object, aim

Of itself, the term may indicate the conclusion of a literary work, such as a book or play. In moral theology, the *finis* refers to the "end" or goal of an action in itself, or the end or goal intended by the one who performs the action. In this regard, see *Ea (eorum) quae sunt ad finem*, *Finis operis*, and *Finis operantis*.

Finis coronat opus
The end crowns the work

"End" has a double meaning in this phrase: both as the terminus of a work, as well as the overall aim or goal of the work. Therefore, the goal of an undertaking gives value to the work itself, as well as the fact that the undertaking is actually finished.

Finis enim dat speciem in moralibus
The end gives the species in moral matters

An expression that appears many times in the works of St. Thomas Aquinas and refers to the "end" or "object" of the moral act which is key in determining the act's moral meaning, i.e., its moral "species." See also *Ea (eorum) quae sunt ad finem*, *Finis est causa causarum*, *Finis operis*, *Finis operantis*, and *Voluntarium directum/indirectum*.

Finis est causa causarum
The end (goal) is the cause of all other causes

Refers to the final cause and intention as the key determining factor in evaluating both causality and the moral meaning or species of an action. See also *Causa finalis est prima inter omnes causas*, *Ea (eorum) quae sunt ad finem*, *Finis enim dat speciem in moralibus*, *Finis est nobilior iis quae sunt ad finem*, *Finis operis*, *Finis operantis*, and *Qui vult finem vult media*.

Finis est nobilior iis quae sunt ad finem
The end (goal) is more important than the means (to the end)

Axiom that highlights the greater importance of the *finis operantis* than the means chosen or used by the agent in evaluating the moral meaning of a given action (*finis operis*). See also *Causa finalis est prima inter omnes causas*, *Ea (eorum) quae sunt ad finem*, *Finis enim dat speciem in moralibus*, *Finis operis*, *Finis operantis*, and *Qui vult finem vult media*.

Finis medius
Intermediate end (aim)

Refers to the intermediate or more remote end of an action, as distinguished from an action's immediate aim or purpose. See *Finis proximus*.

Finis operantis
End ("intention" or "will") of the (moral) agent

Refers to the moral agent's own motive for doing a particular action, and in this sense is distinguished from the finality ("end") of the action itself (the *Finis operis*, q.v.). Thus, a person who gives a large sum of money to the poor merely *in order that* she or he receive praise of others performs an action which in itself is good (i.e., the *finis operis* is good) but whose motive (the *finis operantis*) is bad (seeking vainglory). Thus, for the moral agent her/himself this is a morally bad action. There remains an ongoing debate among moralists about the precise understanding of what constitutes the actual moral distinction between *finis operis* and *finis operantis* in certain actions which have both good and bad effects. See also *Ea (eorum) quae sunt ad finem*, *Licet corrigere defectus naturae*, *Praeter intentionem*, and *Voluntarium directum/indirectum*.

Finis operis
> End (purpose) of the work (or action)

Refers to the "end" or "goal" of the action itself as distinguished from the moral agent's own motive for doing such an action (the *Finis operantis*, *q.v.*). See *Finis operantis* for a further discussion of this important distinction. See also *Accelaratio partus*, *Ea (eorum) quae sunt ad finem*, *Licet corrigere defectus naturae*, and *Voluntarium directum/indirectum*.

Finis proximus
> Proximate (immediate) end (aim)

In reference to a particular moral act, the *finis proximus* is the immediate or direct aim of the act. For example, cooking a meal has as its *finis proximus* the preparation of food, which in turn may serve a further aim (*finis medius* or *remotus*) of satisfying one's hunger. These ends in turn may be directed to an overall aim (*finis ultimus*) which is the ultimate aim, such as sustaining one's individual life in order to do good in this world. See also *Ea (eorum) quae sunt ad finem*, *Finis operis*, *Finis operantis*, and *Voluntarium directum/indirectum*.

Finis remotus
> Remote (intermediate) end (aim)

See *Finis proximus*, *Finis medius*, and *Voluntarium directum/indirectum*.

Finis ultimus
> Ultimate end (aim)

Aristotelian term which when taken over into theology, especially in the system of Thomas Aquinas, refers to God as the final end which is the goal toward which all creation moves for its completion or perfection. Cf. ST I, q. 44, a. 4. See *Finis proximus* for a further description of this term's meaning and significance. See also *Exitus et reditus*, *Gratia supponit naturam et perficit eam*, and *Summum bonum*.

Flagrante delicto
> While the crime is burning

Refers to being caught in the midst of the criminal act while it is being committed, i.e., to be caught red-handed. See also *Corpus delicti* and *Graviora delicta*.

Fons et culmen
> Font (source) and summit

For example, the Eucharist is described as both the source of the church's life as well as its summit since the community gathered in communion around the table of the Lord experiences not only union with the Lord Jesus and one another, but also sanctification and divinization of the individual members.

Fons vitae
> Font of life

Ultimately, this would refer to God, or Christ, and often is expressed in symbols such as the heart of Christ.

Fontes moralitatis
Sources (fonts) of morality

Refers to the three factors which taken together constitute the traditional understanding of the objective content of a moral action: (1) the end of the action itself (the "object" of the action); (2) the circumstances surrounding the agent in the commission of the action; and (3) the intention, purpose, or motive of the agent in committing said action. See also *Actus non facit reum, nisi mens sit rea*; *In se sed non propter se*; and *Intrinsece malum*.

Forma Antiquior
Older form

This expression is often used interchangeably with *Usus Antiquior* (*q.v.*) to refer to the pre–Vatican II Latin Tridentine Mass. Pope Benedict XVI issued his 2007 *Motu proprio* (*q.v.*) **Summorum Pontificum** which allowed for a more liberal celebration of this Rite, calling it a *Forma extraordinaria* (*q.v.*) of the liturgy. See also *Ad orientem, Cappa magna, Coram Cardinale/Coram Episcopo, Coetus fidelium, Missale Romanum, Novus Ordo, Nulla Veritas sine Traditione*, **Sacrosanctum concilium**, **Summorum Pontificum**, *Quidquid latine dictum sit altum videtur, Tu Es Petrus*, **Universae Ecclesiae**, *Usus Antiquior*, and *Versus populum*.

Forma extraordinaria
Extraordinary form

Though this is a literal translation of a common ecclesial concept, this translation may be misleading in English. "Extraordinary" in theological language refers to something that is distinguished from that which is normal or obligatory and usually termed "ordinary." Thus, in the health care arena treatments which are considered morally obligatory are termed "ordinary" whereas those that are supplemental are termed "extraordinary." This expression was also used by Pope Benedict XVI in his 2007 *Motu proprio* (*q.v.*) **Summorum Pontificum**, in which he extended permission to all priests in the Latin Rite to celebrate the *Missale Romanum*, the Tridentine Latin Mass, as a *forma extraordinaria*. See also *Ad orientem, Cappa magna, Coram Cardinale/Coram Episcopo, Coetus fidelium, Forma Antiquior, Missale Romanum, Novus Ordo, Nulla Veritas sine Traditione*, **Sacrosanctum concilium**, **Summorum Pontificum**, *Tu Es Petrus*, **Universae Ecclesiae**, *Usus Antiquior*, and *Versus populum*.

Forma mentis
Form of the mind

Refers to a mind-set, worldview, or general way of perceiving an issue or larger concept.

Forum externum/internum
External/internal forum

The external forum (outward sphere) is oriented primarily to objective law, whereas the internal forum (inward sphere) refers primarily to the interior acceptance by a person in the freedom of his or her conscience. This concept has great importance in canon law, and especially in confessional situations. In case of some conflict between the two spheres, the inward attitude signified by the internal forum is judged to be of greater importance since it aims at acceptance by a person's conscience, the deepest and most privileged forum of law.

Fractio panis
Breaking of the bread

Refers to the Fraction Rite in which the consecrated eucharistic bread is broken during the liturgy prior to distribution in Holy Communion. This Fraction Rite symbolizes that the Body of Christ has been broken for us. The Fraction Rite comes as the community prays the *Agnus Dei (q.v.)*, the Lamb of God.

Fraternitas
Fraternity

Refers to a spirit and/or principle of egalitarianism, in distinction to a hierarchical principle of organization. For example, St. Francis of Assisi would refer to his band of friars as a *fraternitas*. See also *Cursus honorum*.

Fuga mundi
Flight from the world

An aspect of desert and/or monastic spirituality which stressed the monastic life as a separation from the cares and concerns of the secular life. See also *Extra mundum nulla salus*.

G

Gaudet Mater Ecclesia
Mother Church Rejoices

The October 11, 1962, Opening Address of Vatican II delivered by Blessed Pope John XXIII in which he critiqued "prophets of doom who are always forecasting disaster" while encouraging the council fathers "to use the medicine of mercy rather than the weapons of severity" in their pastoral approach. See also *Gaudium et spes*.

Gaudete
Rejoice

Expression used to mark the Third Sunday of Advent, usually called *Gaudete Sunday*, and symbolically marked by a rose-colored candle in the four-candle Advent wreath as well as the optional wearing of rose-colored vestments in place of the deep purple worn on the other days of Advent. These vestments can also be worn on the Fourth Sunday of Lent, called *Laetare Sunday*. However, since these vestments are worn only on two days in the entire liturgical year many parishes opt not to incur the cost of procuring these optional vestments. The special meaning of these "Rose" Sundays is to indicate to the Christian community that their period of waiting is coming to an end, either with Christmas in Advent or Easter in Lent, and thus they should be encouraged to continue in their preparations to welcome the Lord by redoubling their efforts at penance and renewal. See also *Adventus*, *Gaudium et spes*, *Gaudium de veritate*, and *Laetare*.

Gaudium
Joy

Depending on the context used, this term can have a positive or negative meaning. Joy, of course, is normally understood in positive terms, but the expression was also used in manualist moral theology to denote the perverted enjoyment in recollecting sins already committed. In this latter context, see also *Delectatio morosa* and *Desiderium*.

Gaudium de veritate
Delight in the truth

Reference to 1 Corinthians 13:6 as well as to the Augustinian definition of real happiness or beatitude. See also *Gaudete* and *Laetare*.

Gaudium et spes
Joy and hope

Vatican II's Pastoral Constitution on the Church in the Modern World (1965). At the Council there was a sharp debate over the initial words of this constitution since that word choice would determine the common "title" of the document and would give an initial "spin" on the document's thrust. Some church fathers preferred the document begin instead with *luctus et angor* (*q.v.* "griefs and the anxieties") but ultimately the more positive pair carried the day. See also *Gaudete*, **Gaudet Mater Ecclesia**, and *Laetare*.

Generaliter
Generally

E.g., holds as a general rule (to be true, binding, etc.), though not necessarily in each and every instance. See also *Semper sed non pro semper* and *Sic et simpliciter.* See also *Totaliter.*

Generatio prolis
Generation of offspring

Generatio prolis refers to the biological generation or production of offspring. The moral concept of the *bonum prolis* (*q.v.*) refers rather to the end of marriage as a union of love out of which children are conceived, brought into the world, nurtured and raised. See also *Sine prole.*

Genus moris/morum
Moral genus

Refers to the moral nature or structure of a given act, which is found by looking at not only the act itself but also the intention and circumstance (the so-called "fonts of morality" [*fontes moralitatis, q.v.*]). The *genus morum* is distinguished by the *genus naturae* which looks primarily to what is actually accomplished in the act itself. This basic distinction is

closer related to the notions of *finis operis* and *finis operanatis* (*q.v.*) and thus also to concepts of "direct" and "indirect" in terms of moral intentionality. See also *Ea* (*eorum*) *quae sunt ad finem*, *Obiectum actus*, and *Voluntarium directum/indirectum.*

Genus naturae
The natural genus (of an act)

Refers to what is actually accomplished by a certain action. See *Genus morum* above and the related terms in that discussion.

Gloria Dei vivens homo
The glory of God is the human person fully alive

Irenaeus, *Against Heresies* (*Adversus Haereses*, bk. 4, ch. 20, sec. 7), and refers to the theological principle which holds that which most gives God praise and glory is genuine human flourishing. Therefore, that which promotes true human values will at the same time give God glory and best express God's will for humankind. The full treatment of this axiom though indicates a relational reciprocity, namely that likewise our human "end" or purpose will be to see God and ultimately be united with Him. Therefore, we are exhorted to act and become truly human so we can more fully and easily reach our proper end. See also *Deus non impossibilia non iubet.*

Gloria in excelsis Deo
Glory to God in the highest

Opening words intoned by the priest of the hymn in the Latin Eucharist. The hymn itself is often referred to simply as the *Gloria*. These words come from the Latin Vulgate's translation of Luke 2:14, recording the words spoken by the angels to the shepherds in announcing Jesus' birth.

Gloria Patri
Glory be to the Father

Opening words of the doxology, *Gloria Patri et Filio et Spiritui Sancto. Sicut erat in principio, et nunc et semper, et in saecula saeculorum* (Glory be to the Father, the Son, and the Holy Spirit. As it was in the beginning, is now and ever shall be, world without end).

Gratia
Grace

The commonest theological translation of *gratia* is "grace," but the Latin word has a wide variety of other meanings and usages, such as "charm," "loveliness," "thanks," "gratitude," "cause," "reason," "motive," and many more.

Gratia data
Grace given

Refers to that which is freely given by God as a special gift or grace to an individual. Not every person receives the exact same set of graces or gifts, but they all come from the same Holy Spirit and are to be exercised for the benefit of the community (cf. 1 Cor 12:10-11).

Gratia Dei non est alligata sacramentis
God's grace is not confined to the sacraments

This adage indicates that God's grace and action are not limited to the seven sacraments but may be found in a variety of other occasions and means.

Gratia elevans
Elevating grace

Aspect of what is sometimes called "actual grace," i.e., that part of God's grace which raises us above the level of natural reason and morality and helps us so that we might reach the true end God has ordained for us. See also *Gratia operans*, *Gratia sanans*, and *Gratia supponit naturam et perficit eam*.

Gratia increata
Uncreated grace

Refers to God as God-self, as distinguished from created grace, i.e., sanctifying grace, which is shared by God with humanity. See also *Gratia elevans*, *Gratia operans*, *Gratia sanans*, and *Gratia supponit naturam et perficit eam*.

Gratia non tollit naturam, sed perficit
Grace does not destroy nature, but perfects it

Essentially the same idea expressed in the adage *Gratia supponit naturam et perficit eam*. Grace builds on human nature, and therefore does not obliterate human nature, but rather moves human nature to its completion, wholeness, and perfection—which is its *Summum Bonum* (*q.v.*), namely full union with God. See also *Exitus et reditus*, *Finis ultimus*, *Gratia elevans*, *Gratia operans*, *Gratia sanans*, and *Gratia supponit naturam et perficit eam*.

Gratia operans
Grace which is operating/working

Augustinian concept of grace which was further elaborated upon by Thomas Aquinas (cf. especially *Summa Theologiae I–II*, Question 111) which indicates that grace builds upon our human nature and works to perfect or complete that nature. See also *Gratia elevans, Gratia sanans,* and *Gratia supponit naturam et perficit eam.*

Gratia sanans
Healing grace

Aspect of God's grace which heals our broken and sinful human nature. See also *Gratia elevans, Gratia operans,* and *Gratia supponit naturam et perficit eam.*

Gratia supponit naturam et perficit eam
Grace builds on nature and perfects it

Essentially the same idea expressed in the adage *Gratia non tollet naturam, sed perficit (q.v.).* See also *Gratia elevans, Gratia operans, Gratia sanans,* and *Gratia supponit naturam sed perficit.*

Gravamen
Heaviness, burden, hardship, trouble, or complaint

Referred to the use of knowledge obtained in the confessional which might be "harmful" or "burdensome" to the penitent. Such use was forbidden and falls under the seal of the confessional, even if use of such knowledge might prevent a more serious harm to the penitent. For example, if a priest learns through an individual's confession that the marriage she or he is planning would be invalid due to some impediment, the priest cannot act publicly in any way to prevent that marriage from taking place. He could, however, counsel against the marriage in the confessional forum itself. See also *Cum gravamine poenitentis (paenitentis)* and *Prodere peccatorem, Proditio peccatoris.*

Graviora delicta
Most grave crimes

This expression is used in canon law to refer to "delicts" or "crimes" of a more serious nature and which therefore call for special adjudication and/or penalties. For example, the crime of using the sacrament of reconciliation or the place of the confessional to solicit someone for sexual purposes is one of these *Graviora delicta.* As such, and in connection with the sexual abuse crisis which came to light in the church in the 1990s, Pope John Paul II issued in 2001 a special document, *motu proprio (q.v.),* titled **Sacramentorum Sanctitatis Tutela** *(q.v.,* Safeguarding of the Sanctity of the Sacraments), which established procedural norms for handling of the reporting and follow-up of charges of sexual abuse by priests. In July 2012, Cardinal Raymond Burke, prefect of the *Apostolica Signatura (q.v.),* included leaking Vatican correspondence among these crimes. See also *Corpus delicti,* **Crimen sollicitationis,** *Delicta graviora,* **Epistula de delictis gravioribus,** *Graviora delicta, Graviter et dolose, In flagrante delicto, Peccata criminalia,* **Sacramentorum sanctitatis tutela,**

Secretum pontificium, Sub secreto pontificio, and *Sub rosa*.

Graviore culpa, graviore poena
The greater the offense the heavier the penalty

Basic legal axiom that corresponds with our adage "let the punishment fit the crime." See also *Actus non facit reum nisi mens sit rea, Corpus delicti,* **Crimen sollicitationis,** *Delicta graviora,* **Epistula de delictis gravioribus,** *Graviore culpa graviore poena, Graviter et dolose, In flagrante delicto, Peccata criminalia,* and **Sacramentorum sanctitatis tutela**.

Gravis neccessitas
Grave necessity

A somewhat subjective concept often found in canon law and/or moral theology that refers to mitigating or extenuating circumstances which would come into consideration in the application, or non-application, of a general norm and particular law. Thus, Canon 961 of the 1983 Code states that general absolution normally cannot be given *unless* one or more of a variety of circumstances are present, such as "grave necessity" such as a large number of penitents without a sufficient number of confessors available. This concept should be read in conjunction with the general canonical principle of *Odia restringi, et favores convenit ampliari* (*q.v.*), namely that "Burdens (odious things) are to be restricted, and favors (privileges) are to be multiplied (or extended)," a basic principle of canon law interpretation which holds that burdens or strictures are to be interpreted in a narrow sense of application, while on the other hand favors are to be widely applied. See also *Exceptio firmat regulam; Notaria non egent probatione;* and *Odia restringi, et favores convenit ampliari*.

Gravissimum educationis
The gravity (importance) of education

Vatican II's Declaration on Christian Education (1965).

Graviter et dolose
Gravely and maliciously

Expression which brings together at least two of the three traditional criteria for mortal sin, namely grave (very serious) matter and sufficient knowledge (and possibly consent). I.e., an action which is very seriously sinful in terms of its object and which is also done willfully ("maliciously"). This expression is found in canon law as an interpretative guide in determining juridical culpability for an action performed. For example, if an individual did not perform an action with either full knowledge and/or consent, which otherwise might be considered to be seriously sinful, this lack of "maliciousness" would render him/her less culpable in terms of being subject to certain penal sanctions. An example from the 1983 *C.I.C.* (Code of Canon Law) is expressed in canon 1041 §5 which indicates that a man incurs an impediment to receiving sacred orders if he "has mutilated himself or another gravely and maliciously (*graviter et dolose*). . . ." See also *Contra naturam, Graviora delicta, In flagrante delicto, Intrinsece malum in se, Materia levis (gravis),* and *Peccata contra naturam sunt gravissima.*

Gremiale
Lap cloth

Refers to a small cloth which is placed on the bishop's lap in an ordination ceremony to protect his vestments from stains during the anointing of the hands of a priest during the ordination rite. *Gremiale* is also rendered as *gremial* in English.

H

Habeas corpus
You may have the body

Common expression in civil law which refers to a safeguard against illegal detention or imprisonment. According to a writ of *habeas corpus*, a prisoner must be brought before the court to be formally charged or else released.

Habemus Papam
We have a pope

Ritual expression used to announce the election of a new pope to the waiting world at the conclusion of a papal conclave. The announcement is made from the central logia of St. Peter's Basilica to the waiting crowd gathered in the square below (and those watching on television throughout the world). Following this announcement the new pope delivers his first discourse and his first papal blessing, *urbi et orbi* (*q.v.*), to the city of Rome (*urbi*) as its new bishop and to the whole world (*orbi*) as the new head of the universal church. See also *Sede vacante* and *Urbi et orbi*.

Habitus
Habit

Though "habit" is the most obvious English cognate for this Latin term, the Latin concept carries a range of meaning difficult to translate into a single English word. *Habitus* can refer to a moral habit, such as a virtue or vice (i.e., "good" or "bad" habits), but on a deeper level *habitus* refers to the moral nature of human beings which is oriented to moral action and which in turn allows individual "habits" to be fostered. Thus, *habitus* refers more properly to the grounding of human moral striving. See also *Habitus acquisitus*.

Habitus acquisitus
Acquired habit

Based on the intrinsic moral quality of human nature, called *habitus* (*q.v.*), certain dispositions can be deepened by constant repetition. If the disposition acted upon is good then the *habitus acquisitus* would be a virtue, if the disposition acted is bad then the *habitus acquisitus* would be a vice.

Habitus infusus
Infused habit

A supernatural virtue, such as faith, hope, or charity, which is not "acquired" through repetition of an act, but is graciously infused (given directly) by God to the human person so that he or she can have the very ability to perform acts which correspond to that particular virtue (e.g., to believe in faith, to hope, and to love).

Hanc igitur
This therefore

Opening words ("This therefore") of the presider's prayer during the Latin Eucharist recited immediately before the institution narrative of the consecration. At the words *hanc igitur* a bell was rung by the altar server to alert the congregation to the oncoming consecration of the host and wine into the Body and Blood of the Lord. *Hanc igitur* became a shorthand expression for both this prayer and moment in the Eucharist.

Hic est enim calix Sanguinis Mei
This is the chalice of my blood

In the institution narrative of the Latin Eucharist these are the initial words of blessing spoken by the presider over the wine. The institution narrative refers to Jesus' own words used at the Last Supper, which are used as the words of blessing which change the bread and wine into the Body and Blood of Christ.

Hic et nunc
Here and now

This expression denotes something that is to be done now and/or refers to the concrete situation at hand.

Hic sunt dracones
Here there be dragons

Used by medieval cartographers to label unknown parts of the world and metaphorically employed since to highlight fear of the unknown or resistance to change. See also *Semper idem*.

Hierarchiam veritatem
Hierarchy (ordering) of truths

Expression used in Vatican II's Decree on Ecumenism *Unitatis redingratio* #11 (*q.v.*) which refers to the long-standing principle of Catholic dogma that there is a relative importance among the various truths of the faith. For example, the names of the twelve apostles would be far less important than the fact of the resurrection. This is a helpful principle to keep in mind not only in ecumenical and interreligious dialogue but also in any disputes or disagreements about particular approaches to theology. See also *Charisma veritatis*; *De fide definita*; *Depositum fidei*; *In necessariis unitas, in dubiis libertas, in omnibus caritas*; *Magisterium*; *Obsequium religiosum*; *Odium theologicum*; *Quaestio disputata*; *Sensus fidelium*; *Sententia probata*; *Status quaestionis*; *Theologice certa*; and *Unitatis redingratio*.

Hoc est enim Corpus Meum
This is My Body

In the institution narrative of the Latin Eucharist, these are the concluding words of blessing spoken by the presider over the bread. See also *Hic est enim calix Sanguinis Mei*.

Homo
Human being

This is a very common Latin word which refers to the human being as a person. In older (and noninclusive) translations, *homo* was usually rendered as "man." The Latin word *homo* does **not** refer to an individual's sexual orientation to members of the same sex;

this use of the term *homo* is derived instead from the Greek, and in the Greek *homo* means to be the "same" or "similar." Thus, a "homosexual" would be one whose primary sexual orientation is directed toward members of the "same" sex.

Homo assumptus

Christological heresy which denies the dual nature of Jesus Christ (both human and divine) and posits instead that the Divine Son did not actually take on human nature but merely "assumed" an already existing human being. This expression appeared in the critique by the Congregation for the Doctrine of the Faith of Jon Sobrino's "low Christology." See also *Communicatio idiomátum.*

Homo homini lupus
The human person is as a wolf to other humans

Rather pessimistic traditional adage about the savage and adversarial social aspect of human behavior in which one person "devours" another.

Homo ludens
The human person as one who plays

This refers to an important dimension of being a human, namely that leisure and recreation are essential and indispensible elements of human existence.

Homo novus
New person

Pauline concept of the human person as a new creation in Christ. The expression comes from the Latin Vulgate's translation of expressions such as "new person" (cf. Eph. 2:15) and/or "new creation" (cf. 2 Cor 5:17 and Gal 6:15).

Homo sapiens
The human knowing person

The standard scientific designation for the human species, i.e., the subgroup of the genus *homo*, which is distinguished by its rational powers that other animals in the same genus lack.

Homo unius libri
A person of one book

Refers to the Protestant Reformation position on the supremacy and finality of biblical authority, i.e., to need recourse just to "one book" (the Bible). Can also be used ironically to refer to someone who is not widely read and relies on just one source or influence for his or her thought. See also *Sola scriptura.*

Homo viator
A wayfarer

See *Viator.*

Homoexualitatis problema
The problem of homosexuality

Official Latin title of the Congregation for the Doctrine of the Faith's 1986 Letter to Bishops on the Pastoral Care of Homosexual Persons, which outlined serious concerns in pastoral leniency in dealing with gay men and women but which confirmed the earlier position of **Persona humana** #8 (*q.v.*) that sexual orientation is not usually a matter of personal choice or the result of personal sinful actions.

Honoris causa
For the sake of honor

Refers to something, such as an academic degree, awarded as an honor and in recognition for some special achievement. Thus, "Catholic University awarded a doctorate *honoris causa* to Dorothy Day" in recognition of her service to the church through the Catholic Worker Movement (rather than as an "earned" degree in some academic subject).

Hospes venit, Christus venit
(When) a guest comes, Christ comes

Traditional maxim of hospitality, derived from the Rule of St. Benedict, that indicates that in receiving guests one should receive them as if Christ himself had come. Occasionally this maxim is altered to *hospes venit, hostis venit* (When a guest comes, an enemy comes) to refer to either cold hospitality or the difficulties associated with hosting unwanted guests.

Hostis humani generis
Enemy of the human race

Expression used by some to justify suspension of rules of warfare, such as the Geneva conventions, or proscriptions against torture if the individual being subjected to "enhanced interrogation techniques" were considered to be a terrorist capable of harming or killing a large number of people. This expression is also tied to creating supposed exceptions to the considerations of the Just War Theory, especially the *ius in bello* criterion. Though this category was employed by the the George W. Bush administration (2001–9) as legitimization for torture of al Qaeda suspects in the "War on Terror," the Catholic moral tradition would *not* condone such an interpretation. See also *Tyrannus in titula, Tyrannus in regimine.*

Hucusque vigens
In force until now

Expression often used to mark a change in law in policy which had been in force until the present but which is now being abrogated, superceded, or modified. See also *Donec aliter provideatur, Ius vigens, Lex non obligat nisi promulgata,* and *Vacatio legis.*

Humanae vitae
Of human life

Paul VI's encyclical On the Regulation of Births, in which the traditional ban against any use of artificial means of contraception is reiterated (1968), pronouncing such usage to be an *intrinsice inhonestum* (q.v., intrinsically dishonest), though not an *intrinsece malum* (q.v., intrinsically evil). This pronouncement has continued to be the locus of much debate and disagreement, and though Paul VI reigned another ten years as pope, this was his last encyclical.

Humani generis
The human race

Encyclical of Pope Pius XII that strongly criticized certain new theological trends such as the *nouvelle theologie* which originated in France. Moreover, this encyclical contained an affirmation that whenever the pope pronounces on a theological point which has been under debate the debate is closed and no further contrary opinion should be voiced (1950).

Humano modo
In a human mode (or way)

Philosophical expression of human anthropology which indicates that humans can only be expected to act and meet moral obligations in a human manner, which will be necessarily limited and to some degree imperfect. An example given in some moral manuals was that of permanent commitments made in religious vows, clerical celibacy, or marriage. It was argued that since only absolute beings (like God) could make absolute commitments, the best that humans could do would be to make permanent commitments in *humano modo*, which recognized that not every possible set of circumstances could be foreseen in advance, some of which might render the fulfillment of the commitment impossible or even immoral. The expression also refers to the particularly "human" way certain actions should be performed, respecting the humanity of the individual(s). Thus, while marital rape might be open to procreation and the partners sacramentally married to each other, if force or violence were employed then this would violate the *humano modo* moral criterion of the act. Church teaching has evolved over the years to appreciate this last point. See also *Agere sequitur esse, Deus impossibilia non iubet, Lex sequitur esse, Lex spectat naturae ordinem, Operari sequitur esse, Quidquid percipitur ad modum percipientis percipitur, Quidquid recipitur ad modum recipientis recipitur*, and *Ultra posse* (or *vires*) *nemo obligatur*.

I

I.a.
　Among others

Latin abbreviation for *inter alia* (among other things) or *inter alios* (among other persons), and is used to denote a grouping together of similar items, persons, etc. Thus, "important contemporary moral theologians, *i.a.* Häring, Fuchs, McCormick, hold that this position is untenable" means that a number of moral theologians, including the examples named, hold this position.

Ibid.
　In the same place

Latin abbreviation of *ibidem*, and refers to a citation that is found in the same text, work, or location as the citation immediately prior to the citation in question. For the correct usage of *ibid.* and related scholarly terms such as *idem*, *loc. cit.*, and *op. cit.*, it is important to consult an accepted manual of style, such as *The Chicago Manual of Style*.

Ibidem
　In the same place

See *Ibid.*

Id est
　That is

See *I.e.*

Idem
　The same

Occasionally abbreviated as *id.*, this term is used in scholarly works to refer to works written by the same author. For correct usage, see an accepted manual of style, such as *The Chicago Manual of Style*.

I.e.
　That is

Common abbreviation of *id est*, which is used in English to clarify further a statement made. Thus, "At the foot of the Cross stood Mary, *i.e.*, the mother of Jesus, along with Mary Magdalene and Mary, the wife of Clopas." (Cf. John 19:25). See also *E.g.*

Ignorantes
　The ignorant ones

Theologically, this term is usually used to refer to individuals who do not know a truth of the faith or morals, usually through no fault of their own. See the longer discussion under *Sine culpa*, as well as the related terms of *Extra ecclesia nulla salus* and *Ingnorantia invincibilis*. See also *Limbus* and *Mens rea*.

Ignorantia elenchi

Ignorance (or ignoring) of the rules of logical refutation or proof (elenchos, ελεγχος in Greek)

This term is usually used to critique someone or some argument that either overlooks key elements or which otherwise seems to violate the basic tenets of logic. See also *Ex scientia praesumitur consensus*; *Facta non praesumuntur sed probantur*; *Falsus in uno falsus in omnibus*; and *Parvus error in principiis, magnus error in conclusionibus*.

Ignorantia invincibilis

Invincible ignorance

This term has two primary theological usages. First, it can refer to those who through no fault of their own have not had the Gospel message effectively preached to them and so cannot respond in faith to the truth of the Christian faith. For a further discussion of this point see especially *Extra ecclesia nulla salus* and *Sine culpa*. The second usage relates to conscience and moral theology in which an individual is required always to follow one's "certain" judgment of conscience, even if this should be in objective error. The error in this instance is explained as being due to invincible ignorance. For a fuller discussion of this point see **Gaudium et spes** #16 as well as the **Catechism of the Catholic Church** #1790, which states "A human being must always obey the certain judgment of his conscience. If he were

deliberately to act against it, he would condemn himself. Yet it can happen that moral conscience remains in ignorance and makes erroneous judgments about acts to be performed or already committed." See also *Culpa*; *Extra ecclesia nulla salus*; *Ignorantia legis neminem exusat*; *Ignorantes*; *Limbus*; *Mens rea*; *Sine culpa*; and *Ubi non est culpa, ibi non est delictum*.

Ignorantia legis neminem exusat

Ignorance of the law excuses no one

This adage is similar to our Anglo-American juridical principle of "Ignorance of the law is no excuse," though in canon law certain penalties, e.g., *latae sententiae* (*q.v.*), do *not* hold if the individual was inculpably aware of them (cf. *C.I.C.* #1323–24). Similarly, in moral theology *ignorantia invincibilis* (*q.v.*, "invincible ignorance") does "excuse" one from moral culpability (cf. *CCC* #1793).

IHS

Jesus

Comes from the first three letters of Jesus in Greek (ΙΗΣΟΥΣ) and thus is *not* Latin, as is often mistakenly believed. See *In hoc signo vinces*.

Imago Dei

Image of God

Basic Judeo-Christian tenet of theological anthropology. We are made in the image of God (cf. Genesis 1:26), and thus in our being and action we are called to image God's own holiness. The *imago Dei* furnishes a basic theological symbol and grounding for human dignity and the rights of persons. Because humans are created in the image of God they are to be treated with dignity and accorded basic rights. See also *Similtudo Dei.*

Imitatio Christi
The imitation of Christ

Maxim associated with spirituality which stresses the meditation on the life of Christ and modeling of Christian discipleship upon the human portrait of Jesus found in the Gospels. See also *Devotio moderna, Sequela Christi,* and *Via Dolorosa.*

Impedimenta libertatis
Impediments to freedom

Those conditions or factors which are understood to reduce or block one's freedom, both morally and physically. One's moral responsibility for a given action or state of affairs can be thus reduced or eliminated due to these *impedimenta libertatis.* See also *Liberum arbitrium* and *Moralis impossibilitas.*

Impossibilium nulla obligatio (est)
Nothing impossible can oblige

It is important to remember that in moral theology this "impossibility" is not just that which is physically impossible (such as flying unaided) but also that which was termed "morally impossible" and interpreted to mean that which would be very difficult or repugnant to do, short of heroic virtue. See also *Deus impossibilia non iubet, Humano modo, Lex non intendit impossibile, Lex spectat naturae ordinem, Nemo potest ad impossibile obligari,* *Nemo tenetur ad impossibile, Qui tenetur ad finem tenetur ad media,* and *Ultra posse* (or *vires*) *nemo obligatur.*

Imprimatur
Let it be printed

See *Nihil obstat.*

Imprimi potest
It can be printed

See *Nihil obstat.*

In absentia
In (one's) absence

Something that is done when the person in question is not physically present but which still carries effective force. Thus, "the student was awarded her degree *in absentia*" means the student officially graduated, even though she was not physically present to receive her diploma.

In abstracto
In the abstract

Argument based on abstract or speculative considerations, which may yield different conclusions if considered from the viewpoint of concrete, real-life circumstances. See also *In concreto.*

In aeternum
In eternity

Forever and ever, without end.

In articulo mortis
In the moment of death

Refers to the imminent danger of death (usually due to illness or serious injury). See also *Articulum mortis, In extremis,* and *In periculo mortis.*

In casibus urgentioribus
In more urgent cases

This expression usually is found in the context of interpreting certain restrictions in canon law. For example, while a certain practice might generally be forbidden (like giving general absolution) it can be given *in casibus urgentioribus*. Exactly what constituted legitimate "urgency" was a matter of some debate, and certainly anything seen to be in danger of death (*in periculo mortis*) would be a clear example, but most canonists and moral theologians would interpret this axiom much more widely, e.g., when it would be subjectively difficult for penitents to remain without benefit of individual confession even for a period of some few days. See also *In extremis*; *In periculo mortis*; and *Odia restringi, et favores convenit ampliari*.

In concreto
In the concrete

Refers to the concrete, real situation, rather than an abstract or speculative position. See also *In abstracto*.

In credendo falli nequit
Cannot fail in belief

Expression found in **Lumen gentium** #12 (*q.v.*) which speaks of the share of the people of God in Christ's prophetic office and which group as a whole cannot fail in their belief in the Word of God. See also *Auditus fidei*, *Fides qua/ Fides quae*, *Fides quae creditur*, *Fides quarens intellectum*, *Indefectabiliter adhaeret*, *Intellectus fidei*, and *Sensus fidelium*.

In dubio factum non praesumitur sed probatur
In doubt a fact is not presumed but must be proved

This axiom is applied in both moral theology and canon law to refer to cases in which the "law" might be doubtful as to whether it actually applies in a particular case or not. Thus, if there is genuine doubt about the "facts" that would ground the obligation then one cannot simply "presume" the facts as a way of removing the doubt, but one must actually prove the facts before removing the doubt about the obligation of the law. See also *Da mihi factum, dabo tibi ius*; *Dubium facti*; *Dubium juris*; *Lex dubia non obligat*; *Melior est conditio possidentis*; and *Sententia incerta non valet*.

In dubio favores sunt amplificandi, odiosa restrigenda
In matters of doubt favors are given a broad interpretation (or application) and burdensome things a strict (and narrow) interpretation (or application)

This axiom is essentially the same as the *Odia restringi, et favores convenit ampliari* (*q.v.*) found in canon 18 of the 1983 Code of Canon Law (cf. canon 68 of the 1917 Code). See also *Cessante fine cessat lex*, *Consuetudo optima legum interpres*, *Dubium facti*, *Dubium juris*, *In dubio factum non praesumitur sed probatur*, *Lex dubia non obligat*, *Melior est conditio possidentis*, and *Sententia incerta non valet*.

In dubio melior est conditio possidentis

See *Melior est conditio possidentis*.

In dubio pars tutior sequenda
In matters of doubt the safer part is to be followed

This was a practical axiom in moral theology that addressed issues of doubt as to the applicability of a certain law or discipline. In cases of practical doubt, and where no harm would be done by following a stricter course of action, one should follow this "safer" course. For example, if one were in doubt about whether one were bound to abstain from meat on a given day, and if the doubt could not be clarified, then prudently one should abstain from meat, since nothing would be lost by doing so. However, see also *In dubio factum non praesumitur sed probatur*, *Lex dubia non obligat*, *Melior est conditio possidentis*, and *Sententia incerta non valet*.

In extrema necessitate omnia, societati humanae destinata, sunt communia
In extreme necessity all goods, destined for a human society, are common

This position builds on Thomas Aquinas' understanding that private property is not an absolute right, but only relative. The purpose of material goods is for the creation of a truly human society, and thus if there is extreme need or want on the part of any individual or group, then this situation would indicate that the proper end of the material goods was not being met. In such a situation it would then be considered morally legitimate to take those necessary goods, even if the owner were unwilling (or unaware) of their appropriation in these circumstances. Marcelino Zalba, SJ, articulated this position in his moral manual, *Theologiae Moralis Summa* II, #1532–36 (Madrid: Biblioteca de Autores Cristianos, 1957): pp. 683–95. A contrasting position, *Permissum est furari non solum in extrema necessitate sed etiam in grave*, held that it was not required to have "extreme" need but only "grave" need. This position was ultimately condemned by Pope Innocent XI. See also the larger discussion under *Quod in necessitate sunt omnia communia* and *Epikeia*, *Necessitas est lex temporis et loci*, *Necessitas non habet legem*, and *Quod non licitum est in lege necessitas facit licitum*.

In extremis
In an extreme (situation)

Refers to any extreme situation, e.g., at the point of death, or when one is in a desperate situation. Also used in canon law to designate extraordinary circumstances in which an otherwise illicit action may be performed. For example, common absolution may be given *in extremis* when there are insufficient numbers of priests available to confess a large number of penitents or in the case of extreme emergency (such as war, an accident, etc.). See also *Articulum mortis* and *In periculo mortis*.

In fide, unitas; in dubiis, libertas; in omnibus, caritas
In faith, unity; in doubt, liberty; in all things, charity

Attributed to St. Augustine, this is an important principle of Christian discernment: unity in faith is important, but in cases of doubt a plurality of opinions and practices should be allowed, and the overriding principle must always be charity toward each other. See also *In necessariis unitas, in dubiis libertas, in omnibus caritas* and *Odium theologicum.*

In flagrante delicto
In blazing (obvious) crime

Refers to someone caught red-handed or while clearly in the process of committing some offense. See also *Corpus delicti* and *Graviora delicta.*

In forma communi
In common (usual) form

This expression refers to the usual way in which Vatican curial documents are received by the pope and subsequently published. The expression *in forma communi* indicates that the pope has reviewed it and orders it to be published, but the document itself retains the juridical weight of the particular curial dicastery which has formulated the document and does *not* carry the added weight of a papal document or papal act. However, if the pope were to approve a curial document *in forma specifica* (*q.v.*) the particular document then does carry the weight of a formal papal document or act. To carry the added weight of *in forma specifica* the document must carry this precise formula: *in forma specifica approbavit*; otherwise the document would be understood to be approved *in forma communi*. See also *In forma specifica.*

In forma specifica
In specific form

This is a legislative term associated primarily with canon law. An ecclesial document or act or law (e.g., which comes from some Vatican dicastery, such as the Congregation for the Doctrine of the Faith) that is given *in forma specifica* means that the pope has approved this document, act, or law in a special way, such that no further appeal to the pope directly is possible (unless the pope himself should specifically mandate such an appeal). The expression *in forma specifica* indicates that the pope has reviewed the document and makes it his own by express approbation, and thus the document acquires the canonical force of a formal papal act (cf. *C.I.C.* canons 1404 and 1405, §2). To carry the added weight of *in forma specifica* the document must carry this precise formula: *in forma specifica approbavit*; otherwise the document would be understood to be approved *in forma communi* (*q.v.*). The 1997 Vatican instruction On Certain Questions Regarding Collaboration of the Non-Ordained Faithful in the Sacred Ministry of the Priest was signed by the Cardinals Prefect of eight different Vatican dicasteries (including the Congregation for the Doctrine of the Faith, etc.) and was issued *in forma specifica*. The text of this Vatican instruction can be found in *Origins* 27 (27 November 1997): 397; 399–409. For an excellent article analyzing this particular document and a fuller explanation of the relevant canonical terminology, see John M. Huels, "Interpreting an Instruction Approved *in forma specifica*," *Studia canonica* 32 (1998): 5–46. See also *In forma communi* and *Prima sedes a nemine iudicatur.*

In globo
In a ball

Refers to something taken together as a group, or "globally," rather than individually.

In hoc signo vinces
In this sign you shall conquer

Refers to the vision which Constantine saw in heaven prior to his successful Battle of the Milvian Bridge in AD 312, in which he established his power as Roman Emperor. Based on his vision that "in this sign you shall conquer" (Ἐν τῷ νικα in Greek), Constantine inscribed on the soldiers' standards the first two letters of "Christ" (**ΧΡΙΣΤΟΣ**) in Greek (**X** [*Chi*] and **P** [*Rho*]). The monogram of this superimposed *Chi-Rho* has become a familiar symbol for the name of Christ, and Constantine's usage came to be known as the *Labarum* (for "standard" in Latin). The Latin version of Ἐν τῷ νικα ("in this sign you shall conquer") is *in hoc signo vinces*, and the first three letters of the Latin phrase, "IHS," is commonly, though *mistakenly*, thought to be an abbreviation of *in hoc signo vinces*. ("IHS" is actually the first three letters in Greek for the name of "Jesus" [**ΙΗΣΟΥΣ**]).

In loco Dei
In the place of God

Refers *not* to idolatry, but to someone or something that takes or acts in the place of God. A common example given traditionally is the priest who in the sacrament of reconciliation acts to a certain extent *in loco Dei* in ministering God's forgiveness to the penitent.

In loco parentis
In the place of a parent

Refers to some person or institution which has the responsibilities of a parent in the care of a child. A university may have presumptive guardianship *in loco parentis* of its students who are under the legal age of adulthood and therefore may be held responsible for certain actions committed by these students while they are on campus.

In memoriam
In the memory of

Often found in dedications, inscriptions, etc., of some monument or work of art done in memory of a deceased person.

In necessariis unitas, in dubiis libertas, in omnibus caritas
In essential (necessary) matters unity, in doubtful matters freedom (liberty), in all matters charity

Well-known theological saying of Augustine which is used as a principle for authentic ecumenism and as an antidote to theological controversy. See also *In fide, unitas; in dubiis, libertas; in omnibus, caritas*; *Libertas est inaestimabilis*; and *Odium theologicum*.

In nobis sine nobis
In us, without us

Expression which refers to something that humans can possess in a human way, such as the infused theological virtues of faith, hope, and charity, but which have their origin outside of us, i.e., as gifts of God. See also *Gratia supponit naturam et perficit eam*.

In paradisum
To paradise

Refers to the first words of the hymn which is traditionally sung at the end of a funeral liturgy as the body is taken out of the church, praying that the deceased be welcomed by the angels into heaven. See also *Dies Irae* and *Lux Aeterna.*

In pectore
In the breast (heart)

Refers to something held in secret. Occasionally the pope will name a cardinal *in pectore*, which means that this person has been bestowed the dignity of the cardinalate, but for some reason (e.g., political persecution) it is inopportune that this bestowal become public.

In periculo mortis
In danger of death

This term has an important legal distinction in that it applies not only to those who are physically near death, but also includes those who, due to circumstances like war or natural disasters, might also be in some danger of death. Thus, in canon law when someone is "in danger of death," certain impediments and censures may be absolved more easily, or by virtually any validly ordained priest, or certain privileges more easily granted, such as general absolution without individual confession. See also *Articulum mortis, In articulo mortis*, and *In extremis.*

In persona Christi
In the person of Christ

Standard theological expression for the sacramental role played by the ordained priest in the community of the church, i.e., one who stands in place of Christ in presiding at the Eucharist, etc. One of the theological arguments used against the possibility of the ordination of women is that a woman could not stand *in persona Christi* since her gender would preclude the necessary symbolism of the role of a priest (i.e., "maleness" is seen in this view as *essential* to acting *in persona Christi* in the faith community). See also *Alter Christus,* **Inter insigniores**, and **Ordinatio sacerdotalis**.

In rebus fidei et morum

(The church can authoritatively teach) "in matters of faith and morals."

See *De rebus fidei et morum, De fide definita*, and *Ecclesia docens.*

In se
In, of itself

Refers to the essential or inherent quality of something. In moral matters an act that is *intrinsece malum in se* would be an act inherently evil "in itself," i.e., of its very nature (and irrespective of extenuating circumstances and/or motives).

In se et non in alio
In itself and not in something else

Refers to the characteristic of individual uniqueness.

In se sed non propter se
In itself, but not because of itself

Expression which refers to "toleration" or "intention" of some premoral or ontic evils, such as amputation of a diseased organ, which "evil" (the amputation) would be "intended" but not as an end in itself (*propter se*) but as a means to some good end (recovery of health). This axiom is related to the principle of the double effect. For example, one could fully "intend" to commit an act, which under different circumstances could be considered "evil" (such as amputation of a gangrenous limb). However, in this case the action of amputation is not intended "for itself" *because* (*propter se*) it is an amputation, but the evil is tolerated for some other end (such as saving the patient's life). This is an important principle in the evaluation of moral actions. See also *Actus non facit reum, nisi mens sit rea*; *Fontes moralitatis*; and *Intrinsece malum*.

In situatione
In the (concrete) situation (or circumstances)

This expression is used often in moral theology to refer to one of the three "fonts" of morality (cf. *Fontes moralitatis*) of moral action, namely, the act in itself, the intention of the moral agent in performing the act, and the circumstances in which the agent and the act are located. This expression recognizes that moral actions must take into account the concrete circumstances of an action in order to come to a proper moral evaluation of the act and the agent's intentions. See also *Finis operis*, *Finis operantis*, *Intrinsece malum in se*, and *Voluntarium directum/indirectum*.

In toto
In totality

Refers to something in its entirety, or taken completely, on the whole, altogether.

In vestimentis non stat sapientia mentis
Wisdom (of the mind) does not lie in clothing (vestments)

Proverb which points to the fact that true human wisdom is not necessarily found in rich clothing, vestments, or the acquisition of offices. In other words, donning a miter does not *ipso facto* confer added wisdom to one's words or decisions. See also *Ordo sapientiae* and *Sapienti sat*.

In Vetere Novum (Testamentum) latet, et in Novo Vetus patet
In the Old (Testament) the New (Testament) lies hidden, and in the New (Testament) the Old (Testament) is unfolded

Theological axiom which refers to the integral connection between the Old Testament and the New Testament. For Christians neither the Old Testament or the New Testament can be read and interpreted apart from a consideration of the biblical message of the other Testament. See also *Praeparatio evangelica*.

In via
On the way

Refers to something in process, not yet finished, or someone who has not yet reached the terminus of his or her journey. For Christians life on earth will always have a bit of a transitory character until creation is completed in the Second Coming. See also *Via* and *Viator*.

In vino veritas
In wine, truth

Refers to the fact that people under the influence of alcohol are less inhibited and therefore more likely to tell the frank truth about what they feel or believe.

In vitro
In the glass (i.e., test tube)

Common expression related to some sort of artificial setting, such as laboratory experimentation and/or technology. For example, "in vitro fertilization" refers to the process by which an egg is fertilized by sperm in an artificial ("test-tube") environment, and then implanted in the uterus where the pregnancy is then carried to term in the normal fashion. In vitro fertilization was the subject of **Donum vitae**, the 1987 document of the Congregation for the Doctrine of the Faith, and its follow-up in 2008 **Dignitas personae** (*q.v.*).

Inaestimabile donum
Inestimable gift

Congregation for Divine Worship's instruction on Certain Norms Concerning the Eucharist (1980).

Incarnationis Mysterium
The Mystery of the Incarnation

Papal bull of indiction of John Paul II issued on 29 November 1998, which gives the formal decree for the Jubilee Year of 2000 (which began on 24 December 1999 and concluded on 6 January 2001). In this bull the pope also decreed certain special indulgences which could be gained during the Jubilee Year. The text of the bull can be found in *Origins* 28 (10 December 1998): 445; 447–53. See also *Per modum suffragii*, *Totaliter*, and *Toties quoties*.

Inclinationes naturales
The natural inclinations (tendencies to an end)

Term associated with a certain understanding of the natural law which holds that one must always follow the "natural end" of a certain faculty in order to correspond to God's creative intention and will (cf. *Deus nihil facit inane*). Following this view, for example, the marriage act, in its use of the sexual "faculty," must always, in each and every instance, be "open" to the possibility of the transmission of new life (cf. *bonum prolis*). See also *Appetitus rectus*.

Inconsideratio regulae
Lack of consideration of the rule [of right reason]

St. Thomas Aquinas' expression for the nature of sinful acts. That is, acts which fail to consider adequately in the light of right reason that which is to be done (the good) or avoided (the evil).

Indefectabiliter adhaeret
Unfailingly adheres (to the faith)

Expression used in **Lumen gentium** #12 (*q.v.*) to describe a key theological characteristic of the church as the people of God, namely that the whole people of God "cannot fail in belief" (*in credendo falli nequit, q.v.*) and in receiving and adhering to the Word of God "penetrates it more deeply through right judgment, and applies it more fully to daily life." See also *Auditus fidei*, *Fides qua/Fides quae*, *Fides quaerens intellectum*, *In credendo falli nequit*, *Intellectus fidei*, and *Sensus fidelium*.

Indicativa oboedientiae
Indication of obedience

Protestant position on the so-called "third use of the law" put forward by Melancthon, which held that the law might indicate to the believer those moral actions which were in conformity with the will of God and therefore which required obedience. See also *Usus legis*.

Ineffabilis Deus
Ineffable God

Encyclical of Pius IX defining the dogma of the Immaculate Conception in 1854. Considered to be the first example of a papal pronouncement given in an *ex cathedra (q.v.)* format, which explicitly invoked infallibility. See also **Munificentissimus Deus**.

Infamia iuris et facti
Infamy according to law and facts

See the discussion under *Iuris et/vel facti*.

Infra
Below, beneath

Common Latin preposition.

Inhonestum
Dishonorable

The Latin word also carries connotations of disgrace and dishonor. In moral theology an *inhonestum* usually refers to something that is counterproductive to a moral good or *bonum honestum (q.v.)*. Thus, in paragraph 14 of Pope Paul VI's 1968 encyclical **Humanae vitae** *(q.v.)*, any artificial means of birth control is labeled an *intrinsece inhonestum*, i.e.,

essentially disordered or counterproductive to the good end envisioned by the conjugal act performed in the context of marriage. See also *Partes inhonestae*.

Inquisitio
Search, inquiry, investigation

Often this term is paired with *auctoritas (q.v.)* to express complementary roles in theological investigation and authoritative teaching. In this latter example, *inquisitio* refers to the role of theologians to "investigate" a theological position and allows them to advance certain opinions that may be considered but which do not carry with them the claim of the "authoritative" teaching of the pope and bishops who exercise the magisterium. The magisterium, in this sense, then exercises the charism of the *auctoritas* of authoritative teaching while the theologians exercise the charism of the *inquisitio*, or exploratory theological investigation. See also *Auctoritas, Ecclesia discens, Ecclesia docens, Magisterium, Magisterium cathedrae pastoralis & Magisterium cathedrae magistralis, Magisterium docens, Munus, Officium*, and *Peritus*.

I.N.R.I.
Jesus of Nazareth, King of the Jews

Latin abbreviation for *Iesus Nazarenus Rex Iudaeorum*, the inscription placed by Pilate over the cross upon which Jesus was crucified. See also *Adonai* and *Rex Gentium*.

Instantia prima (secunda, tertia)
(Court of) first (second, third) instance

In canon law proceedings (usually involving marriage cases) there are three possible levels of adjudication: in the first instance at the tribunal in one's diocese, in the second instance at the level of a court of appeal (usually held at a different diocesan tribunal), and in the third instance at the ultimate level of appeal to the Roman Rota of the Vatican.

Instinctus rationis
Rational instinct

"Instinct" in this phrase refers to the innate human power of reasoning which is part of the natural human moral sense. "Instinct" should not be understood as some sort of moral ESP or ethical sixth sense. See also *Instinctus Spiritus Sancti*.

Instinctus Spiritus Sancti
Instinct of the Holy Spirit

Refers to the ways in which the Holy Spirit acts in human hearts through donation of the so-called "gifts of the Spirit." The *instinctus Spiritus Sancti* neither opposes nor overrides the *instinctus rationis* (q.v.) but would build on this rational moral sense and elevate it to perfection.

Instrumentum laboris
Working instrument

Refers to a draft document, or an initial version which may be used as a working, or preparatory, document for a commission, meeting, etc. This expression is often found in reference to Roman documents for meetings such as special synods and the like. See also *Lineamenta*.

Intellectus fidei
Understanding of the faith

Refers to the act or process by which the Christian faith is understood. This term was methodologically paired with *auditus fidei* (q.v.) by Pope John Paul II in his 1998 encyclical **Fides et ratio** (q.v.), in which the pontiff stated that the concept of *auditus fidei* (hearing of faith) referred to the process by which "theology makes its own the content of revelation as this has been gradually expounded in sacred tradition, sacred Scripture and the church's living magisterium," while the second methodological principle of *intellectus fidei* refers to the process by which "theology seeks to respond through speculative inquiry to the specific demands of disciplined thought" (**Fides et ratio**, #65). See also *Auditus fidei, Congregatio fidelium, Fides qua/Fides quae, Fides quae creditur, Fides quarens intellectum, In credendo falli nequit, Indefectabiliter adhaeret*, and *Sensus fidelium*.

Intellege ut credas. Crede ut intellegas
Understand so that you may believe; believe so that you may understand

Refers to the reciprocal relationship necessary between faith and reason.

Intentio
Intention

Usually refers to the moral intention of an action. See also *Finis operantis, Fontes moralitatis*, and *Obiectum actus*.

Inter
Between, among, during

Common Latin preposition.

Inter alia
Among other things

See *I.a.*

Inter alios
Among other persons

See *I.a.*

Inter insigniores
Among other characteristics

Congregation for the Doctrine of the Faith's (CDF) 1976 Declaration On the Question of the Admission of Women to the Ministerial Priesthood advanced a number of arguments in support of the ban, principally that Jesus Christ did not will the ordination of women and that women themselves because of their gender could not adequately represent Jesus Christ *in persona Christi (q.v.)*. The document was issued after the Pontifical Biblical Commission (PBC) had responded to a Vatican request for biblical evidence supporting the thesis that women could not be ordained. The PBC found there was no convincing biblical evidence to support that conclusion but the CDF's Declaration affirmed the traditional ban on women priests which was found in the 1917 Code of Canon Law (#813 §2) and would be repeated in the 1983 Code (*C.I.C.* #1024), as well as subsequently in Pope John Paul II's 1994 apostolic exhortation **Ordinatio sacerdotalis** (*q.v.,* On the Ordination of Priests). See also *Alter Christus, Ex convenientia, Mulier taceat in ecclesia,* **Mulieris dignitatem**, and *Responsum ad dubium.*

Inter mirifica
Among wonders

Title of the Vatican II Decree on the Means of Social Communication, issued in 1963.

Inter nos
Among us

Refers to something meant confidentially, or something to be kept secretly between or among ourselves, akin to the French expression *entre nous*, which is often used in English as well.

Inter pares
Among equals

For example, the pope, as metropolitan or patriarch of Rome, was often termed *Primus inter pares*, "first among equals" (of the other ecclesial patriarchs), i.e., primacy in terms of order, but not in terms of essence. See also *Collegium* and *Collegialis affectus.*

Intra
Within

Common Latin preposition.

Intra nos
Among us

See *Inter nos.*

Intrinsece inhonestum
Intrinsically disordered (dishonest)

Expression use in paragraph 14 of Paul VI's **Humanae vitae** (*q.v.*) to condemn artificial contraception. See **Casti**

connubii Inhonestum, *Bonum hones-*
tum, and *Intrinsece malum.*

Intrinsece malum in se
Intrinsically evil in itself

Traditional expression for an action
which of its very nature was always,
and in every instance, morally evil (regardless of the intention and circumstances of the moral agent). A much
debated and nuanced point in contemporary moral theology, and is intimated
related to the understanding of the object of a moral act (*finis operis, q.v.*) as
intended or chosen by a moral agent
acting with knowledge and freedom
(*finis operantis, q.v.*). See also *Actus*
non facit reum, nisi mens sit rea; *Contra*
naturam; *Ex toto genere suo grave*;
Finis operis; *Finis operantis*; *Fontes*
moralitatis; *Genus morum*; *In se sed*
non propter se; *Inhonestum*; *Intentio*;
Ius naturae est immutabile; *Obiectum*
actus; *Praeter intentionem*; and *Volun-*
tarium directum/indirectum.

Ipsissimum/a verbum/a
The very word(s)

Verbatim. In theological usage, this expression usually refers to the purported
very words of God or Jesus Christ.
Some of the discussion concerning the
historical Jesus is centered around trying to ascertain what might be the *ips-*
sissima verba of Jesus found in the
Gospels. See also *textus receptus.*

Ipso facto/Ipso iure
By that very fact/By the very law

Automatically or absolutely. If a certain
crime carried with it only one penalty,

such as death, then conviction of the
crime would *ipso facto* condemn the
criminal to death. Another example
might be that if an individual were to
put his or her hand into strong acid the
hand would be burned *ipso facto*. *Ipso*
facto is related to, but distinguished
from, the legal term *ipso iure* (by the
law), which means that something follows legally upon some other action
such as in canon law when a legitimate
superior accepts an endowment and as-
signs it to some purpose this endowment acquires *ipso iure* a certain
juridical character. The creation of a
trust might be an example more easily
understood in the secular arena. See
also *Iuris et/vel facti.*

Ite Missa Est
Go the Mass is (ended)

Final words of the presider uttered at
the conclusion of the Latin Eucharist,
to which the congregation responds *Deo*
Gratias (*q.v.*, "Thanks be to God").
Missa seems to have been a late Latin
word for *missio* (mission) and thus in
this phrase refers to the "mission" to
live and preach the Gospel which is
given to the community at the conclusion of the eucharistic celebration. In
time *missa* came to refer to the entire
rite of the eucharistic celebration, i.e.,
the "Mass."

Iudicium de actu ponendo
Judgment (of conscience) con-
cerning the act to be undertaken

In the manualist tradition of moral theology there was a distinction drawn
between two kinds of judgment made
in conscience. The first judgment refers

primarily to the "objective" nature—the rightness or wrongness of the moral act in itself—and was referred to as *iudicium de actu ponendo*. However, the individual moral agent could be in "error" about his or her judgment of this act. This error in turn could be totally non-culpable (i.e. invincibly ignorant), or more or less culpable (thus, vincibly ignorant—i.e., able to have been overcome). This basic distinction is key to the church's traditional teaching on sanctity of conscience, the necessity for good formation of conscience, and the notion of an erroneous conscience and vincible and invincible ignorance. See also *Iudicium de positione actus*.

Iudicium de positione actus
Judgment (of conscience) about the position of the act

Coupled with the notion of *Iudicium de actu ponendo* discussed above, this was the second type of moral judgment made in conscience by a moral agent. This second judgment is related more closely to the subjective judgment of the moral agent that this or that act will be "right" and therefore "good" (i.e., the "position" of the contemplated moral act in relation to one's life and the good as one sees it). In traditional moral theology, this distinction about the two types of judgment allowed for the possibility that one could "err" about the objective moral nature of an act and yet still be acting in good faith (or sometimes called good conscience). The "error" would be an error of judgment *de actu ponendo*. In acting in good faith, though, one could not "err" in the second sort of judgment through *de positione actus*. Thus, in summary, we could say that the person believes that doing "X" is morally good: this is the *iudicium de positione actus*. If the person believed that "X" was not morally good but did it anyway, this would be malicious. However, this "judgment" so far only has taken into account the "subjective" judgment of the moral agent about the action. The action itself could in fact be morally (or "objectively") wrong. This "objective" moral judgment is the *iudicium de actu ponendo* (judgment concerning the act to be undertaken). In sum, for a person acting in good faith, his or her *iudicium de actu ponendo* (judgment concerning the act to be undertaken) can be "erroneous" while the *iudicium de positione actus*, (judgment about the position of the act) could not in principle be erroneous—i.e., a person who is acting in good faith will always try to do what she or he judges to be right. See also *Iudicium de actu ponendo*.

Iura et bona
Rights and values (goods)

Declaration of the Congregation for the Doctrine of the Faith on Euthanasia (1980).

Iure divino
By divine law

Important distinction in moral theology and canon law, since that which is held to be *iure divino* cannot be changed, abrogated, or dispensed, inasmuch as it purports to be the expression of God's specific will. That which binds differently, as according to *iure ecclesieastico* (*q.v.*), could be modified, abrogated, dispensed, or replaced. See also *Lex aeterna* and *Lex naturalis*.

(De) Iure ecclesiastico
(According to) ecclesiastical law

Refers to something established by a legitimate ecclesiastical authority and whose observance would be required by those bound by the law and subject to this ecclesiastical authority. *Iure ecclesiastico* is often distinguished from *iure divino* (divine law, *q.v.*), since that which is established merely by ecclesiastical authority (such as the practice of Friday abstinence from meat) could be changed by later competent church authorities, while that which is based on divine law (*iure divino*) is seen as coming from God (such as the indissolubility of marriage) and therefore cannot be changed by human authorities.

Iuris et/vel facti
(By) Law and/or fact

This expression is widely used in canon law and the manualist moral tradition to indicate a distinction that arose either because of a violation of a penal law (*iuris*) or because the transgression itself led to certain natural consequences. One example given in the manuals was the notion of "infamy" that could be incurred by an individual who had violated some serious precept, such as desecration of the sacred species. Since this was a clear violation of canon law, the transgression was called *infamia iuris* (infamy according to law). One canonical penalty would be incurring an irregularity which would bar the individual from some other rights or actions (like receiving holy orders). However,

infamia facti would arise when an individual's own actions led to the loss of his or her good name or reputation in the eyes of the community. The transgressions of many politicians against the sixth commandment might illustrate this notion of *infamia facti*. See also *Dubium iuris vel facti*.

Ius
Justice, Legal system, Subjective right

This Latin word has no precise equivalent in English, so special care must be taken as to the context in which it is used, as well as the words which may modify it, such as *ius canonicum* (canon law) or *ius ad rem* (juridical right to a certain thing). See also the entries connected with *Lex* and also *De bono et aequo, Ius ad rem, Ius et titulum, Iustitiam subsidiariam*, and *Reddere suum cuique*.

Ius ad bellum
Justification for war

Term used to designate the moral calculus employed for ascertaining whether sufficient grounds exist to justify the use of force, i.e., to go to war. See also *Bellum iustum*; *Casus belli*; *Ius in bello*; *Ius post bellum*; and *Si vis pacem, para bellum*.

Ius ad rem
Right to a thing

Principle that recognizes one's presumed juridical right to a certain object, etc., as in ownership and control, (in this context see *Ius utendi, fruendi, abutendi, q.v.*) but which is open to expansion, e.g., right to goods one does not own in cases of extreme necessity. See the discussion under the principle *Quod in necessitate sunt omnia communia.* See also *Ius et titulum* and *Iustitiam subsidiariam.*

Ius canonicum
Canon law

Refers to church law in the sense that it has its own legal system, code of laws, juridical tribunals, and the like.

Ius commune
Common law

In canon law, that which pertains to all the laws and legitimate customs and practices of the whole church, including those of the Oriental Rites. See also *Ius particulare.*

Ius communicationis
Right to communion

Refers primarily to the right of the faithful to partake in the sharing of the Eucharist, which is the symbol of full participation in the Christian community. Someone who loses this right then would be "excommunicated" from the church. In ancient practices of the sacrament of reconciliation, the penitents were restored to eucharistic assembly after the time of their (public) penance and regained therefore the *ius communicationis.* See also *Pax ecclesiae.*

Ius et titulum
Rights and title

Likewise in this context see *Ius utendi, fruendi, abutendi.* Again, this right is open to expansion, e.g., right to goods one does not own in cases of extreme necessity. See the discussion under the principle *Quod in necessitate sunt omnia communia.* See also the various entries under *Dubium* as well as *In dubio factum non praesumitur sed probatur, Ius ad rem, Iustitiam subsidiariam,* and *Melior est conditio possidentis.*

Ius Exclusivae
Right of Exclusion

In ecclesiastical politics this anticipatory veto power was used in papal conclaves by the cardinals of key Catholic countries such as Austria, France, and Spain to indicate on behalf of their respective monarchs potential papal candidates which would be undesirable (termed *personae minus gratae, q.v.*) if elected pope. Though rejected officially by several popes, this practice was nevertheless used on several occasions through the early twentieth century and was last used in the papal conclave of 1903 to block the election of Cardinal Rampolla by Polish Cardinal Jan Puzyna de Kosielsko from Kraków on behalf of the Austro-Hungarian Emperor Franz Josef Hapsburg, leading to the ultimate election of Giuseppe Sarto (St. Pius X). It is no longer in force today.

Ius gentium
Law of the nations

Refers in general to human laws, and often understood as referring more particularly to international law, though different philosophers and theologians have employed this term in differing ways. To be fully and truly just, human laws must correspond to the natural law. See also ***Corpus Iuris Civilis.***

Ius in bello
Justice in [the conduct of] war

Refers to the justifiable "laws" of war once the "just war" has been undertaken. Thus, *ius in bello* aims ultimately at a restraint in prosecuting the just war. See also *Ius ad bellum* and *Pax Dei*.

Ius in corpus (corpore)
Right to the body

Concept in traditional marriage law which meant that each spouse had "rights" over the body of the other spouse for purposes of sexual intercourse. See also *Debitum*.

Ius in se
A right itself

Refers to the right considered in itself.

Ius naturae est immutabile
Natural justice (law) is unchangeable

Since the natural law is understood as being ordained by God and ordered to human moral flourishing, its precepts are viewed as being both unchanging and not admitting of any possible exceptions. Violations of the natural law would be considered to be *contra naturam (q.v.)* to the *Summum bonum (q.v.)* and proper end of human beings, and thus also *intrinsece malum (q.v.)* and would not admit exceptions that otherwise might be found in human laws. See also *Lex naturalis* and *Lex valet ut in pluribus*.

Ius particulare
Particular law

In canon law, that which pertains to the laws and legitimate customs and practices of a particular church and therefore distinguished from the *ius commune (q.v.)*, which would include the universal church.

Ius positum
Positive law

This term refers usually to human laws that are promulgated (i.e., "posited" or placed) for those bound by the law to follow. A speed limit would be an example of positive law. The term "positive" should *not* be understood as the opposite of "negative," but rather has something put into place. The *ius positum* is distinguished from *Lex aeterna (q.v.)*, which is God's eternal law (and which under certain limited circumstances could also include instances of a divine *ius positum* that God ordains for a given individual). Similarly, *ius positum* should not be confused with *Lex naturalis (q.v.)*, which is the natural law or something like the *Lex naturae (q.v.)*; the laws of nature; or the *Lex creationis (q.v.)*, the law of creation. When there is some legitimate doubt about the meaning or scope of a *ius positum* the concepts of *Epikeia (q.v.)* and *Lex dubia non obligat (q.v.)* come into play in interpreting and/or applying the *ius positum*. See also *Statuta sunt stricte interpretanda*.

Ius post bellum
Justice after the war

More recent expression added to the traditional concept of Just War Theory (*bellum iustum, q.v.*), whose traditional component parts were an analysis of the reasons for going to war, *ius ad bellum (q.v.)*, followed by the just conduct of the war itself, *ius in bello (q.v.)*. *Ius post bellum* is an expression of restorative justice which acknowledges the necessity of the repair of damages and restoration of public order that suffered during the war. See also *Si vis pacem, para bellum.*

Ius primae noctis
Rights of the first night (of marriage)

Expression which refers to the putative "rights" that a European lord supposedly enjoyed over all the newly wed brides in his domain. Though this expression can be found in certain medieval myths and legends, its basis in historical practice is highly questionable.

Ius utendi, fruendi, abutendi
Right to use, enjoy, or abuse.

Maxim from Roman law which indicates a rather absolute right of the owner of private property to use, or abuse, one's own property in whatever way she or he pleases. See also *Bonum utile, Dominium utile, Res frutificat dominum,* and *Uti et frui.*

Ius vigens
Law in vigor (living)

Refers to a law which is currently in force and therefore binding. This is an important concept in canon law, since a law that has fallen into desuetude (disuse) is understood to be nonbinding, even if it is technically still on the books. See also **Acta Apolostolicae Sedis**, *Donec aliter providetur, Hucusque vigens, Lex non obligat nisi promulgata,* and *Vacatio legis.*

Iustitiam subsidiariam
Subsidiary justice

Principle that recognizes that "justice" (*ius*) is a somewhat complex concept and that there is a hierarchy of values which must be assessed prior to determining just which principle of justice should be applied. For example, the principle of restitution would normally require that goods that had been taken without payment or permission should be restored to the owner. However, the principle of *Iustitiam subsidiariam* would recognize that if this were a case of extreme need then the obligation to restitution would cease (cf. the discussion under the principle *Quod in necessitate sunt omnia communia*).

Iustum
Right/Just (as a thing)

This refers to moral analysis of an act whose ethical "rightness" or "justice" is revealed by a consideration of the traditional moral fonts (*fontes moralitatis, q.v.*) of the act itself, the intention, and circumstances. See also *Finis operis, Fontes moralitatis,* and *Obiectum actus.*

Iuxta
Next to, nearby, according to, with

An adverb or preposition frequently used in conjunction with other word(s) to express some modification of a concept, term, or idea. For example, *Placet* by itself means "it pleases me" (I'm in favor of this), while *Placet iuxta modum* means "I'm in favor of this if some amendment(s) could be added." Another example could be *iuxta legem* (in accordance with the law) which is used in the interpretation of canon law in speaking of a custom which might not actually be in the Code of Canon Law but which nevertheless is in accord with the spirit of the written law and also enjoys widespread acceptance (see *Consuetudo optima legum interpres* on this point). Depending on circumstances, *iuxta* can be contrasted with *praeter*, which means "outside of," "beyond," or "not included" as in *praeter intentionem* (*q.v.*), which refers to a foreseen but morally unintended effect of another action.

Iuxta legem
    In accord with the law

See the discussion under *Iuxta* above. See also *Consuetudo optima legum interpres*.

J

**NB: *"J" is usually rendered as "I" in Latin; in those cases where a Latin word beginning with a "J" is found, look for it as if it were spelled with an initial "I" instead. Thus, for "Jus" look instead under "I" for "Ius."*

J.C.D.
Doctor of Canon Law

Latin abbreviation for *Juris Canonici Doctor*, i.e., one who has a doctorate in canon law. The *J.C.D.* is the highest ecclesiastical academic degree in canon law. See also *J.C.L.*

J.C.L.
License in canon law

Latin abbreviation for *Juris Canonici Licentia*, one who has a licentiate in canon law. The license, like the *J.C.D.*, is an ecclesiastical academic degree and in this case "licenses" one to teach canon law in a pontifical faculty, such as a seminary. See also *J.C.D.*

Juris Canonici Doctor
Doctor of Canon Law

See *J.C.D.*

Juris Canonici Licentia
License in Canon Law

See *J.C.L.*

J.U.D.
Doctor of both laws

Latin abbreviation for *Juris Utrius Doctor*, and refers to one who possesses academic degrees in both canon and civil law. See also *J.C.D.*

Juris Utrius Doctor
Doctor of both laws

See *J.U.D.*

K

NB: Very few words begin with "K" in Latin, often alternate spellings use the letter "C".

L

Labarum
Banner, Standard

Refers to the monogram of the superimposed *Chi-Rho,* the first two letters of "Christ" (**ΧΡΙΣΤΟΣ**) in Greek (**X**[*Chi*] and **P** [*Rho*]), which Constantine inscribed on the soldiers' standards prior to the Battle of the Milvian Bridge in AD 312 which established his power as Roman Emperor. See also *In hoc signo vinces.*

Labor
Labor, work, effort

Labor refers to the work or effort which must be expended in order to achieve a desired effect, as distinguished from *opus* (*q.v.*), which refers to "work" in the sense of an entity or creation.

Labor vincit omnia
Work conquers all

Expression of Virgil which suggests through hard work all adversity can be overcome. See also *Omnia vincit labor,* and for a play on Virgil's phrase see also *Amor vincit omnia.*

Laborem exercens
Exercising labor

Encyclical of John Paul II on human work (1981) on the ninetieth anniversary of Leo XIII's groundbreaking social encyclical ***Rerum novarum*** (*q.v.*).

Lacuna legis
Gap (lacuna) in the law

Important concept in canon law which refers to something missing in the written code of the law which therefore leaves uncovered a relevant aspect of a case or situation, and therefore the decision regarding this case or situation must be rendered using other principles and laws.

Laetare
To gladden [e.g. to lift up your spirits]

Expression used to mark the Fourth Sunday of Lent and symbolically marked by the optional wearing of rose-colored vestments in place of the purple worn on the other days of Lent. These rose vestments can also be worn on the Third Sunday of Advent, called *Gaudete Sunday.* However, since these vestments are worn only on two days in the entire liturgical year many parishes opt not to incur the cost of procuring these optional vestments. The special meaning of these "Rose" Sundays is to indicate to the Christian community that their period of waiting is coming to an end, either with Christmas in Advent or Easter in Lent, and thus they should be encouraged to continue in their preparations to welcome the Lord by redoubling their efforts at penance and renewal. See also *Advent* and *Gaudete*.

Lamentabili
Lamentable

Decree of the Holy Office (today the Congregation for the Doctrine of the Faith, cf. *DS* 3401–66) condemning certain "errors of modernism," which same movement was condemned later in the same year by Pope Pius X in his encyclical **Pascendi Dominici gregis** (*q.v.*) (1907).

Latae sententiae
By imposed sentence

In canon law, a penalty imposed *ipso facto* by one who knowingly and willfully commits a particular offense, such as procuring an abortion (canon 1398). A penalty *latae sententiae* is contrasted with one *ferendae sententiae* (*q.v.*), which must be formally imposed by the competent juridical authority in order to be considered binding. Though *latae sententiae* is often translated as "automatic," this would not be entirely accurate in canon law, since the same code indicates a number of conditions that would prevent or mitigate incurring a *latae sententiae* penalty (cf. Code of Canon Law canons 1323 and 1324 for a listing of these factors which either block or mitigate canonical penalties). Most penalties in the 1983 Code of Canon Law are *ferenedae sententiae* rather than *latae sententiae*. See also *Notaria non egent probatione*; *Odia re-*

stringi, et favores convenit ampliari; and *Sub poena*.

Lauda Sion
Praise O Sion

Liturgical sequence written by Thomas Aquinas around 1264 which tells of the institution of the Eucharist and is recited or sung after the Epistle on the Solemnity of Corpus Christi (*q.v.*). This is one of only four medieval sequences that were preserved in the reform of the *Missale Romanum* (*q.v.*) published in 1570. The other three are the *Victimae Paschali* (*q.v.*) for Easter, the *Veni Sancte Spiritus* (*q.v.*) for Pentecost, and the *Dies Irae* (*q.v.*) for the Requiem Mass.

Laudate Dominum
Praise the Lord

Common expression found in hymns and psalms, such as *Laudate Dominum, omnes gentes* ("Praise the Lord, all you peoples").

Laus Deo
Praise be to God

Common expression in Latin liturgy and prayer formulae.

Laus Perennis
Endless praise

Refers to a monastic custom whereby teams of monks would take turns chanting the Divine Office, with the goal of having it sung continuously throughout the day in the monastery. The practice began in the sixth century and was much practiced by Celtic monasteries before falling into desuetude, though the custom of perpetual eucharistic adoration and Forty Hours Devotion to some extent is inspired by this same motive of constantly giving praise to God. See also *Coram Sanctissimo.*

Lavabo
I will wash

Refers to the part of the liturgy in which the priest washes his hands after the offering of the gifts on the altar. In the traditional Tridentine Mass the first lines of the prayer are *Lavabo inter innocentes manus meas: et circumdabo altare tuum Domine* [I will wash my hands among the innocent and will walk around your altar O God]. *Lavabo* also was used to designate this whole part of the washing ritual.

Lectio continua
Continued reading

Refers to the practice of ongoing reading of a text, and usually refers to the sequential reading of the Bible. Thus, the Sunday Lectionary is a *lectio continua* over a three-year period of most of the Scripture. In the Sunday Lectionary, the first reading is taken from the Old Testament (except during the Easter Season) and is selected to complement thematically the Gospel passage of the given Sunday. However, the second reading in the Sunday Lectionary is generally a *lectio continua* of a given New Testament Letter, so that over a period of a number of weeks most of the entire Letter is read. Since the second reading is a continuous reading of the Letter it usually is not related thematically to the first reading and the Gospel. As a theological principle, *lectio continua* refers to the need to be in continual contact with the *whole* of Scripture in some systematic fashion in order to hear the entire biblical message of revelation, and to act against the natural tendency to create a "canon-within-the-canon" of elements of Scripture which one holds central to one's faith life and yet which may tend to neglect or ignore other scriptural elements which may modify or call into question some of those scriptural assumptions.

Lectio divina
Holy (spiritual) reading

Method of prayer based on a meditative reading of Scripture or some other spiritual reading, either individually or communally, prominent in the Benedictine tradition. The term may also be used to refer to the time or practice of this spiritual reading. See also *sacra pagina.*

Lex
Law

Also can be used figuratively to refer to a norm or principle.

Lex aeterna
The eternal law

Refers to God's law, or the will of God. In the classic understanding, the natural law is the human participation in the *lex aeterna.* See also *Contra ordinem* and *Lex naturalis.*

Lex creationis
The law of creation

Concept tied especially to the Lutheran theology of the orders of creation which sought in a fashion somewhat analogous to the natural law tradition to come to an understanding of the moral law, as derived from the doctrine of God as the Creator. See also *Contra ordinem.*

Lex dubia lex nulla
A doubtful law is no law

See *Lex dubia non obligat* and *Ubi ius incertum, ibi ius nullum.*

Lex dubia non obligat
A doubtful law does not oblige

Important principle in both canon law and moral theology; in the latter discipline it is often tied to the use of probabilism. If a legitimate doubt exists as to the fact of a given law's existence, or whether the law was meant to apply in this or that particular situation or case, then the law is "doubtful" and would not apply in such an instance. See also *Ad literam*; *Da mihi factum, dabo tibi ius*; *De minimis non curat lex*; *Dubium facti*; *Dubium juris*; *Epikeia*; *In dubio pars tutior sequenda*; *In dubio factum non praesumitur sed probatur*; *Ius positum*; *Melior est conditio possidentis*; *Praesumitur ignorantia ubi scientia non probatur*; *Sensum, non verba spectamus*; *Sententia incerta non valet;* and *Ubi ius incertum, ibi ius nullum.*

Lex Ecclesiae Fundamentalis
Fundamental Law of the Church

Paul VI (1963–78) proposed establishing a *Lex Ecclesiae Fundamentalis* which would serve somewhat like a constitution to ground canon law and other ecclesial legislation, as well as to give the principal interpretation for the documents of Vatican II. This proposal ultimately was not accepted by his successors when the revision of the 1917 Code of Canon Law was promulgated in 1983 by John Paul II (1978–2005).

Lex indita non scripta
Law inscribed (in the human heart) and not written down

Basic affirmation of the nature of the natural law, i.e., innate moral knowledge that each person has and can come to understand in a given situation through the exercise of right reason (*recta ratio, q.v.*). Thus, one responds in conscience to what one understands God is calling him/her to do. This is the notion of conscience contained in Vatican II's Pastoral Constitution on the Church in the Modern World **Gaudium et spes** (cf. Paragraph #16). See also *Ens rationis, Lex interna/lex externa, Lex naturalis, Lumen naturale, Ordo rationis, Per modum cognitionis/Per modum inclinationis,* and *Recta ratio.*

Lex iniusta non est lex
An unjust law is not a law

Expression that indicates that true laws must always be ordained to justice and the common good, and if they are not then such laws are not only unjust but lack the character of true laws and may be disobeyed or ignored. See also *Deus impossibilia non iubet*; *Dura lex sed lex*; *Impossibilium nulla obligatio; Lex non intendit impossibile; Lex semper intendit quod convenit rationi; Nemo tenetur ad impossibile; Non omne quod licet honestum est; Salus publica suprema lex; Sententia facit ius; Ubi ius, ibi remedium;* and *Ubi ius incertum, ibi ius nullum.*

Lex interna/lex externa
Internal law/external law

Concepts connected with the Thomistic axiom of *lex indita non scripta (q.v.)* which distinguish the natural moral law as an internal law written in conscience on the human soul from an external law formulated in the sense of a positive law that is imposed on individuals. See also *lex indita non scripta.*

Lex lata in praesumptionne periculi communis
Law imposed (established) on the presumption of common (universal) danger

Justification for the imposition of a "positive" law since, even if a particular proscribed action does not threaten in each and every instance, there is a reasonable and well-grounded fear that if individuals were allowed to undertake such an action they might well pose a threat to the common good. E.g., in times of drought it is legitimate to forbid campfires absolutely (even if it could be argued that striking such a fire might remain safe). See also *Latae sententiae, Praesumptio hominis,* and *Salus publica suprema lex.*

Lex moralis (praecipiens vel prohibens)
Moral law (that commands or prohibits)

Lex moralis can be taken simply as the moral law itself, and also is used to refer to Decalogue.

Lex naturae
Law of nature

Strictly speaking, this term refers to the physical order of the universe, etc. The "law of nature" is *not* identical to the natural moral law, though at many periods in history this term has been used to refer to the natural moral law in such a way that what was found in "nature" was considered to be illustrative of what was meant to be "moral" and conversely that which was not seemingly found in "nature" was considered to be "against nature" (*contra naturam, q.v.*) and therefore "immoral." This tendency to "read" the natural moral law from what is found/not found in "nature" is called physicalism, and this theory is quite problematic for a correct understanding of ethics. See also *Ius naturae est immutabile, Lex naturalis,* and *Natura nihil facit inane.*

Lex naturalis
Natural law

Related to how we are to live according to our nature, i.e., the natural moral law. Humans come to an understanding of the natural moral law through the use of *recta ratio (q.v.),* and according to St. Thomas Aquinas the most basic principle of the natural law is *Bonum est faciendum et prosequendum, et malum vitandum* ("The good is to be done and fostered, and evil avoided," *q.v.*). See also *Contra ordinem, Contra natruam, Ens rationis, Ius naturae est immutabile, Lex aeterna, Lex indita non scripta, Lex naturae, Lumen naturale, Ordo rationis, Per modum cognitionis/Per modum inclinationis,* and *Recta ratio.*

Lex non distinguit
Law does not distinguish

Latin expression for "justice is blind," i.e., that it makes no distinctions in favor of the rich or poor, etc. However, there are many other situations in which it is quite important to make the proper distinctions, as articulated in the adage *Qui bene distinguit bene cognoscit* (*q.v.*, "The one who distinguishes well knows well"). See also the entries connected with *Ius* and also *De bono et aequo* and *Reddere suum cuique*.

Lex non intendit impossibile
Law does not intend (command) the impossible

Legal principle that reflects the moral principle that no one is ever obligated to attempt to do that which is "impossible," though in moral analysis the notion of "impossibility" is more nuanced than in law or science. See also *Deus impossibilia non iubet, Humano modo, Impossibilium nulla obligatio, Lex iniusta non est lex, Lex semper intendit quod convenit rationi, Lex spectat naturae ordinem, Nemo potest ad impossibile obligari, Nemo tenetur ad impossibile, Qui tenetur ad finem tenetur ad media*, and *Ultra posse* (or *vires*) *nemo obligatur*.

Lex non obligat nisi promulgata
The law does not oblige unless promulgated

This expression refers to human laws, since it is understood that the natural law is inscribed on the human heart by God (*lex indita non scripta, q.v.*). Some laws also require a certain waiting period (*vacatio legis, q.v.*) before they can be applied, even if they have been duly promulgated. This is often the case with canon law. On this point see Thomas Aquinas (cf. ST I–II, q. 90, a. 4). See also *Lex non valet extra territorium* and *Lex semper intendit quod convenit rationi*.

Lex non valet extra territorium
The law does not hold outside its territory

Any human law requires the authority of governance which is usually limited to a specific region. For example, the legislature of the Commonwealth of Massachusetts could not make laws binding on the citizens of New Hampshire, etc. On this point see the treatment of Thomas Aquinas (cf. ST I–II, q. 90, a. 3). This is an important legal principle, especially in canon law since the rules or laws laid down by one bishop or conference of bishops would not necessarily be binding outside of their territory unless this were a law similarly enacted by the proper authority of the other regions, or if it were a law of the universal church, etc. For example, in some dioceses of the United States the Solemnity of the Ascension is celebrated as a holy day of obligation on the Thursday forty days after Easter, whereas in other dioceses this celebration is transferred to the Sunday following Ascension Thursday.

Lex nova
The new law

Refers usually to the law of the Gospel, proclaimed by Jesus, which replaced the *lex vetus* (*q.v.*), namely the Mosaic Law of the Old Testament.

Lex orandi, lex credendi
Law of prayer is the law of belief

Traditional axiom going back to St. Prosper of Aquitane (ca. 390–ca. 463) affirming that liturgy is the norm of faith, i.e., how the church prays witnesses to what the church believes. The fuller form of the axiom is *Legem credendi lex statuat supplicandi* (Let the law of prayer establish the law of belief).

Lex parsimoniae
Law of parsimony

This is the Latin aphorism for what is called "Ockham's Razor" in English, namely that when one is confronted with competing hypotheses or positions that seem equal in most other respects, it is best to choose the one that makes the fewest new assumptions and is therefore more succinct, economical, or "parsimonious" in its supporting argumentation.

Lex poenalis
Law that punishes

In general, a "penal law" can describe a law which does not necessarily oblige in conscience (depending on circumstances and the particular nature of the law in question) but which nevertheless carries a "penalty" if the law is not obeyed. For example, some traffic laws may not always bind "morally" but would still bind in the "penal" sense. In the church's canon law, *lex poenalis* refers to laws in the Code of Canon Law which have a punitive purpose, such as censures and/or sentences of excommunication. See also *Lex praemians*.

Lex praemians
Law that rewards

Refers to laws in canon law which give privileges. *Lex praemians* is distinguished from penal laws. See also *Lex poenalis*.

Lex scripta
See *lex indita non scripta*.

Lex semper intendit quod convenit rationi
The law always intends that which is in accord with reason

This expression follows a key point in the classic definition of Thomas Aquinas (cf. ST I–II, q. 90), namely that it be an ordinance of reason aimed at the common good and duly promulgated by a competent authority. Laws which do not meet these basic criteria would be either unjust or nonbinding (or both). See also *Deus impossibilia non iubet, Humano modo, Impossibilium nulla obligatio, Lex iniusta non est lex, Lex non obligat nisi promulgata, Lex spectat naturae ordinem, Nemo potest ad impossibile obligari, Nemo tenetur ad impossibile, Qui tenetur ad finem tenetur ad media, Salus publica suprema lex,* and *Ultra posse* (or *vires*) *nemo obligatur.*

Lex sequitur esse
Law follows being

Principle which indicates that all law is predicated on the nature of the being(s) regulated by the law. A just law for humans can never command that which is either against the "being" of humans (i.e., true human dignity), and/or that which is "impossible" to follow. See also *Agere sequitur esse, Deus impossibilia non iubet, Humano modo, Impossibilium nulla obligatio, Lex iniusta non est lex, Lex spectat naturae ordinem, Operari sequitur esse, Quidquid percipitur ad modum percipientis percipitur, Quidquid recipitur ad modum recipientis recipitur,* and *Ultra posse* (or *vires*) *nemo obligatur.*

Lex spectat naturae ordinem
The law observes (or respects) the natural order

Principle that shows that human laws must always be grounded in reality and especially that natural human relations, such as in families, must be respected in law. This is an important point because in human history many laws (such as during the period of slavery) were not respectful of these basic natural order relationships. See also *Impossibilium nulla obligatio, Lex iniusta non est lex, Lex semper intendit quod convenit rationi, Nemo potest ad impossibile obligari, Nemo tenetur ad impossibile,* and *Qui tenetur ad finem tenetur ad media.*

Lex talionis
Law of retaliation

The law of "an eye for an eye, a tooth for a tooth," given expression in the Old Testament, as well as in other legal traditions of the Ancient Near East. It should be kept in mind, though, that this *lex talionis* was meant to limit the amount of retribution or punishment that could be exacted and was *not* originally understood as a moral imperative to exact the fullest possible punishment allowed.

Lex valet ut in pluribus
The law holds in most cases

Expression found in Thomas Aquinas ST I–II, q. 94, a. 2, indicating that not every moral norm in the natural will be binding in every instance. See *Ut in pluribus* and *Valet ut in pluribus* for the fuller discussion of this term. See also *Ad literam; Cessante fine cessat lex; Ex facto ius oritur; Exceptio firmat regulam; Odia restringi, et favores convenit ampliari; Quod omnes tangit ab omnibus approbetur; Sensus fidelium; Sensum, non verba spectamus;* and *Unicum.*

Lex vetus
The old law

Refers to the Mosaic Law of the Old Testament which stood in force until the proclamation by Jesus of the *lex nova* (*q.v.*).

Liber Antiphonarius
Book of Antiphons

See the entry under *Liber Gradualis.*

Liber Gradualis
Book of the Gradual Prayers

Name given to the medieval liturgical book which contained responsorial chants and Gospel Alleluia verses sung by the *Schola cantorum* (*q.v.*) or soloists in the Mass. This liturgical book was also sometimes referred to as the *Liber Antiphonarius* (Book of Antiphons) and often included the *Cantatorium* or collection of chants.

Libertas est inaestimabilis
Liberty is priceless

While the Catholic moral tradition does not view liberty as the *Summum bonum* (*q.v.*) for humans, it does put a high value on freedom since without this one cannot act morally. See also *In neces-*

sariis unitas, in dubiis libertas, in omnibus caritas.

Libertatis nuntius
Bringing word (or warning) of liberty

Congregation of the Doctrine of the Faith's 1984 instruction On Certain Aspects of the "Theology of Liberation," which sharply criticized liberation theology. A follow-up instruction ***Libertatis conscientia*** (Liberty of Conscience) issued in 1986 was somewhat less severe, and while acknowledging liberation theology had some legitimate concerns and positive contributions, it was still marked by a number of "ambiguities" and negative aspects. Both documents came during the pontificate of John Paul II who had struggled with Communism in Poland and were signed by the then Cardinal Prefect of the CDF, Joseph Cardinal Ratzinger (later Benedict XVI).

Liberum arbitrium
Free will (or choice)

Refers to the moral freedom with regard to particular choices and acts. The precise meaning of this term has been much debated and discussed by theologians over the centuries. In contemporary moral theology, *liberum arbitrium* is the type of freedom which is related to categorical acts and would be contrasted with the transcendental freedom exercised in the choice of one's most basic stance toward God, which is often termed the fundamental option in contemporary moral theology. The classic definition of this freedom was given by the medieval theologian Peter Lombard

(ca. 1100–1160): *Liberum arbitrium est facultas rationis et voluntatis* (Freedom of the will is the faculty [power] to reason and to will [intend]). As a basic concept for any understanding of moral agency the individual must have *liberum arbitrium* in order to make and act on moral choices. Conversely, anything which impedes this freedom also would diminish (or eliminate) moral responsibility for the acts performed. See also *Impedimenta libertatis* and *Moralis impossibilitas.*

Libri paenitentiales
Penitential books

Term used to designate the manuals prepared to guide confessors in the assigning of proper penances for various sins. These books grew in popularity from the time that individual penance became the primary mode of reception of the sacrament of reconciliation (i.e., from about the sixth century). See also *Casus conscientiae, Summa Casuum Conscientiae,* and *Summae confessariorum.*

(Non) Licet
Licit (or not)

Technically is a legal term, but often is understood to refer to moral (im)permissibility of an action. See also *licet corrigere defectus naturae.*

Licet corrigere defectus naturae
It is licit (morally permissible) to correct defects of nature

Moral principle enunciated by Pope Pius XII in his 1958 Address to the Seventh International Congress of Hematology in which he indicated that the use of the progesterone pill to remedy ("correct") maladies of the uterus or menstrual cycle would be legitimate under the principle of the double effect. This same principle was confirmed in Paul VI's 1968 encyclical On the Regulation of Birth, *Humanae vitae* (*q.v.*), in paragraph 15. Pius XII did stress, though, that this principle could be applied too broadly and that it would be key to the moral liceity that the person using such medication would be doing so *not* for contraceptive reasons but for the purpose of treating or correcting this physical malady. See also *Finis operis*, *Finis operantis*, and *Intentio*.

Ligamen
Bond (ligament)

In canon law of marriage a *ligamen* refers to the bond of a prior marriage which would be an impediment to an attempt at another marriage. The impediment of a *ligamen* would therefore have to be resolved by obtaining an annulment or decree of nullity before another marriage could licitly take place. See also *Affinitas non parit affinitatem*, *Defensor Vinculi, Ligamen, Non constat de nullitate, Ratum, Ratum et consummatum*, and *Super rato*.

Limbus
Limbus infantium
Limbus patrum
Limbus pervulorum
Limbo (hem, fringe, edge)

The Latin term refers to the edge of something, and in theology the term came to denote a place outside the boundary of heaven where those who died either in friendship with God or who had not committed personal sin but still had stain of original sin on their souls existed in a state of perfect natural happiness, though without directly enjoying the beatific vision which is the *Summum bonum* (*q.v.*) of human nature. The latter group encompassed young children who died without baptism but also without having committed personal sin. This version of Limbo was called either *Limbus infantium* (Limbo of infants) or *Limbus puerorum* (Limbo of the children). *Limbus patrum* (Limbo of the Patriarchs [or Fathers]) referred to those who died in friendship with God, but before Christ's resurrection, and therefore had to await Christ's coming to open the gates of heaven. Another general term employed was *Limbus pervulorum*, which means "those who inhabit the place on the edge." While the notion of Limbo was commonly held for centuries, in the post–Vatican II church this tradition is given far less credence. In 2007 the International Theological Commission published with Pope Benedict XVI's approval a study on "The Hope of Salvation for Infants Who Die without Being Baptised." See also *Extra ecclesia nulla salus, Ignorantes, Ingnorantia invincibilis*, and *Sine culpa*.

Lineamenta
Outline

Refers usually to an outline document, often related to a working, or preparatory, document for a commission, meeting, etc. Expression is often found in reference to Roman documents for meetings such as special synods and the like. See also *Instrumentum laboris*.

Littera gesta docet, quid credas allegoria, moralis quid agas, quid speres anagogia

The letter teaches (the facts of) events; allegory, what you are to believe; moral, what you are to do; and anagogic, what you are to hope for.

Dictum of thirteenth-century theologian Augustine of Dacia which distinguished the levels of interpretive meaning found in the Scriptures, i.e., historical "factual" information of events recorded in the Bible; an allegorical mode of interpretation oriented to faith belief; a moral interpretation oriented to ethical praxis; and an anagogic, or eschatological, interpretation oriented to the hope in the ultimate truth of salvation contained in the biblical message.

Loc. cit.

In the place cited

Latin abbreviation for *loco citato*, and used in scholarly works to indicate reference to a citation which has come before in the text, though *not* in the citation immediately prior to the citation in question. Thus, *loc. cit.* differs from *ibid. (q.v.)*, but is used in the same way as *op. cit. (q.v.)*. For correct usage see an accepted manual of style, such as *The Chicago Manual of Style*.

Loci

Locations, places

Plural form of *locus*, and can be used to denote literal and figurative "places" where something is found or done. Thus, biblical *loci* refer to scriptural texts that speak about a certain theme,

such as justification. See also *loci theologici* and *locus classicus*.

Loci receptionis

Places (locations) of reception

Refers to the various places and modalities of reception of revelation and doctrine. For example, theologically one can speak of the reception of a magisterial teaching by the larger church community, or the reception of God's self-communication by humanity, or reception of various dogmas among the churches, and so on. See also *Congregatio fidelium*; *Quod ubique, quod semper, quod ab omnibus, creditum est*; and *Sensus fidelium*.

Loci theologici

Theological loci (locations, places)

The *loci theologici* generally refer to the clusters of organizing principles that help determine the focus of theology. Thus, various biblical themes such as sin, redemption, justification, grace, etc., furnish some of the *loci theologici* for systematic theology. *Loci theologici* can also refer to the sources from which theologians draw the material for their reflection. In this sense Scripture, tradition, liturgy, the experience of the faithful, local churches, etc., become important *loci theologici*.

Loco citato

In the place cited

See *Loc. cit.*

Locum tenens

One holding the place

Legal term used for someone who temporarily occupies the office of another, such as a priest or doctor who substitutes for a pastor or another doctor who is away on vacation.

Locus classicus
Classic location (place)

Refers to a proof-text or authoritative reference for a certain doctrine or the usual textual reference given to demonstrate a certain point. E.g., the *locus classicus* for the New Testament expression of the natural law is Romans 2:12-15. See also *Dicta probantia*.

Locus in quo
The place in which

Refers to the place (physical or figurative) in which something has occurred.

Locus theologicus
Singular form of loci theologici (q.v.).

Locutio contra mentem
Speech against what one is in fact thinking

Traditional manualistic definition, and condemnation, of lying, based on a reading of the "faculty" of speech. Any violation of the "nature" of such a "faculty" would be in itself an *intrinsece malum* (*q.v.*, intrinsically immoral) and could never be justified due to extenuating circumstances and/or otherwise good intentions. See also *Mentalis restrictio*.

Luctus et angor
Griefs and the anxieties

Second pair of terms found in *Gaudium et spes* (*q.v.*), the Vatican II Pastoral Constitution on the Church in the Modern World. At the council there was a real debate over which pair of terms the constitution should lead off with, but ultimately the more positive pair of "joy and hope" was chosen to indicate the council's basic attitude toward the modern world.

Lumen fidei
Light of faith

See the discussion under the contrasting term *Lumen naturale*. See *Cognitio aenigmatica* and also the entries under *Credo* and *Fides*, especially *Crede ut intelligas*, *Fides qua/Fides quae*, *Fides quaerens intellectum*, and *Fides ratione illuminata*.

Lumen gentium
Light to the nations

Vatican II's Dogmatic Constitution on the Church (1964) which established the people of God and the Pilgrim Church as primary ecclesial metaphors. At the council there was a big debate over what trait should come first, the hierarchical nature of the church or the church as the people of God. The council fathers rejected the original schema which privileged the "hierarchical" nature of the church and decided instead to put forth first the notion of the church as the whole people of God, all of whom are called to holiness (cf. chapter 5 of **Lumen gentium**). These developments have caused some tensions within the church since the close of the council. In this context see also **Dominus Iesus**, *Elementa ecclesiae*, *Extra ecclesia nulla salus*, *Nota praevia*, *Obsequium religiosum*, and *Subsistit in*.

Lumen naturale
Natural light (or reason)

This term does *not* refer to sunlight but rather the ability that all humans possess to come to some level of moral knowledge of the natural law through use of our innate faculty of right reason (*recta ratio, q.v.*). *Lumen naturale* then would be contrasted with the *Lumen fidei*, or light of faith, which as an infused theological virtue given as part of God's grace allows us to comprehend that which otherwise would be beyond our reasoning ability or human knowledge. See also *Ens rationis, Lex indita non scripta, Lex naturalis, Ordo, Ordo bonorum, Ordinatio rationis,* *Per modum cognitionis/Per modum inclinationis,* and *Recta ratio.*

Lux Aeterna
Eternal Light (or Flame)

While this term can be used to indicate any "eternal flame" (usually found in grave sites of personages like President John F. Kennedy), in Roman Catholic circles it refers to a canticle often employed in Requiem Masses for the dead. It comes from the prayer, "Eternal Rest Grant Unto *Him/Her/Them* O Lord, and Let Perpetual Light Shine Upon *Him/ Her/Them*. See also *Dies Irae* and *In paradisum.*

M

Magis
> The greater

Refers to the Ignatian principle of discernment in which one seeks to do that which will be more for God's greater glory. See *Ad majorem Dei gloriam.*

Magister
> Master

This term has the nuance of "master" in the sense of teacher, expert, or director. The Latin word does not carry the meaning of "master" in the sense of being an owner or overlord (which would be *dominus, q.v.*). See also the various entries under *Magisterium.*

Magister Sacrae Paginae
> Master of the Sacred Text

Refers usually to a theologian, who is to be an "expert" in Scripture (the Sacred Page or Text), inasmuch as Scripture is to be the "soul" of theology. This expression was used primarily in the Middle Ages. See also *Sacra Pagina.*

Magisterium
> Authority of the master/teacher

In its generic form this concept refers to the authority granted to one by his or her "mastery" of a position, art, trade, or discipline. Thus, the *magisterium* of a ship captain depends on both position as head of the crew and mastery of the art of sailing. Thomas Aquinas spoke of a twin *magisterium* (*magisteria*): the pastoral *magisterium* of the bishops and the professional *magisterium* of theologians. In more recent centuries the term *magisterium* is usually reserved to the authoritative teaching role of the hierarchy (bishops and pope). See also *Authenticus*, **Christus Dominus**, *Ecclesia discens*, *Ecclesia militans*, *Fides implicita*, **Lumen gentium**, *Magister*, *Magisterium authenticam*, *Magisterium cathedrae pastoralis* & *Magisterium cathedrae magistralis*, *Munus*, *Obsequium religiosum*, *Officium*, *Potestas docendi*, and *Sensus fidelium.*

Magisterium attestans
> Magisterium (teaching office) attesting or bearing witness

The neoscholastic manuals spoke of two aspects of the *magisterium* (*q.v.*): this *magisterium attestans*, which was exercised primarily by the pope and bishops in bearing witness to and safeguarding the "deposit of faith," or *depositum fidei* (*q.v.*), and the other, termed the *Magisterium docens* (*q.v.*)

or "teaching magisterium" which consisted primarily of the scholars and whose teaching authority depended on the proper exercise of the discipline of theology and coherence and weight of the mode of argumentation employed. Thus, this term and its pair, *magisterium docens*, implied that the notion of the magisterium had two authorities, that of the pope and bishops on one hand and that of the scholarly theological community on the other. In this respect see especially *Authenticus and De fide definita*. See also *Depositum fidei, Diffinimus, Ecclesia docens, Ex cathedra, Magisterium, Magisterium attestans, Magisterium authenticam, Magisterium docens, Magisterium cathedrae pastoralis & Magisterium cathedrae magistralis, Munus, Obsequium religiosum, Officium, Potestas docendi,* and *Sensus fidelium*.

Magisterium authenticam
Authentic, authoritative magisterium

In a theological or ecclesial context this would refer to some teaching or document that comes from an official magisterial source, e.g., an individual pope or bishop, or some established ecclesial institution such as the Congregation for the Doctrine of the Faith. See also *Authenticus*, **Christus Dominus**, *Ecclesia docens, Ex cathedra, Magisterium, Magisterium attestans, Magisterium cathedrae pastoralis & Magisterium cathedrae magistralis, Magisterium docens, Munus, Munus docendi, Obsequium religiosum, Officium, Potestas docendi,* and *Sensus fidelium*.

Magisterium cathedrae pastoralis & Magisterium cathedrae magistralis
Juridical Magisterium Chair and Teaching Magisterium Chair

These two terms were used more widely in the Middle Ages to differentiate the juridical (pastoral) power of the hierarchical magisterium (*cathedrae pastoralis*) from the teaching magisterium invested in the professors on the theology faculties of the various universities in Europe (*cathedrae magistralis*). Since the Council of Trent, the term magisterium has increasingly referred solely to the members of the official hierarchy of the college of bishops in communion with the pope (as bishop of Rome). See also the other entries under *Magisterium* as well as the entries under *Munus*. Also see *Auctoritas, Ecclesia dicens, Ecclesia docens, Obsequium religiosum, Peritus, Potestas docendi, Quaestio disputata, Sensus fidelium, Sententia probata, Status quaestionis,* and *Theologice certa*.

Magisterium docens
Teaching authority

See first the discussion above under the term *Magisterium attestans*. As used in the neoscholastic manuals, the *magisterium docens* was not seen primarily as a charism of office but rather as an acquired expertise that would be the result of serious study, teaching, discussion, and publication. Thus, those who exercise the *magisterium docens* primarily were the professional theologians. In this respect see especially, *Auctoritas, Ecclesia dicens, Ecclesia docens, Inquisitio,*

Magisterium, Magisterium attestans, Magisterium cathedrae pastoralis & Magisterium cathedrae magistralis, Obsequium religiosum, Peritus, Potestas docendi, Quaestio disputata, Sensus fidelium, Sententia probata, Status quaestionis, and *Theologice certa.*

Magnum opus
(A/The) Great work

Usually refers to one's principal book or masterpiece which best indicates the author's thought or the artist's talent.

Mala fide
In bad faith

The opposite of *bona fide* (*q.v.*), that is, something done in bad faith is done with a bad or evil intention.

Mala in se
Bad in itself

See *Intrinsece Malum* and *In se.*

Mala intrinseca
Intrinsically bad

See *Intrinsece Malum.*

Mala moralia and mala praemoralia
Moral and premoral (ontic, physical) evil(s)

Basic terms to distinguish between evil which is moral (and therefore sinful) and evil which lacks any moral culpability and therefore is not sinful. These terms are generally used in the principle of the double effect and this distinction is very important in the theory of proportionalism. Not all evil is moral evil; premoral (ontic) evil can be permitted and even caused for a *proportionately* greater reason (than for not doing, permitting, this premoral evil). For example, in order to save the life of a person with a gangrenous foot it is morally permissible to amputate the foot so that the person will not die from gangrene. In this case the amputation is an ontic or physical evil, not a moral evil, since the preservation of life is proportionately greater than the "evil" suffered by the loss of the foot. However, if someone were to amputate his or her foot in order to elicit sympathy, or for some other "disproportionate" reason, the amputation would be equivalent to the moral evil of self-mutilation and should not be done. In this latter case, even though some "good" might result from the amputation (e.g., sympathy won), the "good" obtained is not proportionate to the evil suffered. Thus, since there is a clear lack of proportionate reason, the evil of the amputation in this second case would not be ontic or physical evil but rather moral evil. See *Pars propter totum.*

Male sonans
Evil sounding

Though this might seem to express something "ominous," the expression was usually used to highlight something which might well be true but which would likely offend pious folk (cf. the longer entry under *Piarum aurium offensiva,* "offensive to pious ears"). See also *Delectatio morosa* and *Scandalum pusillorum.*

Malum in se
Bad in itself

See *Intrinsece Malum* and *In se.*

Malum non est faciendum ut eveniat bonum
>Evil is not done so that good may result

In other words, the end does not justify the means. Nevertheless, it is important to recognize that in fact in the Catholic moral tradition it is the "end" that justifies the means and not vice versa. The point of this axiom, though, is to counter a utilitarian or consquentialist ethic which might hold that any "good" would justify even a morally evil means. See also *Bonum est faciendum et prosequendum, et malum vitandum*; *Causa finalis est prima inter omnes causas*; *Cooperatio in malum*; *Ea (eorum) quae sunt ad finem*; *Finis enim dat speciem in moralibus*; *Finis est nobilior iis quae sunt ad finem*; *Finis operis*; *Finis operantis*; *Minus malum*; and *Qui vult finem vult media.*

Malum physicum and malum morale

See *Mala moralia* and *mala praemoralia.*

Malum quia prohibitum
>Wrong because prohibited

This contrasts with *prohibitum quia malum*, "forbidden because wrong"; i.e., in the former instance something is wrong simply because it is "forbidden," not because it is wrong in itself. In the latter case of *prohibitum quia malum*, "forbidden because wrong," something is forbidden because it is being perceived as wrong and therefore is not to be done.

Mandatum
>Commandment, mandate

Usually refers to the foot-washing ritual which takes place in the liturgy of Holy Thursday, and is based on Jesus' command given in John 13:14 that, just as Jesus washed the disciples' feet, they ought to do likewise. Based on this *mandatum* the Holy Thursday liturgy is sometimes called "Maundy Thursday." This expression is also used to refer to the seal of approval given by a local bishop to university-level Catholic teachers of theology and philosophy called for in the *Ordinationes (q.v.)* of **Ex corde ecclesiae** (q.v.). See also *Mandatum novum* and *Missio canonica.*

Mandatum novum
>New commandment

Refers to the "new commandment" given by Jesus in John 13:34 that the disciples are to love one another. See also *Mandatum.*

Mane nobiscum Domine
>Give to Us, Lord

Apostolic letter of Pope John Paul II of 7 October 2004.

Mare magnum
>Great sea

Referred to the comprehensive grants of pastoral prerogatives given to certain religious orders.

Massa damnata
>Condemned throng

The effect of original sin is that all of humanity is born into a fallen state.

Only through God's grace can humans be saved. Cf. Augustine's *Enchiridion, 26: PL 44, 450. Massa* itself can carry the metaphor of a lump (*massa*) of clay in the hands of a potter and thus is a metaphor in which God is the potter and humanity the clay. See also *Prorsus indebitum.*

Mater Dolorosa
The sorrowful mother

Usually refers to the depiction of the Blessed Virgin Mary holding the dead body of Jesus after it has been taken down from the cross. The *Dolorosa* enjoys a very popular cult in certain areas of the world, such as Italy. See also *Stabat Mater Dolorosa.*

Mater et Magistra
Mother and teacher

Social encyclical of Pope John XXIII On Christianity and Social Progress (1961), in which he indicated that the state has a legitimate role and must at times act in health care, education, and housing.

Materfamilias
Mother of a family

Though the Latin translates literally as a "mother of a family," the nuance is more of a matriarch. See also *Paterfamilias.*

Materia circa quam
The matter around which

Expression in scholastic theology that refers to the "matter" about which an action or faculty moves, or can also refer to the object of an action and its corresponding faculty. As Thomas Aquinas states in the section of his ***Summa Theologiae*** (*q.v.*), which deals with human acts, the (moral) "object is not the matter out of which, but the matter about which (*materia circa quam*), and stands in relation to the act is its form, as it were, through giving it its (moral) species." ST I–II, q. 18, a. 2, ad. 2. See also *Secundum quid.*

Materia levis (gravis)
Light (serious) matter

Refers to the objective "matter" of sin. Some "matter," such as murder would be "grave" (serious), and if accompanied by the more subjective elements of sufficient consent and sufficient freedom on the part of the moral agent, would be considered as "mortal" sin. If the "matter" were "light" (i.e., not of such a serious nature, such as uttering an expletive upon hitting your finger inadvertently with a hammer), the resulting "sin" would be considered "venial." See also *Graviter et dolose, Parvitas materiae in Sexto,* and *Sub levi.*

Mea culpa
Through my fault

Expression which comes from the *Confiteor* (*q.v.*) in which the penitent pronounces the words "*mea culpa, mea culpa, mea maxima culpa*" (through my fault, through my fault, through my most grievous fault"). *Mea culpa* can be used to indicate both guilt and apology. However, by itself *culpa* has a technical meaning in canon law, which points to an oversight rather than a premeditated violation. See also *Culpa, De defectibus, Dolus,* and *Sanatio in radice.*

Mediator Dei
Mediator of God

Pope Pius XII's encyclical On the Sacred Liturgy (1947), which called for active participation of the faithful in the Eucharist.

Melior est conditio possidentis
Better (stronger) is the condition (status, right, etc.) already in possession (or force)

Axiom which relates to adjudicating claims about doubtful laws or facts. This is somewhat akin to the legal principle of "possession is nine-tenths of the law," which means that in disputes over ownership the person in actual possession of the object has the stronger legal claim, unless proven otherwise. In terms of moral theology and/or canon law *melior est conditio possidentis* means that in cases of doubt whatever has enjoyed the previous right or interpretation—whether in terms of a presumed law or liberty—is presumed to stand in this disputed case as well, unless it is disproved by a stronger case. See also the various entries under *Dubium* as well as *In dubio factum non praesumitur sed probatur, Ius ad rem, Ius et titulum, Iustitiam subsidiariam, Lex dubia non obligat,* and *Possessio non est juris sed facti.*

Melius est dare quam accipere
It is better to give than to receive

While this aphorism is common also in English, the Latin can be used to indicate that having a perfection is superior to just being able to receive it (presuming in that case that the recipient lacks the perfection). In conjunction with this

latter sense see also *Nemo dat quod non habet.*

Memento mori
Remember (you will) die

Expression which means "remember that you will someday die." The expression can be used to put one's life in a larger perspective, as well as to indicate an implicit call to conversion and a life of moral rectitude so as to avoid the pains of hell.

Memoria liberationis
Memory of liberation

Refers usually to the salvation history of liberation, e.g., the recollection of the Exodus event, which is a formative narrative for the faith community. The Exodus story is recounted during the Passover Seder service in which the head of the celebration responds to the youngest child's ritual question "Why is this night different from all other nights?" (cf. Deut 6:6, 20-25). The concept of *memoria liberationis* is key to the theological understanding of the covenant and is widely used in liberation theology as well.

Mens legislatoris
The mind of the legislator

Principle for interpreting the true meaning of a law, such that one "reads" the law as if the legislator were present to give the proper application of the law. This principle is used both in canon law and in moral theology to elucidate the fuller meaning of the law which looks to similar laws in different contexts or which seeks to discern the grounding reasons or the so-called "spirit of the law," as opposed (at times) to the "letter of the law." For example, in the case of a serious medical emergency one might presume, invoking the *mens legislatoris*, permission to exceed the posted speed limit (and presuming that public safety were not otherwise endangered, etc.). See also *Epikeia*.

Mens rea
Guilty mind (evil intent)

Basic principle in criminal law which indicates for a true crime one needs not only an unlawful act (*actus reus, q.v.*) but also an accompanying evil intent to commit the crime. If the intent is not there or cannot be proven then the accused should be acquitted or possibly convicted of a lesser crime (e.g., involuntary manslaughter instead of murder). The full principle is *actus non facit reum nisi mens sit rea* ("act does not make one guilty unless the mind [intent behind the act] would be guilty"). See also *Absolutus sententia judicis praseumitur innocens*; *Actus reus*; *Onus probandi*; *Nulla poena sine culpa*; *Sententia facit ius*; *Sententia incerta non valet*; *Sine culpa*; and *Ubi non est culpa, ibi non est delictum*.

Mens sana in corpore sano
A sound mind in a sound body

Usually this expression stresses the necessity of keeping one's body physically fit, though the Latin would indicate also the need for mental development.

Mensa Episcopalis
Revenue (literally, "table") of a bishop

Canonical term which includes the benefice of the bishop's office, namely all of the ecclesiastical goods and income that he enjoys by right of his episcopal office (and apart from anything he may own as a private individual, such as a family legacy). The *Mensa Episcopalis* in canon law is a juridical entity somewhat like a corporation would be in civil law.

Mensura non mensurata
A non-measured measure which measures (everything else)

Cf. *Norma normans non normata*.

Mentalis restrictio
Mental reservation

This expression refers to the casuistical principle which sought to justify certain forms of deception which otherwise would appear to be outright lies. This usage often amounted to a form of equivocation which deliberately chose words that either could be misleading or have a double meaning, such that the speaker might technically be telling the "truth" but is clearly aiming at not being correctly understood by the hearer. See also *locutio contra mentem* and *stricte mentalis*.

Meum
Mine

Often used in conjunction with *tuum* (yours). Thus, a basic principle of justice is to render to me what is mine and to you what is yours.

Minima de malis
See *Minus malum*.

Minima non curat praetor
The magistrate does not treat small matters

The purpose of the legal system is not to deal with each and every possible situation, especially those that cover minor matters. Another variation on this adage is *De minimis non curat lex* (*q.v.*, "The law does not treat small matters"). See also *Ad literam*; *Epikeia*; *In necessariis unitas, in dubiis libertas, in omnibus caritas*; *Lex dubia non obligat*; *Libertas est inaestimabilis*; and *Quod raro fit non observant legislatores*.

Minus malum
Lesser evil

If one is faced with a dilemma in which the only concrete possibilities of action both have evil effects, one is to choose the action which will have the "lesser evil." The classic phrase, attributed to Thomas à Kempis, is *"De duobus malis, minus est semper eligendum"* ("In matters concerning two evils, the lesser is always to be chosen," *q.v.*). This expression also would correspond logically to Thomas Aquinas' understanding of practical right reason (*recta ratio*, *q.v.*) in responding to his first principle of the natural law, namely that *Bonum est faciendum et prosequendum, et malum vitandum* (*q.v.*, "The good is to be done and fostered, and evil avoided"). If we cannot always and in every instance "avoid" evil entirely, then it makes logical sense at least to reduce the evil caused if this be in our power. See also *Cooperatio in malum*; *Ens rationis*; *Lex aeterna*; *Lex indita non scripta*; *Lex naturae*; *Lumen naturale*; *Malum non est faciendum ut eveniat bonum*; *Non facias malum, ut inde fiat bonum*; *Ordo rationis*; *Per modum cognitionis/Per modum inclinationis*; and *Recta ratio*.

Mirabile dictu
Wonderful to relate

However, the *nuance* is one of astonishment, often meant ironically, at hearing news of a certain event or occurrence, e.g., "He passed his exams, *mirabile dictu!*"—which might be said of someone who had not studied very diligently and who was not an especially gifted student.

Mirabilia
Wonders

Usually refers to miracles and/or things which astonish.

Miramur
We are surprised

Though this word is technically a verb, in theological circles it often functions as a noun to refer to a letter given by some official hierarchical organ, such as the Congregation for the Doctrine of the Faith, which expresses some puzzlement or critique of a theologian's writing or teaching. The expression comes from the opening line of the letter, *miramur*, "We are surprised . . . (that you would hold this position)." A theologian who receives a *miramur* may wish to clarify or change his or her opinion on the matter in question, but a *miramur* can also be used as a sort of censorship or control, as well as serve as an initial step in a more thorough investigation of one's theological teachings. See also *Monitum*.

Mirari vos
(It) amazes you (pl.)

Gregory XVI's encyclical condemning indifferentism in religion and the supposed individual's freedom of conscience in choice of religion (1832). This same position was echoed in Pius IX's *Quanta cura* (1864) and the accompanying *Syllabus of Errors*. Nevertheless, there is some tension with this position dating from Roman times through Thomas Aquinas, who held contrary views. *Dignitatis humanae*, Vatican II's Declaration on Religious Liberty, ultimately enshrined the position of Thomas Aquinas, who held that that no one should ever be forced to act against his or her conscience, and even if this is done the person should resist: "anyone upon whom the ecclesiastical authorities, in ignorance of the true facts, impose a demand that offends against his clear conscience, should perish in excommunication rather than violate his conscience" (Thomas Aquinas, 4 Sent. 38, q. 2, a. 4, Expos. Text). See also **Dignitatis humanae**, *Nisi enim sponte et ex animo fiat, execratio est*, **Quanta cura**, and **Quod aliquantum**.

Miserere
Have mercy

Usually refers to Psalm 51, the best known of the seven penitential psalms, which begins in the Latin Vulgate's translation with the words *Miserere mei, Deus* ("Have mercy on me, O God"). This psalm is recited every Friday in the *Lauds* (Morning Prayer) of the breviary and is used in other liturgical services as well. This expression can also be used to indicate sorrow and repentance for one's sins, as well as a prayer to God for their forgiveness. See also *De profundis*.

Missa
Mass

Latin word for the celebration of the Eucharist. See also *Ite Missa Est*.

Missa Cantata
Sung Mass

A Mass in which various parts of the celebration are sung by the presider, but without the participation of a deacon (and subdeacon), which would be required for a *Missa Solemnis* (*q.v.*).

Missa Solemnis
Solemn Mass

Refers to a very solemn liturgy, sung with a deacon (and subdeacon), often called a "High Mass" in the pre–Vatican II church. Also refers to musical works composed for performance at such liturgies. See also *Missa Cantata*.

Missale Romanum
Roman Missal

As a proper noun, when used in Latin this term usually refers to the 1570 reform of the Tridentine liturgy by Pope Pius V and used until the Second Vatican Council, though technically it could refer to any missal officially recognized by the Holy See. Some individuals who resisted the liturgical changes of Vatican II preferred to celebrate the Latin Mass of this Missal and permission was given to all priests to celebrate it by Pope Benedict XVI in his 2007 *motu proprio* (*q.v.*), **Summorum Pontificum** (*q.v.*).

See also *Ad orientem, Coetus fidelium, Forma extraordinaria, Missale Romanum, Novus Ordo, **Summorum Pontificum, Universae Ecclesiae**,* and *Versus populum.*

Missio canonica
Canonical mission

Refers to an office or position (such as a bishop, professor in a pontifical faculty of theology, etc.) whose exercise of that office depends on either the ecclesiastical nomination (e.g., for a bishop) or confirmation in office (e.g. obtaining the *nihil obstat* for a professor). A *missio canonica* can also be withdrawn by the same competent ecclesiastical authority (as has happened occasionally and been threatened somewhat more often). See also *Auctores probati* and *Mandatum.*

Missio Dei
Mission from God

The ultimate "mission of God" is the salvation of all human creatures. The church's own mission is derived ultimately from this universal salvific will of God. See also *Visio Dei.*

Modo speciali
In a special mode or manner

For a fuller discussion of this concept, especially as it is employed in canon law, see the entry *Specialissimo modo.*

Modus operandi
Manner of working

Refers to a certain pattern of behavior or action. E.g., a criminal's "M.O." is his or her *modus operandi*, or usual way

of committing the crime. A philosophical axiom that builds on this notion is *Modus operandi sequitur modum essendi (q.v.).*

Modus operandi sequitur modum essendi
The manner of operating follows the mode of being

Metaphysical and moral principle that underscores it is the agent rather than the act that is the key determining factor in evaluating both nature and moral acts. See also *Agere sequitur esse, Operari sequitur esse,* and *Quidquid recipitur ad modum recipientis recipitur.*

Modus procendi
Way of proceeding

Refers to a process or approach to a problem, issue, study, etc.

Modus vivendi
Way of living

Usually refers to a certain degree of compromise as a principle of adaptation in order to live peacefully in what might be otherwise a difficult situation.

Monitum
Reminder, warning

In ecclesiastical circles a *monitum* may be issued by a competent authority, such as a Vatican congregation, as an admonition for a canonical offense or irregularity, as a preventive penalty warning against some anticipated action, or as a warning against the teaching of a certain opinion. For example, the traditionalist archbishop, Marcel Lefevre, received an official *monitum* from the Vatican in 1988 prior to his announced, but unauthorized, ordination of new bishops for his Society of St. Pius X. Archbishop Lefevre ignored the *monitum* and was excommunicated *ipso facto* (*q.v.*) upon completion of the unauthorized episcopal ordination (cf. canon 1382). For an example of a moral *monitum*, in 1952 the Holy Office (institutional precursor to the Congregation for the Doctrine of the Faith) issued a *monitum* which warned moral theologians not to "describe, praise, and urge *amplexus reservatus*" (*q.v.*).

Moralis impossibilitas
Moral impossibility

Factor which prevents or renders very difficult the fulfillment of a law or obligation due to one or more conditions, such as grave fear or psychological impossibility, serious harm to oneself or others, and/or a serious external difficulty which would be involved if the law or obligation would be fulfilled. For example, someone in a remote area would be impeded (and thus excused) by virtue of this "moral impossibility" from fulfilling the obligation to attend Sunday Mass if there were no church nearby. See also *Impedimenta libertatis* and *Liberum arbitrium*.

Mores
Customs, nature, manner, practice, law, etc.

Mores is the plural of *mos*. This is an extremely difficult term to translate adequately into English, and in moral theology it is important to make the distinction between what are "mores" (customs) of a given society and what

truly pertains to morals and morality as such. See also *De rebus fidei et morum*.

Mors tua, vita mea
Your death, my life

Principle of taking another's life so that one might live. Expression might be found in certain biomedical situations, such as organ donation or sacrificing the life of a fetus so that the mother might live (or vice versa).

Mortalium Animos
Minds of mortals

Encyclical of Pope Pius XI On Religious Unity, issued on 6 January 1928. In this encyclical the pope takes a rather dim view of the ecumenical movement and its conventions, meetings, and the like, held among different Christian groups. He calls instead for all people to return to the Catholic Church, which is the one, true Church.

Mortui vivos docent
The dead teach the living

Expression which usually connotes the value of studying the classics and tradition in order to learn. See also *Nihil novi sub sole, Nil nisi bonum de mortuis dicere, Praeparatio evangelica, Quidquid latine dictum sit altum videtur*, and *Traditio*.

Morum disciplina
Ordering (discipline) of mores (right conduct)

Refers to a code of conduct or discipline. See also *Mores*.

Motu proprio [data]
[Given] of one's own accord

In ecclesiastical usage this refers to a personal letter written by a pope either to the whole church, a local church, or some particular group or body. A *motu proprio* is an authentic exercise of the magisterium, but its authority ranks below other forms of the magisterium (i.e., after definitions proposed *ex cathedra*, conciliar decrees, papal encyclicals, apostolic exhortations, and apostolic constitutions). Technically a *motu proprio* indicates an act or instruction, establishment of disciplinary regulations, etc., given on the initiative of the legislator rather than in response to a request. Some recent examples issued by Pope Benedict XVI include his 2011 *Porta Fidei* (*q.v.*) calling for a Year of Faith to commemorate the fiftieth anniversary of Vatican II; his 2009 *Omnium in mentem* (*q.v.*), which amended parts of the 1983 *Codex Iuris Canonici* (*q.v.*), or Code of Canon Law; and his 2007 *Summorum Pontificum* (*q.v.*), which gave all priests the rite to celebrate the pre–Vatican II Latin Tridentine Liturgy as an "extraordinary form" (*q.v., forma extraordinaria*).

Mulier fortis
Strong woman

This expression denotes a woman who is forthright and strong. Positively, it is similar to the ideal wife depicted in Proverbs 31:10-31. Negatively, this expression is somewhat akin to the Asian expression of a "Dragon Lady," i.e., a woman who tries to dominate affairs, especially within the family. See also *Mulier taceat in ecclesia* and **Mulieris dignitatem**.

Mulier taceat in ecclesia
A woman is to keep silent in church.

This is the Latin for Paul's admonitions against women speaking in church (cf. 1 Corinthians 14:34 and 1 Timothy 2:11-15). Obviously, this is an exegetical point that provokes much contemporary controversy. The 1917 Code of Canon Law forbade women as priests (#813 §2) and was repeated in the 1983 Code (*C.I.C.* #1024), as well as in the CDF's 1976 **Inter Insigniores** (*q.v.*, On the Question of the Admission of Women to the Ministerial Priesthood) and Pope John Paul II's 1994 apostolic exhortation **Ordinatio sacerdotalis** (*q.v.*, On the Ordination of Priests). See also Pope John Paul II's 1988 **Mulieris dignitatem** for a more positive assessment of the role of women.

Mulieris dignitatem
Dignity of women

Apostolic letter of Pope John Paul II On the Dignity and Vocation of Women on the Occasion of the Marian Year (1988). See also **Inter Insigniores**, *Mulier fortis*, *Mulier taceat in ecclesia*, and **Ordinatio sacerdotalis**.

Mundus vult decipi
The world wants to be deceived.

Aphorism which indicates that rather than face an uncomfortable truth most people would prefer to be deceived by a less challenging view of reality, even if it should prove to be ultimately false.

Munera
Offices or ministries

Latin plural of *Munus* (*q.v.*). See *Munus* for a discussion of this term, as well as *Authenticus, Ecclesia docens, Magisterium, Munus docendi, Munus gubernandi, Obsequium religiosum, Officium,* and *Potestas docendi.*

Munificentissimus Deus
Most Munificent God

Papal bull of Pius XII promulgated in the Marian Year of 1950 defining the dogma of Mary's assumption body and soul into heaven upon her death. Considered to be the second, and most recent, example of a papal pronouncement given in an *ex cathedra* (*q.v.*) format which explicitly invoked infallibility. See also **Ineffabilis Deus**.

Munus (Plural, Munera)
Mission, ministry, office

Often used in ecclesiastical context to refer to some aspect of the role of the church or an individual (such as a bishop or pastor) in the church's primary mission of teaching, governing, and sanctifying. In a liturgical context *munus/ munera* may mean "gift" or "gifts." See also *Authenticus,* **Christus Dominus***, Ecclesia docens,* **Lumen gentium***, Magisterium, Magisterium authenticam, Munus docendi, Munus gubernandi, Munus santificandi, Obsequium religiosum, Officium,* and *Potestas docendi.*

Munus docendi
Office (or ministry) of teaching

According to Vatican II's Dogmatic Constitution on the Church **Lumen gentium** (*q.v.*) #21, each bishop by virtue of his episcopal ordination receives a share or participation in the ecclesiastical teaching power of the church. This charism of office, though, is not absolute but must be exercised in communion with the pope and the college of bishops. See also *Authenticus,* **Christus Dominus***, Ecclesia docens, Magisterium, Munus, Munus gubernandi, Obsequium religiosum, Officium,* and *Potestas docendi.*

Munus gubernandi (or munus regendi)
Office (or ministry) of governance

In the ecclesiastical context this term refers to those who have jurisdiction or power to govern, and in the current Code of Canon Law this *munus* is restricted to the ordained. This *munus* is distinguished from the other two *munera* of teaching and sanctifying. See also **Christus Dominus***, Ecclesia discens, Ecclesia docens, Magisterium, Munus docendi, Obsequium religiosum, Officium,* and *Potestas docendi.*

Munus Petrinium
Petrine (papal) ministry

This concept is a further specification of the ecclesial notion of *munus* and focuses on the specific functions, powers, and privileges of the papacy in the church that was given to Peter by Jesus. Besides the other entries paired with *Munus,* see also *Primus inter pares; Servus Servorum Dei; Tu Es Petrus; Ubi Petrus, ibi ecclesia, ibi Deus;* and *Vicarius Christi.*

Munus sanctificandi
Ministry of sanctification

Mission of the church to sanctify its members in holiness and governed primarily by the magisterium (*munus gubernandi, q.v.*) and administered by the ordained in the celebration of the Sacraments, etc.

Munus triplex
Threefold ministry

Expression which refers to the work of Jesus Christ as priest, prophet, and king.

Mutatio legis odiosa
Change in the law is odious

Legal principle that indicates that when laws are changed there will likely be resistance and difficulties. Any change, of course, is difficult and institutions, especially of law, need stability. On the other hand, this stability can at times resist the necessary flexibility that is required for appropriate adaptation to changing circumstances and times. See also *Ens rationis*; *Lex aeterna*; *Lex indita non scripta*; *Lex naturae*; *Ordo rationis*; *Per modum cognitionis/Per modum inclinationis*; *Recta ratio*; and *Summum ius, summa iniuria*.

Mutatis mutandis
The necessary changes being made

Refers to the application of a general principle which is expressed in terms of one case and would apply to a second case if minor adjustments are made to take into account the differences and/or particularities of the second case in contrast to the original case.

Mysterium Crucis
Mystery of the cross

Expression for the central mystery of the Christian faith, namely the "folly" of the cross.

Mysterium Ecclesiae
Mystery of the church

Issued on the Feast of St. John the Baptist (24 June 1973) by the Congregation for the Doctrine of the Faith, this "Declaration in Defense of the Catholic Doctrine on the Church Against Certain Errors fo the Present Day" defends the ministerial priesthood and the infallibility of the universal church and the magisterium.

Mysterium fidei
Mystery of the faith

An element, or doctrine, of the faith which because of its sacred and/or supernatural character is difficult to explain completely in rational and/or logical terms and which therefore must be accepted finally on faith. *Mysterium fidei* is also the liturgical invocation uttered by the presider immediately following the consecration ("Let us proclaim the mystery of faith"). **Mysterium fidei** is also the title of Paul VI's 1965 encyclical on the real presence of Christ in the Eucharist.

Mysterium iniquitatis
Mystery of iniquity [sin]

The mystery of sin is seen within the Christian context in the economy of salvation, in which God's grace surpasses sin. As Pope John Paul's 1984 post-synodal apostolic exhortation *Reconciliatio et Paenitentia* (On Reconciliation and Penance in the Mission of the Church Today) expresses this thought, the *mysterium iniquitatis* of sin is fought against by the *mysterium pietatis* (*q.v.*), the mystery of religion.

Mysterium pietatis
Mystery of piety (religion)

Expression found in 1 Timothy 3:16 which refers to the power of religion which will be ultimately victorious over sin and death. This expression was also cited in Pope John Paul's 1984 post-synodal apostolic exhortation *Reconciliatio et Paenitentia* (On Reconciliation and Penance in the Mission of the Church Today) in reference to the *mysterium iniquitatis (q.v.)* of sin which is fought against by the *mysterium pietatis*, the mystery of religion.

Mysterium tremendum et fascinans
"Mystery which inspires awe and fascination"

Description of the religious experience of the sacred used by the religious thinker Rudolf Otto (1869-1937). *Mysterium* referred to that which was totally different from what is found in ordinary life and evokes a reaction of silence. However, this religious experience is also *tremendum* in that its overwhelming power evokes awe or trembling. Finally, religious experience also is *fascinans* in that it presents itself as "fascinating" in the sense of being merciful and gracious. Often the expression is shortened to *mysterium tremendum*.

Mystici Corporis
Mystical Body

Pope Pius XII's encyclical on the Eucharist (1943) and the nature of the Church as the Mystical Body of Christ. See also **Dominus Iesus Lumen gentium**, *Elementa ecclesiase*, *Extra ecclesia nulla salus*, and *Subsistit in*.

N

Natura actus
Nature (form) of the act

In traditional moral theology this refers to the manner in which a certain act, e.g., coitus, is performed. Traditionally, anything that blocked or destroyed the form of the act would be considered immoral. In the development of Roman Catholic sexual ethics, the conjugal act was considered moral, even if performed for the so-called "secondary ends" alone (e.g., pleasure and the unitive dimension) as long as the manner of the conjugal act did not violate the basic form and integrity of the act (i.e., the semen still had to be deposited in the vagina). Cf. *Actus naturae* and *Actus personae.*

Natura humana mutabilis est
Human nature is mutable (changeable)

Refers to a teaching of St. Thomas. If human nature is in some sense changeable, then things which relate intimately to humans, such as laws and customs, will also have to change. The point of debate, however, focuses on what changes and what remains the same. In moral theology this adage is the locus of some controversy over the precepts of the natural law. See also *Lex naturalis.*

Natura nihil facit inane
Nature does nothing in vain

See *Deus nihil facit inane*, though one should not conclude from this expression that everything in nature is somehow divinely ordained (e.g., earthquakes and disease), or that any modification of what is "natural" would be immoral (e.g., artificial light, shelter, etc.). See also *Contra naturam* and *Lex naturae.*

(Ex) natura vel finalitate naturali actus
(From the) nature or natural finality of an act

In moral theology this expression refers to a mode of reasoning which evaluates the moral rectitude of an action by looking at the "nature" and "finality" of a given "faculty" (such as the sexual organs) or individual action (e.g., killing in self-defense or for murder). In this view, for example, the "finality" of the sexual organs is for procreation, and therefore their use must have a procreative intent in order to be judged morally right. Another example that looks to the "finality" of the action would be using force: if the force were justified in the line of self-defense it would be moral; however, if excessive force were used, or intended unjustly to harm or kill someone, then in this case the force would be immoral.

Naturaliter nota
Known naturally (or from the nature of the thing itself)

Somewhat akin to self-evident, or at least able to be known without relying on revelation. Thus, if a moral norm is said to be *naturaliter nota* it would be "accessible" or "knowable" to humans through a natural process of reflection through reason and would not depend on some external source for its knowledge (such as a scriptural insight, revealed norm, etc.).

N.B.
Note well

Latin abbreviation for *nota bene*, and used to emphasize or call attention to something of importance in a text or instructions which must be followed in a specific way.

Ne auf.
Do not remove

Latin abbreviation for *ne auferatur*, commonly placed on objects such as books or magazines that should not be taken away (e.g., from a reading room, etc.). This abbreviation is often used in those religious communities in which Latin once served as a lingua franca.

Ne auferatur
Do not remove

See *Ne auf.*

Ne cede malis
Do not yield to evil

Line taken from book 6 of the *Aeneid* of the advice given to Aeneas by the oracle Sibyl in his descent to the underworld; also used as the motto of the Bronx and a general aphorism to resist evil. See also *Cooperatio in malum* and *Non facias malum, ut inde fiat bonum.*

Ne fides rideatur
Do not let the faith be ridiculed (laughed at)

Saying of Thomas Aquinas that is used to caution against adopting ill-founded positions that either will prove unverifiable or untenable and thus bring by association the faith or the church into scorn. See also *Crede ut intelligas, Credo quia absurdum, Fides quaerens intellectum, Reductio ad absurdum*

Ne plus ultra
Not more beyond

Term which has two basic uses: in the positive sense it refers to a state of perfection (higher than which one cannot achieve); in the negative sense it connotes a prohibition, i.e., to go no further.

Nec minus salutaris quam festivus
No less salutary than festive

Expression applied to Thomas More's *Utopia* and indicates something that is not only helpful but also celebratory.

Necessitas est lex temporis et loci
Necessity is the law of time and place

Expression that indicates that dire need often trumps other concerns and values, including laws. See also *Epikeia*; *In extrema necessitate omnia, societati hu-*

manae destinata, sunt communia; *Necessitas non habet legem*; *Quod in necessitate sunt omnia communia*; and *Quod non licitum est in lege necessitas facit licitum.*

Necessitas non habet legem
Necessity does not have a law

Another of many similar expressions that express the moral concept that in case of dire need human laws may be broken to meet such basic needs as food, clothing, shelter. See *Epikeia*; *In extrema necessitate omnia, societati humanae destinata, sunt communia*; *Necessitas est lex temporis et loci*; *Quod in necessitate sunt omnia communia*; and *Quod non licitum est in lege necessitas facit licitum.*

Negativa non sunt probanda
Negatives are not proven

Basic point of logical argumentation that it is virtually impossible to prove a negative since proof requires some concrete evidence and a negative does not readily offer that possibility. For example, lacking something concrete like a tape recording or other witnesses it would be very difficult to "prove" that a person did not say or think a certain proposition. See also *Nemo potest ad impossibile obligari* and *Nemo ad inutile tenetur.*

Nemo ad inutile tenetur
No one can be obliged to do what is useless

Expression often used in bioethical reasoning to indicate that "heroic means" in patient care are not morally required. Thus, keeping a person on life support who is brain dead would clearly be inappropriate and not morally required. See also *Deus impossibilia non iubet*, *Lex non intendit impossibile*, *Nemo potest ad impossibile obligari*, *Nemo tenetur ad impossibile*, *Qui tenetur ad finem tenetur ad media*, and *Ultra posse* (or *vires*) *nemo obligatur.*

Nemo dat quod non habet
No one gives what one does not have

Besides a basic philosophical principle, this saying was reputedly used on occasion by seminarians and other non-ordained persons when asked in certain pastoral situations to give some sacramental blessing by some other(s) who thought the given individual in question was in fact an ordained priest. Thus, by giving this sort of pseudo-blessing the one who requested the blessing might be "satisfied" while the seminarian could avoid, from a technical view, the impropriety of misrepresentation and thereby avoid the canonical impediment to ordination of a *dolus* (*q.v.*). The expression is also used in philosophy to indicate that no one can give to another a quality or perfection that the individual lacks him/herself. In this latter sense, see also *Melius est dare quam accipere.*

Nemo iudex in sua causa
No one judges in one's own case

Basic legal and moral principle which prevents one who might otherwise have jurisdiction or authority from judging his or her own case. We see this in contemporary jurisprudence, in which a judge is expected to recuse him/herself from a case in which a previous experience or potential conflict of interest could arise.

Nemo potest ad impossibile obligari

No one is obligated to do the impossible

One of several similar aphorisms which indicate that no one is held to do the very difficult or morally impossible. See also *Deus impossibilia non iubet, Nemo ad inutile tenetur, Nemo tenetur ad impossibile, Qui tenetur ad finem tenetur ad media*, and *Ultra posse* (or *vires*) *nemo obligatur*.

Nemo tenetur ad impossibile

No one is held to the impossible

One of several variations of a basic principle in both law and moral discernment. In moral reasoning any moral "ought" or duty is necessarily predicated upon the actual possibility of performing this action, duty, etc. We are not called upon to attempt the impossible. Thus, one who is "constitutionally" homosexual could not be morally "called" to enter into a heterosexual marriage relationship. See also *Deus impossibilia non iubet, Impossibilium nulla obligatio, Lex non intendit impossibile, Nemo ad inutile tenetur, Nemo potest ad impossibile obligari, Qui tenetur ad finem tenetur ad media*, and *Ultra posse* (or *vires*) *nemo obligatur*.

Nihil amatum nisi praecognitum

Nothing is loved unless it is known first

Thomistic aphorism, variations of which are found throughout the **Summa**

Theologiae, that shows the interrelation between the intellect which moves the will toward acquiring the object desired or loved. See also *Summum bonum*.

Nihil consuetudine maius

Nothing is greater than custom

Another expression which underscores the importance of culture and custom in our lives. In legal interpretation, especially in canon law, a similar principle is found: *consuetudo optima legum interpres* (*q.v.*). See also *Traditio*.

Nihil ex nihilo fit

Nothing from nothing comes

See *ex nihilo*.

Nihil innouetur nisi quod traditum est

No innovation except that which is tradition

Aphorism attributed to Pope Stephen (c. 256) which expresses the idea that nothing new is to be introduced (e.g., in the liturgy) which is not based or found in the church's tradition.

Nihil novi sub sole

Nothing new under the sun

Expression that could be the Latin equivalent of "we've seen this all before." It also indicates the importance of tradition. See also *Mortui vivos docent* and *Traditio*.

Nihil obstat

Nothing stands in the way

In theological writings this term refers to the judgment of the censors that in terms of essential orthodoxy "nothing stands in the way" of the text's being printed, and thus it may be given the *imprimi potest* and/or *imprimatur*, i.e., the formal permission given by the appropriate ecclesiastical authority, usually the bishop of the diocese, for the book to be printed. *Nihil obstat* is also used to indicate approval of the election or promotion of some individual to a post that has some ecclesiastical bearing. Thus, the *nihil obstat* is required for the promotion of a theology professor in a pontifical faculty governed by the statutes of **Sapientia Christiana** (*q.v.*). This is given along with the *placet* (*q.v.*), which indicates that the theological writings of said professor "please" the relevant ecclesiastical authorities and so "nothing stands in the way" (*nihil obstat*) of the professor's promotion in rank. See also *Auctores probati, Censor deputatus, Cum approbatione ecclesiastica, Imprimatur, Imprimi potest*, and *Recognitio*.

Nil nisi bonum
Nothing unless good

Usually this refers to the fuller expressions, *De absentibus nil nisi bonum* (*q.v.*) or *nil nisi bonum de mortuis dicere*, which exhort us not to speak (*dicere*) ill of those absent (*De absentibus*) or the dead (*de mortuis*). See also *Beati mortui qui in Domino moriuntur, Bona mors*, and *Mortui vivos docent*.

Nisi
Unless

Important expression in canon law. A given canon holds true in all circumstances, except (*nisi*) in situations where the following factors hold true. These

factors are then indicated in the canon, and this section of the canon is often termed a "*Nisi* clause."

Nisi enim sponte et ex animo fiat, execratio est
"Unless the act is done freely and from the heart, it is an abomination"

Saying of Lactantius in the third century pronouncing against the Roman law which compelled religious sacrifice. This saying corresponds with the teaching of Thomas Aquinas that no one should ever be forced to act against his or her conscience, and even if this is done the person should resist: "anyone upon whom the ecclesiastical authorities, in ignorance of the true facts, impose a demand that offends against his clear conscience, should perish in excommunication rather than violate his conscience" (Thomas Aquinas, 4 Sent. 38, q. 2, a. 4, Expos. Text). See also **Dignitatis humanae, Mirari vos, Quanta cura**, and **Quod aliquantum**.

Nolens, volens
Unwilling, willing

To have to do something somewhat unwillingly and/or out of mere obligation. Something done *nolens volens* is often done in a rather imperfect manner, and thus the expression might also be translated as "willy nilly."

Noli me tangere
Do not touch [cling to] me

The risen Jesus' words to Mary Magdalene in the Latin Vulgate translation of John 20:17. Used rather more frequently as a sign placed on an object that is not to be removed from its current location, e.g., such as one's bag lunch left in the refrigerator!

Nolo contendere
I do not wish to contend

Usually employed in legal proceedings as part of a plea bargain in which the accused party does not directly admit guilt but yet will not offer a defense, and so is then usually given some sort of (reduced) sentence or fine.

Non compos mentis
Not of sound mind

See *Non sui compos.*

Non constat de nullitate
Nullity is not established

Negative decision handed down in marriage cases in which a decree of nullity is not given. In such a case the prior bond of marriage is held to be binding. See also *Defensor Vinculi, Ligamen,* and *Ratum et consummatum.*

Non est imponenda obligatio nisi certo constet
An obligation is not imposed unless it is clearly established

General principle of law and, by extension, morality, that no obligation or duty is to be understood as imposed or required of someone unless the fact that the given obligation or duty binds is itself clearly and certainly established. See also *Lex dubia non obligat, Dubium iuris, Praesumitur ignorantia ubi scientia non probatur,* and *Sententia incerta non valet.*

Non facias malum, ut inde fiat bonum
One does not do evil so that good may come

Basic principle of the moral order that a morally evil means may never justify even a good end. However, in moral theology there are certainly instances in which one may tolerate, cooperate, and even participate in actions which have evil aspects of effects. See *Cooperatio in malum, Finis operis/Finis operantis,* and *Minus malum.*

Non liquet
Not clear (nor proven)

Expression often used to counter an argument that pretends to be self-evident. See also *Facta non praesumuntur sed probantur; In necessariis unitas, in dubiis libertas, in omnibus caritas; Lex dubia non obligat; Onus probandi; Q.E.D.; Res ipsa loquitur;* and *Tantum valet quantum probat.*

Non multa sed multum
Not many but much

Quality rather than quantity. In prayer and spirituality this expression referred to the depth of the prayer experience as being primary, rather than the number of texts meditated upon and the range of insights acquired. This Latin axiom is a translation of a similar Greek phrase, *ou polla alla pollou* (ου πολλα αλλα πολλου).

Non nobis, Domine sed nomini tuo da gloriam
Not to us Lord, but to your name give glory

From the Latin Vulgate translation of the opening words of Psalm 115, and refers to the prayer that the Lord and his glory are the end to be pursued, and not human glory and honor.

Non nomina sed argumenta
Not names but arguments

Principle which states that truth is not found by citing personages or numbers, but rather through the quality of the arguments for a given position.

Non nova sed nove
Not new things, but in a new way

Refers to the fact that the item under discussion is not an innovation in the sense of being a completely new and different thing, but rather is something established traditionally that is now being adapted or done in a new mode. The presumption behind this sentiment is that something truly "new" would be dangerous or suspect in itself.

Non obstante
Notwithstanding

Non omne, quod licet, honestum est
Not everything that is legal is honest

Basic principle of moral reasoning that shows that mere "legality" does not *ipso facto* demonstrate that the action is therefore good or moral. See also *Lex iniusta non est lex.*

Non placet
It does not please

In certain circumstances this is equivalent to a "no" vote; in other circumstances a *non placet* has the force of withholding a *nihil obstat* (*q.v.*), and therefore blocking an item or placing an impediment in its path. See also *Placet* and *Placet iuxta modum.*

Non salus sed voluntas aegroti suprema lex
It is not health, but the will of the patient that is the highest law

Expression of the principle of autonomy in bioethics, i.e., that the desires of the patient are to be followed as the determinative guideline in decisions regarding health care, even if that should lead to an earlier death than if some other therapeutic course of action were to be followed. This principle is especially important in cases regarding a living will and the use of extraordinary medical means.

Non sequitur
It does not follow

Common expression used to indicate a logical fallacy in an argument, in which the conclusion stated cannot in fact be validly drawn from the premises stated. As a shorthand expression, *non sequitur* means that a certain affirmation is illogical, and therefore it and its dependent conclusions are nonsensical and/or false.

Non sui compos
Not in one's own mind

Refers to someone who is "out of his or her mind" and therefore not of "sound mind" and not legally or morally responsible for one's actions or liable for the fulfillment of a given law or obligation.

Sometimes rendered more commonly as *Non compos mentis*. See also *Compos mentis*.

Non ut explicetur, sed ne taceretur
[We speak] not to explain [the mystery] but to not remain silent

Expression originally used by Augustine in speaking of the Trinity—i.e., that we do not seek to explain fully this mystery, but rather we aim simply at not being reduced to silence in addressing questions about God. This saying therefore is a helpful reminder that theological discourse and dogmatic formulations can never have the precision and completeness of scientific definitions but will retain a certain amount of "necessary" ambiguity. See also *Deus absconditus/Deus revelatus*; *Deus semper maior*; and *Si comprehendis, non est Deus*.

Non valet illatio
The inference (conclusion) does not hold

Judgment that an argument constructed by inference lacks sufficient evidence to be considered valid or conclusive. See also *Petitio principii*.

Norma normans non normata
Norming norm not normed by something else

Refers to a principle, etc., that grounds a discussion, etc., since it establishes itself and does not depend on anything else for its basic legitimacy or authority. See also *Articulus stantis et cadentis ecclesiae* and *Mensura non mensurata*.

Norma normata
Norm normed (by some higher norm)

For example, this principle could refer to something like a magisterial teaching, which, though authoritative, is not absolute, inasmuch as it is subject in turn to the ultimate norm of the Christian revelation as contained within the Scriptures. See *Norma normans non normata*.

Norma universalis
Universal norm

Refers usually to a moral norm which would be transcultural and transhistorical, thus binding upon all in all times, places, and circumstance. Thomas Aquinas' first precept of the natural law, *Bonum est faciendum et prosequendum, et malum vitandum* (*q.v.*), would be one such example. Much of the discussion and controversy in contemporary Roman Catholic moral theology concerns just what can and cannot be considered a true *norma universalis* of the natural law. See also *intrinsece malum*.

Nostra aetate
In our age

Vatican II's Declaration on Non-Christian Religions (1965) which struck a more positive chord in terms of interreligious dialogue and attitudes, especially toward Jews, than had been the case before the council.

Nota bene
Note well

See *N.B.*

Nota (explicativa) praevia
　Preliminary (explanatory) note

For example, an introduction, preface, or explanatory note added to a larger document to help explain its context. An example would be the *Nota praevia* on the meaning of the college of bishops attached as an appendix to **Lumen gentium** (*q.v.*), Vatican II's Dogmatic Constitution of the Church.

Notaria non egent probatione
　Notorious things do not require proof

Canonical principle which indicates that if a crime is "notorious" it does not require a formal juridical process to be "proven." This principle, it should be noted, differs substantially from Anglo-American jurisprudence in which all criminals quite obviously guilty of public crimes are still entitled to plead "not guilty" and have their day in court. In ecclesiastical usage this principle is important since there is a relatively high bar for what qualifies as being truly "notorious," and therefore this principle would militate against those that too easily want to excommunicate or bar individuals from the sacraments, especially the Eucharist, under the rubrics established in canon 915 of the 1983 Code of Canon Law regarding those in "manifest grave sin." Here the canonical principle of *Odia restringi, et favores convenit ampliari* (*q.v.*) would be an important aid in interpreting what might or might not constitute *notaria* in a concrete situation. See also *Gravis neccessitas*; *Latae sententiae*; *Odia restringi, et favores convenit ampliari*; and *Quod lege permittente fit, poenam non meretur.*

Novum
　New thing

Refers to something which is an innovation. See also *Non nova sed nove.*

Novum Testamentum
　The New Testament

Refers to the New Testament of the Bible. See also *In Vetere Novum (Testamentum) latet, et in Novo Vetus patet* and *Vetus Testamentum.*

Novus ordo
　New order

Expression commonly employed by ultraconservatives (such as adherents of the movement of schismatic Archbishop Lefevre) to denigrate the post–Vatican II reformed liturgy (i.e., the vernacular) of the Latin Eucharist. Thus, it serves as a certain code word to locate one's theological sensibilities. In another sense *novus ordo* can also refer to any new order, as in the motto of the Great Seal of the United States: *Novus Ordo Seclorum*, "New Order of the Ages." See also *Ad orientem, Forma extraordinaria, Missale Romanum,* **Summorum Pontificum**, and **Universae Ecclesiae.**

Nulla misericordia sine miseria
　There can be no mercy where there is no misery

This expression indicates that those who have suffered themselves are more likely to show mercy than those who have suffered little.

Nulla parvitas materiae in Sexto
No parvity (lightness/smallness) of (sinful) matter in the sixth commandment

See *Parvitas materiae in Sexto* for the discussion of this term.

Nulla poena sine culpa
No punishment (penalty) without culpability (guilt)

Basic legal principle (also applied in canon law) which indicates that where there is no personal guilt or culpability (*Sine culpa, q.v.*) there should be no penalty. This is important since this means that a mere factual transgression of the law (without personal culpability or intent to violate the law) would not justify the imposition of a penalty. Canon law in particular recognizes this principle in the various mitigating or dispensing conditions that affect the imposition of the so-called "automatic" *latae sententiae (q.v.)* penalties. See the *C.I.C.* 1323 & 1324, which lists several factors removing imputability for a *latae sententiae* penalty. The presence of any one (or more) of these factors *removes* canonical imputability, not merely diminishes it. See also *Absolutus sententia judicis praseumitur innocens*; *Actus reus*; *Mens rea*; *Onus probandi*; *Sententia facit ius*; *Sententia incerta non valet*; *Sine culpa*; *Ubi ius, ibi remedium*; and *Ubi non est culpa, ibi non est delictum.*

Nulla Veritas sine Traditione
There is no truth without tradition

Also the name of the international prize awarded by the International Catholic Association *Tu es Petrus (q.v.)*. The recipient in 2011 was Cardinal Raymond Burke who received the award while attired in the pre–Vatican II galero (elaborate red hat) and cappa magna (flowing red silk cape). Thus, the expression, as well as the organization and award are expressive of a certain ideal of Catholicism that values greatly pre–Vatican II liturgical and ceremonial practices, such as the more elaborate vesture associated with the Tridentine Mass. See also *Cappa magna*; *Coram Cardinale/Coram Episcopo*; *Coetus fidelium*; *Novus Ordo*; *Missale Romanum*; **Summorum Pontificum**; *Quidquid latine dictum sit altum videtur*; *Tu Es Petrus*; *Ubi Petrus ibi ecclesia*; *Ubi Veritas, Deus ibi est*; and **Universae Ecclesiae.**

Nullius dioceseos
(Belonging to) no diocese

This term is often appended to "abbot" and abbreviated by not including the word *dioceseos*. In this usage the term refers to the head of a monastery who as the ecclesiastical superior (ordinary) over the Catholics and parishes within a certain prescribed territory surrounding the monastery, much like a bishop would rule over the faithful in his diocese. The practice of abbots having such jurisdictional power has been largely phased out, though, after the Second Vatican Council.

Nullo modo
No way

Shorthand expression to indicate that in no way would this be possible or considered.

Numerus clausus
Closed number

Refers to a quota imposed upon some group. E.g., due to a limited number of available professors, the dean imposes a *numerus clausus* of students admitted into a particular degree program.

Nunc aut nunquam
Now or never

Expression of a certain urgency and/or desperation.

Nunc dimittis
Now you let me leave

From the Latin Vulgate's rendition of Simeon's prayer of praise and thanksgiving upon seeing the infant Jesus recorded in Luke 2:29: *Nunc dimittis servum tuum, Domine* (Now you let your servant depart, O Lord). This biblical prayer is recited as part of Compline each night in the Liturgy of the Hours (breviary). The expression also can be used to indicate someone's having finished a major project, term of office, or even being ready to die.

Nunc pro tunc
Now for then

Refers to something that is performed or given in the present moment with a view to some future effect. For example, at the age of seventy-five the current Code of Canon Law requires that each diocesan bishop submit his resignation to the Holy See. This resignation might be "accepted" but not "enacted" immediately, e.g., the bishop might remain fully in office until some later date in the future when his resignation would be formally accepted and he would step down as residential bishop.

O

O Adonai
O Lord (of Israel)

See also *Adonai*. The second of the "O Antiphons" that mark the octave of anticipation beginning December 17 for preparation for Christmas Eve, which in itself is the vigil of Christ's birth. Each antiphon gives a different title for the Christ taken from the prophet Isaiah, and when arranged in order of recitation in Latin the titles spell out in reverse order an acrostic in Latin for *Ero Cras* (Tomorrow I come). The order of celebration for the seven antiphons is as follows:

Saptientia (Wisdom)
Adonai (Lord)
Radix Jesse (Root of Jesse)
Clavis David (Key of David)
Oriens (Radiant Dawn, Dayspring)
Rex Gentium (King of the Nations)
Emmanuel (God with us)

O tempora! O mores!
Oh the times, oh the morals

Used by Cicero in his attack on Catiline, but repeated by many since who feel that the present times are the worst of times (in distinction to some mythical Golden Age in the not-so-distant past).

Obedientia et Pax
Obedience and peace

Episcopal motto of Angelo Roncalli, later Pope John XXIII (1958–63). *Obedientia* can also be spelled *Oboedientia* (*q.v.*).

Obiectum (objectum)
Object

In moral philosophy and theology *obiectum* usually refers to the moral end or "object" of an action. Frequently this word is used in combination with other terms to specify a specific point, such as (*Ex*) *Defectu obiecti* (*q.v.*). See also *Ea* (*eorum*) *quae sunt ad finem*, *Finis operis*, *Finis operantis*, and *Voluntarium directum/indirectum*.

Obiectum actus
Object of the act

Usually refers to the moral end or goal (i.e. *Obiectum* or "object") of an action. See also *Actus humanus, Ea* (*eorum*) *quae sunt ad finem*, *Finis operis/operantis*, and *Voluntarium directum/indirectum*.

Obiter dictum/dicta
Incidental remark(s)

The plural is *obiter dicta*. In jurisprudence the expression is used to indicate a statement the judge may make on a tangential issue related to the judicial opinion being given but which has no strict legal bearing upon the case in question. More commonly, it refers, for example, to opinions, etc., given by someone like a professor in the course of the lecture but which do not directly concern the subject matter at hand.

Oboedientia
Obedience

While English-speakers may think this is a crystal clear cognate for "obedience," it should be noted that the primary meaning of the Latin actually refers to an active attitude of "hearkening," "hearing," or "attending" to. The secondary meaning is "yield," "obey," or "be subject to." These nuances are important in both theology and canon law so that we can understand properly what is being requested or expected in terms of "obedience." In this vein, see also the larger discussion under the term *Obsequium religiosum* and the other terms cross-listed there.

Obsequium religiosum
Religious submission (of the will)

Referred to in ***Lumen gentium*** #25, the Code of Canon Law canon 725, and ***Donum veritatis***, the 1990 Congregation for the Doctrine of the Faith's instruction On the Ecclesial Vocation of the Theologian. Used just once in ***Lumen gentium***, the full phrase is *religiosum voluntatis et intellectus obsequium*, and the terms *voluntatis et intellectus* refer respectively to the "will" (*voluntas*) and the "intellect" (*intellectus*) or "mind" (*mentem*, which is used in the phrase which follows). The precise meaning and application of this singular phrase is a much debated issue, especially in terms of how one *translates* this phrase, as well as to how one understands and then applies the phrase. While some prefer "submission" to translate *obsequium* (e.g., ***Donum veritatis*** #23) it should be noted that if this were truly the intent of the council fathers they had other Latin terms such as *submissio* (submission) or *oboedientia* (obedience) that would have captured this meaning more precisely. In general, one might understand this "religious submission" to refer to a fundamental attitude of loyal openness to accept and evaluate the teaching of the magisterium, especially that which is not proposed as being explicitly infallible in a solemn *ex cathedra* (*q.v.*) form. Canon #752 states that "although not an assent of faith, a religious submission of the intellect and will must be given to a doctrine which the Supreme Pontiff or the college of bishops declares concerning faith or morals when they exercise the authentic magisterium, even if they do not intend to proclaim it by definitive act; therefore, the Christian faithful are to take care to avoid those things which do not agree with it," and Canon #749 §3 states that "no doctrine is understood as defined infallibly unless this is manifestly evident." Noted canon lawyer Ladislas Orsy, SJ, and longtime Pontifical Gregorian University ecclesiologist Francis Sullivan, SJ, both suggest that "respect" as opposed to "rejection" would better characterize the attitude of *obsequium religiosum* but that this does *not* mean blind acceptance. See also *De fide definita, Depositum fidei, Diffinimus, Ecclesia docens, Ecclesia discens,*

Ex cathedra, Munus, Oboedentia, Potestas docendi, Proxima fidei, Sententia probata, and *Theologice certa.*

Occasionarii
Those in the [proximate] occasion [of sin]

Reference in the traditional moral theology of labeling in a certain class of penitent those who were likely to fall into a certain sin because they found themselves to be in an occasion which enticed them to commit this sort of sin. Thus, related to the concept of *occasionarii* is the term of proximate occasion of sin, namely something (like a person, place, thing, etc.) which, though not sinful in itself, might be a source of temptation to sin. Thus, entering a tavern could be a proximate occasion of sin for a drunkard but not for a person of temperance. See also *Recidivus.*

Octogesima adveniens
The coming eightieth (anniversary)

1971 apostolic letter of Pope Paul VI on the occasion of the eightieth anniversary of **Rerum novarum** (*q.v.*), Leo XIII's social encyclical On Capital and Labor. This document addressed the issue of securing democratic foundations to operate in human society and also introduced the theme of care for the environment.

Odia restringi, et favores convenit ampliari
Odia sunt restringenda, favores ampliandi
Burdens (odious things) are to be restricted, and favors (privileges) are to be multiplied (or extended)

Principle of canon law interpretation which holds that burdens or strictures are to be interpreted in a narrow sense of application, while on the other hand favors are to be widely applied. In the current Code of Canon Law (1983), canon 18 states, "Laws which establish a penalty, restrict the free exercise of rights, or contain an exception from the law are subject to strict interpretation." A shortened form of this axiom is *Favores ampliandi, odia restringenda* (*q.v.*). See also *Ad literam; Cessante fine cessat lex; Consuetudo optima legum interpres; Dura lex sed lex; Exceptio firmat regulam; In dubio favores sunt amplificandi, odiosa restrigenda; Quod lege permittente fit, poenam non meretur; Sensum, non verba spectamus;* and *Statuta sunt stricte interpretanda.*

Odium
Hatred

See below for some particular examples.

Odium Dei
Hatred of God

Refers to a stance of willful disobedience to the will of God.

Odium fidei
Hatred for the Faith

Refers to one who is martyred for the faith (and is thus eligible for canonization).

Odium theologicum
Theological hatred

Refers to the oft-found controversy among theologians concerning their opponents' doctrinal or moral positions. See also *Hierarchiam veritatem*; *In necessariis unitas, in dubiis libertas, in omnibus caritas*; *Quaestio disputata*; *Sensus fidelium*; *Sententia probata*; *Status quaestionis*; and *Theologice certa.*

Officium
Office, service, or duty

Refers primarily to the exercise of "office" in the church through the conferral of minor and/or major orders. Initially these "offices" were conceived primarily in terms of ritual and liturgical functions but subsequently developed to include wider social and economic aspects, especially when linked to benefices. See also *Munus.*

Olea sancta
Holy oils

Refers to the holy oils blessed by the bishop on Holy Thursday and distributed for use throughout his diocese. In many older churches there would be a special storage place for these oils which often would be labeled *olea sancta.*

Omnes ad
All to

Refers to a situation in which everyone is to participate or devote themselves to a certain task.

Omnes gentes
All peoples, all nations

Common expression found in hymns and psalms, such as *Laudate Dominum, omnes gentes* ("Praise the Lord, all you peoples").

Omnes homines aequales sunt
All humans are equal

Basic principle of natural justice. Though the traditional translation of *homines* here would have been "men," the Latin term refers to human beings in the generic sense and not males.

Omnia parata (sunt)
Everything is prepared

In canon law (cf. *C.I.C.* #1080), refers to a situation, such as an impending marriage, in which all the preparations are complete; therefore, if a certain type of impediment is discovered at the last moment that, if it were to become public, would cause difficulty, a dispensation from the said impediment might be granted in view of the state of affairs *omnia parata* in which everything is already prepared and a cancellation or postponement might, for example, unjustly compromise the reputation of one of the parties.

Omnia vincit amor
Love conquers all

Adage which refers to the principle that in difficult situations love enables one to persevere. See also *Amor vincit omnia.*

Omnia vincit labor
Work conquers all things

Expression which highlights the importance of effort and hard work as the practical means to success. In Virgil, the word order of this sentiment is rendered as *Labor omnia vincit.* This can also be taken as a classical antecedent to *Arbeit macht frei* ("Work makes one free"), which was hung over the Nazi concentration camps.

Omnium in mentem
Reminding everyone

Motu proprio (q.v.) of Pope Benedict XVI issued on 29 October 2009 by which he amended several provisions of the 1983 **Codex Iuris Canonici** *(q.v.)*, or Code of Canon Law.

Onus probandi
The burden of proving (proof)

This refers to the fact that the burden of proof lies upon the one who makes a certain charge, assertion, etc., rather than on one who denies the assertion's truth or claim. The legal aphorism that expresses this principle is *Actori incumbit onus probandi,* as well as the common legal expression of the accused being held innocent until proven guilty, and *a fortiori* if in fact found innocent through a formal process the person must be presumed in fact to be innocent (which is referenced in the legal aphorism *Absolutus sententia judicis praeumitur innocens*). See also *Absolutus sententia judicis praeumitur innocens*; *Actori incumbit onus probandi*; *Actus non facit reum nisi mens sit rea Allegatio contra factum non est admittenda*; *Da mihi factum, dabo tibi ius*; *Ex scientia praesumitur consensus*; *Facta non praesumuntur sed probantur*; *Mens rea*; *Non liquet*; *Res ipsa loquitur*; *Testis in uno falsus in nullo fidem meretur*; and *Ubi non est culpa, ibi non est delictum.*

Op. cit.
In the work cited

Latin abbreviation for *opere citato.* Used in scholarly works in much the same way as *loc. cit. (q.v.)* to refer to a citation which has come previously in the text, but not in the citation immediately prior. For correct usage see an accepted manual of style, such as *The Chicago Manual of Style.*

Opera Omnia
All the works

Refers to the complete works of a given author, such as the *opera omnia* of Thomas Aquinas. "Collected works" would probably be a more contemporary translation.

Operari sequitur esse
Action follows being

Important metaphysical and moral principle in which one's moral duties, possibilities, etc., are grounded in one's being. For similar expressions of this same idea, see also *Agere sequitur esse*; *Modus operandi sequitur modum essendi;* and *Qualis modus essendi, talis modus operandi.*

Opere citato
In the work cited

See *op. cit.*

Opportune et importune
Opportune and inopportune

E.g., in season and out of season, or "always" whether appropriate or not.

Optatam totius
Desired by all (entirely)

Vatican II's Decree on the Training of Priests (1965), which decreed that Scripture was to be foundational (literally, the "soul") of the study of all of theology. See also ***Dei Verbum*** and ***Providentissimus Deus***.

Optima legum interpres consuetudo
Custom is the best interpreter of the law

This expression is the same basic meaning of *Consuetudo optima legum interpres* (*q.v.*). See also *Nihil consuetudine maius* and *Optimus interpres rerum usus*.

Optimus interpres rerum usus
The best interpretation of a thing is its use.

Principle of practical reason that focuses on the primary use of an object in order to understand its purpose or meaning. Abuses, therefore, do not *ipso facto* destroy the legitimacy of proper use. See also *Abusus non tollit usum*, *Consuetudo optima legum interpres*, *Nihil consuetudine maius*, and *Optima legum interpres consuetudo*.

Opus
Work, creation

In Latin, *opus* is used to designate some entity or creation and in this sense is distinguished from *labor*, which means "work" in the sense of an effort expended. See also *Labor* as well as the entries immediately below for some well-known usages of *Opus*.

Opus Dei
Work of God

This phrase has two common meanings in the Catholic Church. The first refers to the celebration of the Liturgy of the Hours in monastic communities, while the second refers to the name of the religious movement founded in 1928 by Saint Josemariá Escrivá de Balaguer (1902–75), which is now a secular institution of both clerics and laypeople and since 1982 governed as a personal prelature.

Opus magnum
A great work

Same as *magnum opus* (*q.v.*).

Opus operantis/operatum

See *Ex opere operantis* and *Ex opere operato*.

Opusculum
A little work

For example, a short treatise or monograph on some subject, which is not meant to be the last word on the subject or the author's *opus magnum*. *Opuscula* (plural), being treatises on particular issues, were distinguished from a *summa* (*q.v.*), which would be a broader summary done in a systematic fashion of the whole of a branch of theology.

Ora et labora
Pray and work

Slogan for the monastic life, often used humorously and/or ironically in other contexts.

Ora pro nobis
Pray for us

Formulaic response in Latin litanies of saints, in which a saint's name is invoked by the leader and the congregation responds with "pray for us": e.g.,

Sancta Maria (Holy Mary), Ora pro nobis (Pray for us). See also *Deus donabilis*, *Pro multis*, and *Pro nobis*.

Orans
(One) Praying

Refers to the liturgical posture or gesture of outstretched arms which is used to indicate the act of prayer and/or intercession.

Orate fratres
Pray my brothers (and sisters)

Latin invocation given to the people after the offertory gifts have been prepared but before the offertory prayer is recited ("Pray my brothers and sisters that my sacrifice and yours be acceptable to God the almighty Father"). This expression is sometimes used to "mark" a point in discussing the parts of the eucharistic liturgy, even when the liturgy is celebrated in the vernacular. Other common Latin "markers" in the liturgy are the *Confiteor* for the Penitential Rite, the *Hanc igitur* for the beginning of the Institution Narrative (Consecration), the *Pater Noster* for the Our Father and the *Agnus Dei* for the Lamb of God. See also *Domine non sum dignus*, *Oratio*, and *Oremus*.

Oratio (plural Orationes)
Prayer

Usually used for liturgical prayers, such as the collect or opening prayer in the Mass. An *Oratio imperata* (prayer that is ordered) denoted special prayers mandated by the pope or a bishop for a special cause (e.g., the *oratio imperata* for peace that was said during World

War I). The *Oratio super oblata* referred to the offertory prayer over the bread and wine at Mass (*oblata* is "offerings"). The *Oratio super populum* is the prayer over the people done in solemn blessings at the end of Mass (in English this is designated by the presider's words "Bow down your heads and pray for God's blessing"). See also *Orate fratres* and *Oremus*.

Orbis terrarum
The whole world

This expression comes from the longer dictum of Augustine, *Securus iudicat orbis terrarum (q.v.)*, namely "Secure is the judgment of the whole world," and refers to a broad consensus to confirm that a position is probably true. Of course the whole world can still be in objective error and only a minority (or no one) be in possession of the truth on a certain proposition as expressed in *Consensus non facit veritatem (q.v.,* "consensus does not make truth"). In theological terms *orbis terrarum* is related to the *Consensus fidelium (q.v.)* and was invoked by Blessed John Henry Cardinal Newman, who held that the validity of the First Vatican Council would depend in large part upon the reception of the *orbis terrarum*. See also *Ecclesia docens/Ecclesia discens,* the entries under *Magisterium*, *Sensus fidelium*, *Solus consensus obligat*, and *Urbi et Orbi*.

Ordinatio rationis
Ordering of reason

Expresses a fundamental idea of human moral action, i.e., that which acts in accord with human reason, and thus is ordered to and by reason. All law is meant to conform to this order of reason, and the natural law would be the pre-eminent expression of the order of reason. See also *Ordo*, *Ordo rationis*, and *Ordinatio rationis ad bonum commune*.

Ordinatio rationis ad bonum commune
Rational ordering for the common good

St. Thomas' definition of a proper law. This definition highlights the essential purpose of law itself, namely, that it be for the good of all, and thus the common good itself, rather than the will of the legislator, becomes the evaluative principle for determining when a law is in fact proper. See also *Bonum commune*; *Lex semper intendit quod convenit rationi*; *Ordo publicus*; *Salus publica suprema lex*; and *Ubi cessat ratio legis, cessat ipsa lex*.

Ordinatio sacerdotalis
The ordination of priests

Pope John Paul II's apostolic letter On Priestly Ordination reaffirming the Roman Catholic Church's opposition to women's ordination (1994). See also *Alter Christus*, *Cura animarum*, **Inter Insigniores**, *Dubium*, *Responsum ad dubium*, and *In persona Christi*.

Ordinationes
Those things ordained (ordered)

Often refers to practical directives "ordained" or prescribed from some legal document. Thus, the practical directives governing the relationship of Catholic academic institutions of higher learning would be the *ordinationes* coming out of *Ex corde ecclesiae* (*q.v.*), Pope John Paul II's 1990 apostolic constitution on Catholic Universities. One of these *ordinationes* was the call for Catholic teachers of philosophy and theology to seek a *mandatum* (*q.v.*) from their local bishop to certify that their teaching would be in accord with the official teachings of the church.

Ordines
Orders, arrangements

In liturgical use *ordines* refer to the ceremonial books which contain rules, etc., for the celebration of various liturgical rites, sacraments, etc.

Ordines Sacri
Holy Orders

Refers to ordination to the "major orders" of deacon, priest, and bishop.

Ordo
Order

Besides the liturgical usage of the term, in which *ordo* refers to the liturgical calendar, in theology (and especially in moral theology) *ordo* refers to a basic orientation which affects, directs, and "orders" everything that it touches. Thus, the *ordo amoris* refers to the basic orientation which would animate and direct human life according to the end, goal, or principle of love. See also *Ad libitum*, *Tabula dierum liturgicorum*, as well as the various specifications of *ordo* which follow below.

Ordo amoris
Order of love

That which refers to and is governed by, or in accord with, the principle of love.

Another rendition of this principle is *ordo caritatis* (the order of charity) which views charity as the primary virtue, or that which would provide the highest value in instances of a conflict of values or duties. Thus, in a conflict situation we should do what love seems to require.

Ordo bonorum
Order (or hierarchy) of goods

This principle is related to the fundamental principle of the natural law, namely that the good (*bonum*) is to be done and fostered and evil (*malum*) is to be avoided. Therefore, in one's moral actions in conflict situations, one should seek to choose the good if this is realistically possible, or at least to minimize or choose the lesser of evils. In choosing the lesser of evils one therefore is being guided or governed by the *ordo bonorum*, i.e., one acts in accord with the principle of the order of goods. See also *Bonum est faciendum et proseguendum et malum vitandum*; *Malum non est faciendum ut eveniat bonum*; *Minus malum*; *Non facias malum, ut inde fiat bonum*; *Ordo amoris*; and *Ordo rationis*.

Ordo caritatis
Order of charity

See *Ordo amoris*.

Ordo Missae
Order of the Mass

Refers to the section of the *Missale Romanum* (*q.v.*) that contains the ordinary (e.g., unchangeable part of the Mass) and the eucharastic canon (as distinguished from the Propers of the Missal,

which contain the specific prayers to be said on a given Sunday or feast).

Ordo publicus
Public order

This phrase usually is taken to refer to the necessity of maintenance of the rights and duties of the state and individuals in a society in such a way so as to provide for the common good. Thus, *ordo publicus* would not usually refer to "public order" in the narrow sense of maintaining public decorum. See also *Bonum commune, Ordinatio rationis ad bonum commune*, and *Salus publica suprema lex*.

Ordo rationis
Order of reason

That which governs the human life according to the principle of reason. See also *Ens rationis, Lumen naturale, Ordo, Ordo bonorum, Ordinatio rationis, Per modum cognitionis/Per modum inclinationis*, and *Recta ratio*.

Ordo rectitudinis
Order of rectitude

Refers to the order or plan established by God for creation, an order of righteousness, which has been marred by human sinfulness—both original sin and individual sins committed over the course of time. See also *Ordo* and *Summum iustitia in se*.

Ordo salutis
Order of salvation

Refers to God's saving will and the plan for human justification and salvation. See also *Ordo* and *Processus iustificationis*.

Ordo sapientiae
Order of wisdom

The basic principle which orders human life according to reason and wisdom. See also *In vestimentis non stat sapientia mentis*, *Lumen naturale*, *Ordo*, *Recta ratio*, and *Stultis non succuritur*.

Oremus
Let us pray

Invocation to pray used by the presider in liturgical celebrations. After a brief pause the prayer formula itself is recited. See also *Oratio*.

Oremus pro invicem
Let us pray for one another

Common expression, often used as a closing salutation, among religious and others with some acquaintance of Latin.

Oriens
Radiant Dawn, Dayspring

The fifth of the "O Antiphons" that mark the octave of anticipation or preparation for Christmas Eve, which in it-self is the vigil of Christ's birth. See the fuller discussion under *O Adonai*.

Orientalium Ecclesiarum
Of the Eastern churches

Vatican II Decree on the Eastern Rite Churches in union with Rome (1964).

Orientem, ad

See *Ad orientem*.

Oscula solita
The accustomed kisses

In the church's liturgical tradition this term refers to the ritual kisses given to various liturgical ministers or sacred objects, such as the kiss of peace or the kiss given to the book of the Gospels by the bishop after the Gospel has been proclaimed by the deacon. In some cultures this practice is also extended as a mark of respect, such as the Italian *bacciamano* (literally, "kissing the hand"), which is the term for a courtesy call made to a notable (as was also the custom of kissing the bishop's ring).

P

Pace
> Peace

In English this word connotes "with due respect" in the face of a potential disagreement. Thus, an opinion may be put forth that, "*pace* Rahner," differs from that of the great theologian Karl Rahner.

Pacem in terris
> Peace on earth

Social (and last) encyclical of Pope John XXIII on peace on earth (1963), which was addressed not just to Catholics but to all people of good will. In this encyclical the pope tackled the problems not only of war in general but also contemporary issues such as the Cold War, respect among all nations, and human rights.

Pacta sunt servanda
> Agreements (pacts) are kept (or observed)

Basic axiom of contract law which indicates that legal agreements properly constituted are considered binding on the parties who knowingly and freely entered in upon them.

Pallium
> Cover/cloak

A circular band of white wool worn by the pope and archbishops over liturgical vestments as a sign of office and collegiality with one another. The *pallium* is laid on the tomb of St. Peter in the Basilica of St. Peter's in the Vatican and then is sent by the pope to the archbishop or given to him in a special ceremony in St. Peter's.

Pange Lingua
> Sing my tongue

Title of a traditional Latin eucharistic hymn attributed to Thomas Aquinas, the final two stanzas of which are sung at eucharistic Benediction. The penultimate stanza begins with the words *Tantum ergo Sacramentum veneremur cernui* (Come venerate and bow to this Sacrament).

Panis Angelicus
> Bread of angels

Euphemism for Holy Communion, and also the name given to a hymn written by Thomas Aquinas (and set to a variety of musical tunes and settings) sung at Communion and/or at Benediction.

Pars propter totum.
> Part (is) for the (good of the) whole

Traditional axiom expressing the principle of totality, in which a part may be sacrificed for the good of the whole. For example, in a therapeutic operation on a diseased organ or bodily function it was considered permissible to sacrifice that organ or function when no other possibility existed to secure the well-being of the total organism, for example, to amputate a gangrenous limb which if left untended would cause death of the whole person. A similar idea is also expressed in the adage *Bonum totius (q.v.)*, for the "good of the whole." See also *Mala moralia* and *mala praemoralia*; *Ratio proportionata*; and *Si finis bonus est, totum bonum erit*.

Partes honestae
Honorable parts (of the body)

See *Partes inhonestae* and *Partes minus honestae* for a discussion of this concept.

Partes inhonestae
Dishonest (dishonorable or less noble) parts

Euphemistic expression for the sexual organs, suggested by Paul's expression found in 1 Corinthians 12:23-24 and used in the Latin Vulgate translation of the Bible to translate Greek equivalents for the sexual organs. This expression also indicates a negative view toward human sexuality which unfortunately has had a long history in the theological tradition of the church from the time of Augustine up to very recent times. The *partes inhonestae* were distinguished from the *partes minus honestae* such as the breasts, thighs, upper arms, etc., and these in turn were contrasted with the *partes honestae*, which comprised the rest of the body. See also *Ex toto genere suo, Inhonestum, (In) Re venerea, Materia levis (gravis), Partes honestae, Partes minus honestae*, and **Persona humana.**

Partes minus honestae
The less noble parts of the body

Refers to the parts of the body such as the breasts, thighs, upper arms, etc. For a fuller discussion of this concept see *Partes inhonestae*. See also *Ex toto genere suo, (In) Re venerea, Materia levis (gravis), Partes honestae*, and **Persona humana.**

Particula veri
Particular truths

This expression refers usually to certain things which may have aspects of truth, but the nuance suggests that there also is much in the discussion that is incomplete, false, or misleading. For example, Karl Barth uses this term in his section on casuistry to acknowledge that, while casuistry certainly could illustrate valid points in moral analysis of human acts, overall the casuistical approach (in Barth's view) was fundamentally unacceptable. (Cf. Karl Barth, "The Command of God the Creator" §52 in his *Church Dogmatics*). See also *In vino veritas*; *Ubi Veritas, Deus ibi est*; *Veritas*; and *Vincit veritas*

Parvitas materiae in Sexto
(No) Parvity of (moral) matter in the sixth (commandment)

The full expression would be *Nulla parvitas materiae in Sexto*, though usually the shortened form, without the *nulla* (nothing/no), is more commonly found.

This traditional theological adage held that any sexual sin always contained grave matter, i.e., one of the three requisites necessary for mortal sin (along with sufficient knowledge and consent). If someone would engage in any sexual activity for the purpose of sexual stimulation (even hand-holding or close dancing), the traditional view held that this activity would be mortally sinful. Even more so, in this view (seemingly repeated in recent Vatican documents on sexual ethics such as **Persona humana** and the **Catechism of the Catholic Church**) each act of teenage masturbation *could* be potentially material for mortal sin. See also *Ex toto genere suo*, *(In) Re venerea*, *Materia levis (gravis)*, *Partes honestae*, *Partes minus honestae*, *Partes inhonestae*, **Persona humana***i*, *Rara con tigribus*, *Remedium concupiscientiae*, and *Sub levi*.

Parvus error in initio magnus erit in fine

Small error in the beginning; large (error) will be in the end

See *Parvus error in principiis, magnus error in conclusionibus* as well as *Falsus in uno falsus in omnibus* and *Ignorantia elenchi*.

Parvus error in principiis, magnus error in conclusionibus

Small error in the beginning leads to great error in the conclusion

Adage which points to the vital importance of establishing a good beginning, especially in matters of one's methodological premises and operating principles. A small error in these will lead to larger errors drawn as conclusions. Thomas Aquinas begins his treatise *De entis et essentia* ("On being and essence") with a slightly different version of this axiom: *Parvus error in initio magnus erit in fine* ("Small error in the beginning; large [error] will be in the end"). See also *Falsus in uno falsus in omnibus*.

Pascendi Dominici gregis

Pasturing the Lord's flock

Pope Pius X's encyclical condemning the errors of modernism, and often referred to simply as **Pascendi** (1907). See also **Lamentabili**.

Passim

Here and there

Scholarly reference used to indicate that the cited topic, etc., is found in a variety of places in a certain text. E.g., "p. 23 and *passim*" indicates a principal reference to page 23, but also indicates this same topic is found in a number of other places in the text.

Pastor aeternus

Eternal Pastor

Vatican I's Dogmatic Constitution on the Church of Christ, which included the formulation of the doctrine of papal infallibility (1870). See also *Credenda*, *De fide vel moribus*, *Depositum fidei*, *Ex cathedra*, and *Tenenda*.

Pastor Bonus

Good Pastor

1988 apostolic constitution of John Paul II that reorganized some of the discasteries (offices) of the Roman Curia, such as the Congregation for the Doctrine of the Faith, and articulated the mission or area of competency of the various Vatican organs.

Pastores dabo vobis
I give you (pl.) pastors

1992 post-synodal apostolic exhortation of Pope John Paul II on priestly ministry ("I Will Give You Shepherds").

Pater est, quem nuptiae demonstrant
The (presumed) father is the one shown by the nuptial ceremony

I.e., in cases of contested doubt over paternity the legal presumption was cast in favor of the man legally married to the mother. Contemporary genetic testing, though, has rendered this principle less helpful. See also *Pater semper incertus*.

Pater Noster
Our Father

Opening words of the Lord's Prayer, and often used to indicate the whole prayer itself. See also *Ave Maria* and *Fiat voluntas Tua*.

Pater semper incertus
The father is always

Until the recent advent of genetic paternity tests, this principle was true—i.e., that it was difficult to confirm with absolute certainty who the father might be in cases of doubt or conflict. See also *Pater est, quem nuptiae demonstrant* for an indication of how this doubt was resolved in canon law.

Paterfamilias
Father of the family

A patriarch, a senior male relative, or the male head of a household. The feminine equivalent would be a *materfamilias (q.v.)*.

Pax
Peace

Can be used as a greeting or in combination with other words.

Pax Christi
Peace of Christ

Often used as a greeting in letters written in ecclesiastical or religious circles. Also is the name of an advocacy group for certain social justice issues and causes.

Pax Dei
Peace of God

Medieval practice of immunity from involvement in warfare extended to clerics, religious, and noncombatants, which also included (in theory at least) churches, monasteries, and similar properties. The *Pax Dei* also was extended in certain areas to a cease-fire on Sundays and certain religious feasts. Violators could be punished by interdict by the appropriate ecclesiastical authority. See also *Ius in bello*.

Pax ecclesiae
Peace of the church

Expression linked historically to the sacrament of reconciliation, which originally developed to restore public sinners to the church and at the same time to restore the peace of the Christian community which had been rent by sin. See also *Ius communicationis*.

Pax et bonum
Peace and goodness

May be used as a greeting, blessing, or pious wish. Often associated with St. Francis of Assisi.

Pax Romana
Roman peace

Refers to a somewhat enforced "peace" as a result of the imperial domination of the ancient Roman Empire. In contemporary politics one occasionally speaks of a *Pax Americana*, which is usually meant pejoratively to refer to American superpower domination in the world's affairs.

Pax tecum/vobiscum
Peace be with you (sing./pl.)

Commonly used as a greeting and also in the Roman liturgy as celebrated in Latin. See also *Dominus vobiscum*.

Pecca fortiter
Sin boldly

While at first glance this expression seems diabolical, it is the idea advanced by Martin Luther to underscore that we are saved by God's grace and not by our own actions. Therefore, we are called to place our faith in the saving work of redemption of God's Son, Jesus Christ, and not to obsess with the casuistry that might be employed in trying to figure out degrees of gravity of sin and the like. The full aphorism is *Pecca fortiter sed fortius fide et gaude in Christo* (Sin boldly, but believe and rejoice in Christ more boldly still). See also *Fides fiducialis*, *Peccata contra naturam sunt gravissima*, *Simul iustus et peccator*, *Sola fide*, *Sola gratia*, *Solus Christus*, and *Totus conversus sed non totaliter*.

Peccata contra naturam sunt gravissima
Sins against nature are most gave

See the longer entry under *contra naturam* for an explanation of this term. See also *Intrinsece malum*, *Ius naturae est immutabile*, and *Parvitas Materiae in Sexto*.

Peccata criminalia
Criminal sins

This expression was used to refer to gravely scandalous sins. In the earlier history of the sacrament of reconciliation these sins, because of their serious and public nature, were understood as requiring confession to a bishop or priest so that the individual could be restored to the Christian community and the community itself healed of this injury. As time went on all serious "mortal" sins could be considered *peccata criminalia* and had to be confessed according to number and species in individual confession. See also *Graviter et dolose*, *Graviora delicta*, and *Peccata mortalia*.

Peccata mortalia
Deadly (mortal) sins

Another expression in Catholic theology, similar to *Peccatum mortale* (*q.v.*) to describe those sins which when done with sufficient knowledge and consent would break the individual's relationship with God and deprive him or her of the life of sanctifying grace. Those who died in the state of mortal sin would presumably go to hell for eternity. See also the other entries under *Peccata*.

Peccatum & Peccata
Sin & Sins (singular and plural forms)

Peccatum is the Latin term used to translate the biblical Greek concepts for "sin," though the Latin word carries more of a nuance of "crime" than the corresponding Greek terms found in the New Testament: ἁμαρτια [(*hamartia*) missing the mark], ὑβρις [(*hubris*) pride], and αδκια [(*adikia*) unrighteousness].

Peccatum mortale
Mortal sin

Sin which is considered "deadly" in that it destroys one's graced relationship with God. See *Peccatum veniale*.

Peccatum originale
Original sin

Refers to the sin of the first parents, Adam and Eve, which resulted in the loss of the original nature of human innocence and whose "stain" or effect is transmitted to all subsequent human beings. The sin of Adam and Eve is often called *peccatum originale originans* (the "originating" of original sin), while the original sin and its effects on all humans born subsequently to the sin of our first parents is called *peccatum originale originatum* ("originated" original sin). This distinction between *peccatum originale originans* and *pec-catum originale originatum* is rather difficult to render into good English in a literal fashion.

Peccatum veniale
Venial (pardonable) sin

Sin which is not ultimately destructive ("mortal") of one's life relationship with God through sanctifying grace. *Peccatum veniale* is usually contrasted with *peccatum mortale*, or mortal (deadly) sin, which does destroy the individual's life relationship with God. Though all sin can be forgiven by God, "venial" comes from the Latin *venia* (meaning "pardon") and therefore carries the nuance of being more easily overlooked or pardoned in the sense that it does not cause a definitive rupture in the relationship.

Per
Through, throughout, by, owing to

Common Latin preposition.

Per accidens
By accident

In scholastic terminology an "accident" refers to something that occurs indirectly or which is not essential to the matter itself. In this latter sense, *per accidens* would be contrasted with *per se* (*q.v.*). See also *Accidens*, *Essentia*, and *Per Se*.

Per additionem
By addition

Term used usually to describe how what "materially" might be just a venial sin could become a mortal sin. For example, loose language, which of itself might be "venial," if used to seduce another into fornication might then become mortally sinful.

Per annum
Per year

Refers to something paid down annually or on a yearly basis.

Per ardua ad astra
Through adversity (difficulties) to the stars

Common variant of *Ad astra per aspera* (*q.v.*).

Per capita
Per head

Refers to something taken individually. Also can refer to a rate computed according to each individual who partakes of or uses a certain service, etc. "The *per capita* income of this country is $20,000 *per annum*" means that averaged together the yearly income of each individual is $20,000.

Per diem
Per day

This refers to a daily rate or charge. In some religious congregations *per diem* often refers to the cost-per-day to support an individual in a certain house of the community, or the charge that a guest is expected to pay when visiting a certain house.

Per ipsum
Through him

Opening words of the doxology recited by the presider at the conclusion of the Latin eucharistic canon. The text of the entire prayer is *Per ipsum, et cum ipso,*

et in ipso est tibi Deo Patri omnipotenti, in unitate Spiritus Sancti, omnis honor et gloria. Per omnia saecula saeculorum ("Through him, with him, and in him, in the unity of the Holy Spirit, all glory and honor is yours almighty Father, forever and ever"). The congregation responds with "Amen" to this doxology. The "him" in the prayer refers to Jesus Christ. *Per ipsum* is also a shorthand designation for the entire doxology.

Per mensem
Per month

Refers to something done or computed on a monthly basis.

Per modum absolutionis
By way (manner, mode) of absolution

This expression is generally used to refer to the means by which sins, or the punishment due to our sins, are remitted. In this case, the term refers to forgiveness of sins through absolution by the priest in the sacrament of reconciliation. Often this expression is related to the theology of indulgences as well, i.e., the church's long-standing belief that the merits of Jesus Christ obtained for our salvation are inexhaustible in themselves and that part of the church's sanctifying role is to help administer or mediate these saving merits through the sacraments, sacramentals, indulgences, and so on. See also *Per modum suffragii.*

Per modum cognitionis/Per modum inclinationis
Judgment by means of cognition (intellect)/Judgment by means of inclination

In the beginning of the **Summa Theologiae**, Thomas Aquinas makes a distinction between two kinds of knowledge: that which is acquired through study and is therefore known through the modality of cognition (*per modum cognitionis*) and that which is known by natural inclination (*per modum inclinationis*), which is more of an innate or "connatural" knowledge. The example Thomas uses concerns "virtue"—we could study about virtue and come to some judgment about it as an intellectual property (*per modum cognitionis*), but the more important knowledge in this instance would be the natural inclination to embrace virtue, and this would be done *per modum inclinationis*. However, experience often teaches us that sometimes the intellectual knowledge is insufficient to move us to embrace the corresponding virtue. For example, I "know" *per modum cognitionis* that I have high cholesterol and should limit my intake of cheese, but as a native son of Wisconsin I often find it hard to practice the necessary virtue of dietary restraint. However, if I could train myself in the exercise of this virtue *per modum inclinationis*, then my habit would eventually correspond to follow a proper diet more easily and effectively. See Thomas Aquinas' discussion on this point, which can be found at ST I–I, q. 1, a. 6, reply to obj. 3, and also an important further discussion on the relation of charity to the connatural knowledge of divine things is discussed at ST II–II, q. 45, a. 2. See also *Ens rationis*, *Lex indita non scripta*, *Lex naturalis*, *Ordo rationis*, and *Recta ratio*.

Per modum inclinationis
Judgment by means of inclination

See the discussion above under the title *Per modum cognitionis*.

Per modum suffragii
By way (manner, mode) of support (*suffrage* in ecclesiastical usage)

See *Per modum absolutionis* for an explanation of the relation of this term to the remission of sins. In distinction to *per modum absolutionis*, *per modum suffragii* refers to the remission of temporal punishment due to sin by means of the church's own prayers for the deceased and indulgences. Thus, prayers offered by the living for the dead, such as "Eternal rest grant unto to him/her O Lord, and let perpetual light shine upon him/her," were viewed as earning credit for the temporal punishment due to sins incurred by the individual while living and which may have been forgiven but some of whose temporal punishment effects still remained at the time of death. See also *Ecclesia militans*, *Per modum absolutionis*, and *Toties quoties*.

Per saecula saeculorum
Forever and ever

Common formulaic ending used in liturgical prayers. See also *Gloria Patri* and *Saecula saeculorum*.

Per se
By itself

Refers to the intrinsic nature of something, and often in English *per se* could be rendered as "strictly speaking" and thus is used to qualify a statement. Philosophically and/or theologically, *per se* refers to the essence of a given thing and is distinguished from those nonessential characteristics (identified as being *per accidens*), which of themselves do not change the essential nature of a thing. See also *Essentia* and *Per accidens.*

Per se illicitum, per accidens licitum
In itself (morally) illicit; through certain circumstances ("accidents") licit

Expression that a certain action was usually considered in itself morally illicit (wrong) but that in view of certain extenuating circumstances the action might be morally acceptable in a given particular situation. For example, in the late nineteenth and first half of the twentieth centuries there was a debate that deliberate use of the infertile period by married couples to avoid pregnancy was *per se illicitum* but that a particular married couple, due to certain circumstances (such as disease, etc.), might be able morally to use the infertile period in this way, even though for most married couples this same usage (without the presence of the mitigating circumstances) would have been considered morally illicit.

Per se nota
Known through themselves, not derived, self-evident

Refers to something that is known or self-evident through the normal use of human intelligence and therefore needs no further logical proof or the help of some other middle term to aid in apprehension. See also *Naturaliter nota.*

Perfectae caritatis
Perfect charity

Vatican II's Decree on the Renewal of Religious Life (1965).

Perfectus
Complete, finished, excellent, perfect

This Latin word is widely used in theological vocabulary and is the root of the English word "perfect." However, often this very similarity with the English word can be misleading. *Perfectus* more often bears the connotation of being whole, complete, autonomous, and less frequently the nuance of being without blemish, fault, or imperfection. *Perfectus* was often used to translate the Greek word *telos* (τελος) and/or the Hebrew word *shalom* (שלם). However, these latter two words carry connotations of teleology, being in the process of becoming more whole, complete, fulfilled, accomplished, healthy and at peace, etc. Thus, Jesus' command given in Matthew 5:48, "Therefore be perfect as your Heavenly Father is perfect," the Greek word which is rendered as "perfect" is a form of *telos*. Jesus is not giving an impossible command to be without any blemish, fault, or imperfection, but rather is giving an exhortation to continue along the path of wholeness and completion.

Periculum matrimonii
Danger of marriage

Refers to the perceived danger to contract a civil marriage by someone who is otherwise not "free" to marry, such as a priest, deacon, or professed religious. The *periculum matrimonii* may be cited by a relevant ecclesiastical superior as a reason for giving or expediting a laicization or dispensation from the religious vow of chastity.

Periculum peccandi
Danger of sin

An act which may not be objectively or explicitly sinful in itself but which nevertheless involves courting a near occasion of sin, e.g., reading pornographic literature may lead one into the sin of fornication or masturbation.

Peritus
Expert

Someone who has a special knowledge or competence and who may be called upon for help or expert testimony (e.g., in some canon law marriage cases). Theologians often function as *periti* for members of the *magisterium* (*q.v.*). For example, at Vatican II a theologian who served as a consultant to the bishops was called a *peritus* (pl., *periti*). Even though the *periti* would not have a deliberative vote in the council sessions their input was very important. Several *periti* at Vatican II, such as Yves Congar, Henri de Lubac, and Karl Rahner, were theologians who in the years prior to the council had their work censured or cast under suspicion by certain Vatican offices. See also *Auctoritas, Ecclesia discens, Ecclesia docens, Inquisitio, Magisterium, Magisterium attestans, Magisterium authenticam, Magisterium docens, Potestas docendi, Sensus fidelium, Sententia probata,* and *Theologice certa.*

Permissum est furari non solum in extrema necessitate sed etiam in grave
It is permitted to take the necessary goods not only in extreme necessity but also in grave necessity

See the larger discussion under the axiom *Quod in necessitate sunt omnia communia.* Among moralists, there was a debate as to how much "necessity" was required to make the involuntary theft morally licit, e.g., whether the need had to be "extreme" or merely "grave." While the former position was generally accepted Pope Innocent XI condemned this laxer proposition. See *Denzinger* #1186 for the Pope's condemnation. See also *In extrema necessitate onmnia, societati humanae destinata, sun communia; Iustitiam subsidiariam;* and *Quod in necessitate sunt omnia communia.*

Persona facit opera
The person does the (moral) works

Statement attributed to Martin Luther, which theologically speaking indicates that the key for the moral life is the person who stands behind and "does" the good works. This expression might also be used to indicate the deep connection between one's moral actions and his or her apprehension of the nature of these actions in conscience, or in other words, the status of one's fundamental option. This latter interpretation comes from the work of Josef Fuchs, SJ, who uses Luther's statement in the former's treatment of conscience. Cf. Josef Fuchs, SJ, "The Phenomenon of Conscience: Subject-orientation and Object-orientation," in *Christian Morality: The Word Became*

Flesh, (Washington, DC: Georgetown University Press; Dublin: Gill and Macmillan, 1987), 124.

Persona (non) grata
Person (not) acceptable

Most commonly, this expression is used in the negative, and a *persona non grata* would refer to someone who is considered a pariah or no longer welcome for some reason. See also *Personae minus gratae* and *Promoveatur ut amoveatur*.

Persona humana
The human person

The Congregation for the Doctrine of the Faith's Declaration on Certain Problems of Sexual Ethics (1975). This document was used for the first time in a Vatican teaching that marked the concept of "sexuality" as distinct from sexual activity and also stated in paragraph 8 that the homosexual orientation was not usually freely chosen and therefore should not be equated with personal sin. All masturbation, though, was still regarded as potentially mortally sinful. See also *Ex toto genere suo, (In) re venerea, Materia levis (gravis)*, and *Parvitas materiae in Sexto*.

Persona iuridica
Juridic person

Refers to a legal "person" in law and therefore can refer not only to human persons but also institutes, congregations, and the like, which enjoy legal recognition.

Personae minus gratae
Persons less desirable (plural form of *persona non grata, q.v.*)

In ecclesiastical politics, this expression was tied to the so-called Right of Exclusion (*Ius Exclusivae, q.v.*) exercised in papal conclaves by the cardinals of key Catholic countries such as Austria, France, and Spain to indicate on behalf of their respective monarchs potential papal candidates which would be undesirable if elected pope. This right became a sort of anticipatory veto, though it is no longer in force today.

Petitio principii
Asking the principles (premises); begging the question

In a logical or reasoned argument, this refers to asserting the very principle that one either seeks to prove or which in itself is necessary in order to prove some other position. Thus, this action would be a violation of logic and render the resulting conclusions as suspect at best. See also *Non valet illatio*.

Philosophia perennisis
Perennial (always valid) philosophy

Claim that a certain philosophical approach, such as an Aristotelian or Thomistic system, because of its abstract and "universal" rational basis and language, would be virtually transcultural and transhistorical and therefore valid for all peoples. This philosophical view is often tied to a classicist worldview and a certain approach to the natural law. However, this expression may also refer to a simple statement of a fact and thus in that sense can be called an "enduring" or "perennial" philosophy.

Pia opinio
Pious opinion

Expression used to refer to range of theological "notes" or supposed theological positions or opinions which rank at the lower end of certainty. At the other end would be those tenets of the faith which are solemnly defined. See also *De fide definita*, *Depositum fidei*, *Diffinimus*, *Ex cathedra*, *Obsequium religiosum*, *Proxima fidei*, *Sententia probata*, and *Theologice certa*.

Piarum aurium offensiva
Offensive to pious ears

An expression used in conjunction with *male sonans* (*q.v.*, evil sounding) which denoted something that, though possibly true, was considered indecorous and offensive to the reverent belief of pious believers. Depending on the particular, such an offense might also constitute a sin against charity such as detraction. See also *Delectatio morosa* and *Scandalum pusillorum*.

Pietas
Piety

Besides the literal translation as "piety," in Christian spirituality *pietas* can refer to a general attitude of respect, reverence, and appreciation for God and the spiritual life.

Placet
It pleases

Equivalent to a yes vote, the opposite being *non placet* (*q.v.*). The *placet* is also used as an equivalent to granting the *nihil obstat* (*q.v.*) for the promotion of a theology professor in a pontifical faculty, i.e., the theological writings of said professor "please" the relevant ecclesiastical authorities and so "nothing stands in the way" (*nihil obstat*) of the professor's promotion in rank. See also *Non placet*, *Placet iuxta modum*, and *Recognitio*.

Placet iuxta modum
It pleases with an amendment added

In deliberative votes, such as an ecumenical council, one might be able to vote "yes, but" and indicate that the document or matter under vote is basically acceptable as long as certain amendments or further items are taken into consideration and addressed. For example, in Vatican II most of the final documents came as a result of several drafts on earlier versions which had been approved by the majority *placet iuxta modum*. See also *Placet* and *Non placet*.

Placuit Spiritui sancto et nobis
Pleased the Holy Spirit and us

Expression taken from Acts 15:28 referring to the First Apostolic Council of Jerusalem (AD 70) that indicates a belief that a decision or course of action taken by the leaders of the church, e.g., the church fathers acting in communion in an ecumenical council, is in fact pleasing to the Holy Spirit and thus in accord with the will of God.

Plantatio ecclesiae
Planting, setting in place the church

Expression which indicates that one of the aims of missionary evangelization is the establishment or enlargement of the church in the world, though the principle mission given by Christ remains the *salus animarum (q.v.)*. See also *Extra ecclesia nulla salus.*

Plus minus non mutat speciem
"More" or "less" does not change the "species" of a thing.

Logical expression which asserts that adding or subtracting from a "total" will not change the essence of a matter. For example, a half cup of water and two cups of water will not change the "essence" that is water. This expression is used in theological discourse, such as by Karl Rahner in his essay "The Meaning of Frequent Confession of Devotion," in volume 3 of his Theological Investigations (1967), in which he argues that since venial sins are remitted even by imperfect contrition, then subsequent sacramental confession of such sins would not cause their forgiveness. At the very least, imperfect contrition is a requirement of any valid celebration of the sacrament of confession, and so, using the principle of *plus minus non mutat speciem*, we have to conclude that the venial sins were already forgiven by the presence of the imperfect contrition and not because the penitent went to sacramental confession.

Plus tenetur homo vitae suae providere quam vitae alienae
One is required to take more care of one's own life than that of another

Principle grounded in the moral obligation of the duty of self-preservation articulated by Thomas Aquinas (cf. ST II–II, q. 64, a. 7). This principle is used to justify self-defense as well as the justification for saving one's own life in situations in which otherwise the death of both one's self *and* another would result. The classic example used is that of a good swimmer who would be justified in repelling a drowning person who was dragging him down if it seemed unlikely that the good swimmer could save both himself and the other. Martin Rhonheimer, OD, in his 2009 *Vital Conflicts in Medical Ethics: A Virtue Approach to Craniotomy and Tubal Pregnancies* (p. 117), also references this Thomistic principle as justification for a mother's decision to terminate a pregnancy when it is reasonably foreseen that otherwise *both* the mother and fetus would die but that if the pregnancy is terminated at least the life of the mother could be saved.

Pontifex maximus
Supreme bridge builder

Title for the Roman pontiff (pope) taken over from Roman pagan political theology, which held that the high priest, and later the Roman emperor, was the supreme "bridge builder" between humans and heaven.

Populorum progressio
The progress of peoples

Social encyclical of Pope Paul VI On the Development of Peoples (1967) in which the pontiff stressed that the goods of the world are destined for all people and called for the right to a just wage, the right to security of employment, and the rights to unions and collective bargaining.

Porta Fidei
Portal of Faith

Benedict XVI's apostolic letter, issued *motu proprio* (*q.v.*) on 11 October 2011 for the indiction of the Year of Faith, which would begin on 11 October 2012 to commemorate the fiftieth anniversary of Vatican II and conclude on 24 November 2013, the Solemnity of Christ the King.

Possessio
Possession

Understood as something which is not under *dominion* (*dominium, q.v.*). To possess something in classical Roman law was to "occupy" and/or use it but without having private property rights to it. See also *Melior est conditio possidentis* and *Possessio non est juris sed facti*.

Possessio non est juris sed facti
Possession is not a matter of law but facts

See the discussion on *Possessio* above. This principle is rather self-evident, indicating that actual possession often is simply a matter of who controls something, whether this be lawful or not. See also *Melior est conditio possidentis*.

Post
After, behind

Common Latin preposition; however, it has nothing to do with mail or the mail system, as in the sense that "The post usually arrives by 10:00 AM."

Post factum
After the fact

Vantage point obtained after a given event which can furnish a certain perspective for evaluating progress made, mistakes incurred, etc. See also *Ex post facto*.

Post hoc, ergo propter hoc
After this (event), therefore because of this (event)

A common, though faulty, mode of reasoning in which one concludes from the fact that Event B followed temporally upon Event A that therefore Event B was *caused* by Event A. Thus, if a crow flew away from its perch on a tree and then at that moment an apple fell from the tree, a *post hoc ergo propter hoc* conclusion would be that the crow's flight caused the apple to fall. However, in point of fact the apple's fall may have been merely a coincidence with the crow's flight and not caused by the crow at all.

Post mortem
After death

In English this phrase refers to an autopsy.

Post partum
After birth (bearing)

In English this phrase refers to the period immediately after a woman has given birth to a child. There may also be some physical or psychological problems, such as *post partum* depression, connected with childbirth.

Post scriptum
Written afterward

See *P.S.*

Potentia
Power, potential

In Latin the term *potentia* refers to the efficacy in the sense of a power, ability, or potential to do or complete some activity inherent in a person or thing. Thus, a person with legal jurisdiction over a certain issue, area, etc., would have the *potentia iurisdictionis* regardless of whether this jurisdiction were actually exercised. Similarly, the legal actions of a person who lacked a legitimate *potentia iurisdictionis* would be invalid and not binding. It is an important concept in scholastic philosophy and theology and is often combined with other terms to give a more precise application (for some common examples see the terms which follow immediately). Philosophically, *potentia* refers to the various capabilities inherent in this or that being; thus, humans have a *potentia* for knowledge, irrespective of whether a given individual actually learns this or that. Theologically, *potentia* is often used, among other things, to refer to various divine attributes. See *De potentia Dei absoluta* and *De potentia Dei ordinata*.

Potentia coeundi/Potentia generandi
Ability to engage in coitus/ability to produce offspring

This distinction is important in the church's theology of marriage and in canon law governing marriage. The traditional teaching has held that for a valid marriage (*ratum et consummatum, q.v.*) the couple had to be able to complete the marital act. However, it was not required that the couple actually be physically able to produce children in order to consummate validly the marriage. Thus, while a dysfunction such as an inability on the part of the husband to have an erection that could be maintained to the point of penile insertion into the vagina would be grounds for an annulment (since the marriage could not be physically consummated), the fact that one or the other partner was sterile would *not* jeopardize the canonical recognition of the marriage. See also *Concubitus propter solam procreationem* and *Ratum et consummatum*.

Potentia Dei absoluta/ordinata
Absolute/ordered (ordinary) power of God

See *De potentia Dei absoluta*.

Potentia iurisdictionis
Power of jurisdiction

See also *Cui licet quod est plus, licet utique quod est minus*; *Potentia*; *Potestas*; *Qui potest plus, potest minus*; and *Si iudicas, cognossce; si regnas, iube*.

Potentia Obedientialis
Obediential potency

Refers to the intrinsic aspect of human nature for self-transcendence and receptivity of God's self-gift of supernatural grace. The "potency" refers to this openness to the divine, and the "obedience" highlights the fact that it is God, and not the human, who must initiate the encounter and freely given self-donation of grace. This concept is important in fundamental theology and considerations of the possibilities of human beings to receive and understand God's revelation, as well as to have a certain sense of self-consciousness of oneself and one's relationship to God. See also *Anima naturaliter Christiana*.

Potestas
Power, authority

In Latin there are two principal terms for authority: *potestas* and *auctoritas* (*q.v.*). *Potestas* carries nuances of "power" in the sense of jurisdictional authority or efficacious ability to perform a function, carry out an office, make a decision, etc. *Auctoritas* refers more to the authority of counsel, wisdom, learning, advice, influence, support, etc. However, it is important to keep in mind that neither the authority of *potestas* nor the authority of *auctoritas* is absolute in the sense that it can function or exist with the complementary element of the other. See also *Cui licet quod est plus, licet utique quod est minus*; *Potentia iurisdictionis*; *Potestas docendi*; *Potestas regendi*; *Prima sedes a nemine iudicatur*; *Qui potest plus, potest minus*; *Regiminis*; *Rex non potest peccare*; *Si iudicas, cognossce; si regnas, iube*; and *Summum ius, summa iniuria*.

Potestas delegata non delegatur
A delegated power cannot be delegated (to someone else)

While in general this principle is true and speaks to the nature of *Potestas* (*q.v.*) in point of fact both in civil and canon law, there are delegated powers that under certain conditions can be delegated to another, whereas in other situations the power cannot be subdelegated (cf. *C.I.C.* #135 & #137). See also *Qui delegat, solvit*.

Potestas docendi
Power (authority) of teaching

Expression used to refer to the *munus* (*q.v.*) of the magisterium to teach authoritatively in matters of faith and morals (cf. *De fide vel moribus*). This power is also shared with duly designated assistants to the magisterium, such as the staff workers in the various Vatican dicasteries like the Congregation for the Doctrine of the Faith, even though the majority of these individuals are not themselves ordained into the fullness of the priesthood as bishops. This expression was used explicitly by Pope Benedict XVI in his 2010 Address to the Plenary Session of the Congregation for the Doctrine of the Faith. See also **Christus Dominus**, *Ecclesia docens, Magisterium, Magisterium cathedrae pastoralis & Magisterium cathedrae magistralis, Munus, Obsequium religiosum, Officium, Potentia iurisdictionis, Potestas, Potestas regendi,* and *Prima sedes a nemine iudicatur.*

Potestas regendi
Power of governance

As expressed in canon 129 of the 1983 Code of Canon Law, this expression refers to the power of jurisdiction exercised by church officials by virtue of their presbyteral ordination: "Those who have received sacred orders are qualified, according to the norm of the prescripts of the law, for the power of governance, which exists in the Church by divine institution and is also called the power of jurisdiction (*potestatis regiminis*)." The term is therefore also sometimes just called *regiminis* (jurisdiction). See also *Ecclesia docens, Magisterium cathedrae pastoralis & Magisterium cathedrae magistralis*, *Obsequium religiosum*, *Potentia iurisdictionis*, *Potestas*, *Potestas delegata non delegatur*, *Potestas docendi*, *Prima sedes a nemine iudicatur*, and *Si iudicas, cognossce; si regnas, iube*.

Potestas regiminis
Power of jurisdiction

See *Potestas regendi*.

Praecipuum munus
Principal (or chief or special) office

This term refers to a function or "office" which is the special or privileged function of the one who holds that office. Thus, the Council of Trent designated preaching as the *praecipuum munus*, or special function, of the bishop. See also *Ecclesia discens*, *Ecclesia docens*, *Munus*, *Officium*, and *Potestas docendi*.

Praembula[e] fidei
Preambles of faith

"Preambles" in this expression refer to the preliminaries or presuppositions for human acceptance of God's word in faith, or in other words, to human natural knowledge which is necessarily antecedent to an acceptance and understanding of God's revelation. Faith, though, as an infused theological virtue, is a gift of God and therefore cannot be produced by either the human intellect or will acting alone. Thomas Aquinas used this concept to describe truths of the faith which could also be known by natural reason and which help an individual come to faith or deepen the reasonableness of faith. See also *Fides quaerens* *intellectum*, *gratia supponit naturam et perfecit eam*, and *Quinque viae*

Praenotanda
Prenote

Praenotanda are usually prefatory remarks given at the beginning of a longer document which set out what the document contains and often give a theological summary and/or rationale for the document in question. For example, the new Rite of Penance, promulgated on 2 December 1973, contains a *Praenotanda* of forty paragraphs that explain the new ritual.

Praeparatio evangelica
Preparation for the Gospel

This expression can have a range meanings, and points to what will prepare people to hear and receive the Gospel message. Often the Old Testament had been considered by Christian theologians as a sort of *praeparatio evangelica* for the acceptance of the Gospel message contained in the Scriptures of the New Testament. Others would hold that even "pagan" philosophy, such as that of the Greeks and Romans, should be studied since it is a contribution to order and reason and this sense helps prepare people to receive and/or integrate the Gospel message more fully into their lives and culture. See also *In Vetere Novum (Testamentum) latet, et in Novo Vetus patet* and *Mortui vivos docent*.

Praesumitur ignorantia ubi scientia non probatur
Ignorance can be presumed where knowledge has not (yet) proven

It is important to note here that *scientia* does not mean "science" in English, but rather "knowledge." This expression gives a basic epistemological premise that indicates that in cases where we lack sufficient data to prove or demonstrate a proposition (e.g. in cases like a *Dubium facti* or *Dubium iuris, q.v.*) we may conclude that we are in ignorance over the truth, and act accordingly. Thus, a doubtful law does not oblige (*Lex dubia non obligat, q.v.*) and in situations like this the moral principle of probabilism may be employed. However, once sufficient authority, intrinsic or extrinsic, decides the matter then contrary presumptions should cease (e.g., *Praesumptio cedit veritati, q.v.*).

Praeter

Beyond, except, besides, contrary to, more than

Latin preposition widely used with other nouns to express an idea that usually involves something foreseen but not morally intended, as in *praeter intentionem* below. Though it can be used to indicate "contrary to," the most common meanings carry the nuance of being "outside of" or "beyond." *Contra* is the more common Latin preposition to indicate "contrary to." Another example used in the interpretation of canon law is *praeter legem* or *praeter ius* (more than the law or items not covered by the law) which refers to a custom that is not in strict accordance with the current law (which would be expressed as *iuxta legem* (according to the law), but which is a custom widely established and thus, at least theoretically, could enjoy the force of a new law since

Consuetudo optima legum interpres (*q.v.*) is an established interpretative principle of canon law. See also the discussion under *Iuxta* which functions in a similar way grammatically but with an opposite meaning.

Praeter caritatem

Outside of (not in accord with) charity

Depending on context this expression could mean that which is uncharitable, or that which goes beyond what charity requires. See also *Contra caritatem*.

Praeter finem

Outside of (not in accord with) the proper end

That which is not in accord with a thing or person's proper moral end. See *Contra caritatem*.

Praeter intentionem

Outside (beyond) the (moral) intention

In cases of the double effect a pre-moral (ontic or physical) bad action that is done for a proportionately greater good end is said to be "voluntary" but not "intended" (i.e., *praeter intentionem*). Thus, if one has no choice but to kill an intruder in order to save an innocent child, such killing would be considered "unintentional" from a moral point of view and therefore not "murder" in the moral sense. On this point see Thomas Aquinas, who states that "moral acts take their species according to what is intended, [*praeter intentionem*] and not according to what is beside the intention (*Morales autem actus recipiunt speciem secundum id quod intenditur, non autem ab eo quod est praeter intentionem.* ST II–II, Q. 64, art. 7). See also *Finis operis*, *Finis operantis*, *Genus morum*, *Intentio*, *Licet corrigere defectus naturae*, *Obiectum actus*, *Pars propter totum*, and *Voluntarium directum/indirectum.*

Praeter ius
Beyond (e.g., not covered by) the law (or justice)

See the discussion above on *Praeter*. This particular expression is found in the introductory canons for the 1983 Code of Canon Law (*C.I.C.* #5.2): "Universal or particular customs beyond the law (*praeter ius*) which are in force until now are preserved."

Praeter legem
Outside of the law

Refers to an item which is not regulated by law (and therefore not illegal). Certain customs are considered to be *praeter legem*. *Praeter legem* is distinct from *contra legem* (*q.v.*), i.e., something which would be directly against the law and therefore illegal. Also see *Consuetudo optima legum interpres.*

Praeter ordinem
Outside of (not in accord with) the proper order of things

That which is not in accord with the proper order of things as willed by God, though this would not be quite as serious as something judged *Contra ordinem* or *Contra naturam* (*q.v.*). See *Contra caritatem.*

Predicatio ecclesiastica
Ecclesiastical preaching

Here the literal translation is misleading, as one might conclude this term refers to the sermon or homily given at Mass, when instead the expression usually refers to the transmission of the church tradition from one generation to the next overseen by the magisterium. Prior to Vatican II and the Dogmatic Constitution on Sacred Revelation *Dei verbum* (*q.v.*), it was commonly held (though never formally defined) that church tradition as articulated by the magisterium represented another separate source of divine revelation. *Dei verbum*, though, stated (cf. #8–10) that biblical revelation is the *norma normans non normata* (*q.v.*) and that it stands above even the teaching office of the magisterium. See also *Traditio.*

Presbyterorum ordinis
Of the order of priests

Vatican II's Decree on the Ministry and Life of Priests (1965).

Presumptio cedit veritati
Presumption gives way to truth

Refers to the logical proposition that if one's hypothesis or "presumption" is subsequently demonstrated to be in error, then a commitment to "truth" and objectivity demands that one either drop or reform one's earlier position.

Prima facie
At first sight

"On first consideration," even though a thorough investigation has not been completed, initial evidence suggests a certain inference which will tend to stand unless disproved. Thus, a crib sheet found in a student's possession during an exam can be said to be *prima facie* evidence of cheating.

Prima pars
The first part

Usually refers to the first major section of St. Thomas Aquinas' **Summa Theologiae** (*q.v.*), which deals with the doctrine of God. See also *Secunda pars* and *Tertia pars*.

Prima secundae
First of the second

Usually refers to the first section of the *Secunda pars* (*q.v.*) of St. Thomas Aquinas' **Summa Theologiae** (*q.v.*), which deals with the human person, human acts, moral habits, etc. The *Prima secundae* is often abbreviated as I–II or Ia–IIae.

Prima sedes a nemine iudicatur
The first see is judged by no one

This is canon 1404 of the 1983 Code of Canon Law and expresses the canonical principle that the pope, as the highest law giver, chief executive officer, and supreme judge, enjoys a very great latitude and discretionary power in governance and matters of positive ecclesiastic law. For example, if the pope has the power to make certain liturgical laws requiring some sort of activity, then he would also have the power to dispense or lessen conformance to these same sorts of things. A concrete example would be a papal indult granting the power to impart general absolution to penitents without requiring them to confess their sins individually to a priest. Pope John XXIII granted just such an indult in 1962 to the people of Sudan. See also *Altum dominium*; *Cui licet quod est plus, licet utique quod est minus*; *In forma specifica*; *Qui potest plus, potest minus*; *Rex non potest peccare*; and *Summum ius, summa iniuria*.

Primum est vivere
First is to live

The most important principle is to maintain one's life, i.e., the principle of self-preservation, which trumps other competing values.

Primum non nocere
First, do no harm

Hippocratic dictum in which the first commandment for a health-care giver is to not further injure the patient, i.e., the biomedical principle of non-maleficence.

Primus inter pares
First among equals

Refers to a certain primacy, even among equals. Often used of the pope as patriarch of Rome in relation to the other patriarchs of the church. See also **Apostolos suos**, **Christus Dominus**, *Collegium*, *Collegialis affectus*, *Inter pares*, *Munus Petrinium*, and *Servus Servorum Dei*.

Privilegium
Privilege

However, in theological terms usually refers to a particular right granted in canon law. Several such types of "privileges" are found in canon law, and some of the more common are listed below.

Privilegium fidei
Privilege of the faith

Sometimes rendered more fully as *Privilegium in favore fidei*, i.e., privilege in favor of the faith, and refers to cases in which a nonsacramental bond of marriage between two individuals is dissolved by the appropriate marriage tribunal so that the individual(s) might enter into a sacramental bond of marriage (which would therefore be indissoluble). Thus, if someone were married civilly, got divorced, and then converted and/or wished to marry a Catholic in the church, the first marriage could be declared null on the grounds of the *Privilegium fidei*. It is called such, since this allows one to act in a way that would foster the acquisition and/or maintenance of the faith. The *Privilegium fidei* is further specified as the *Privilegium Paulinum* and *Privilegium Petrinum* (*q.v.*), but taken as a general term in canon law the *Privilegium fidei* also refers to the hermeneutical principle by which in doubtful cases the *Privilegium fidei* enjoys the *Privilegium iuris* (*q.v.*, "privilege of law"), i.e., the law is interpreted in a manner favorable to the convert or baptized person who desires to marry again (cf. canon 1150).

Privilegium fori
Privilege of the (confessional) forum

Expression related to the seal of confession which protects the confessor from having to reveal anything he might have heard in the confessional in some external forum such as a law court or to a religious or ecclesiastical superior, etc. See also *Sigillum*.

Privilegium iuris
Privilege of law

In canon law this refers to a special "favor," such as a dispensation, granted to someone who is a *persona iuridica* (*q.v.*), which is granted either by a special act of the legislator or by an executive authority to whom the legislator has granted such power. See also *Privilegium fidei*.

Privilegium Paulinum
Pauline privilege

In canon law this refers to the dissolution of a marriage between two *unbaptized* parties, one of whom is later baptized and seeks to marry in the church. (Cf. canons 1143–47). See also *Privilegium fidei*.

Privilegium Petrinum
Petrine privilege

In canon law this refers to the dissolution of a nonsacramental marriage between a *baptized* person and an *unbaptized* person, given by the pope (hence "Petrine") in favor of one of the persons so that she or he may marry again in the church. See also *Privilegium fidei* and *Privilegium Paulinum*.

Pro
Before, in front of, on behalf of, in place of, in return for, in view of

Common Latin preposition.

Pro bono (publico)
For the (public) good

Refers to work one does for the common or public good but for which one is not remunerated. Thus, a lawyer may work on a particular case for an indigent client, etc., on a *pro bono* basis, i.e., without receiving the customary fees. See also *Pro bono Ecclesiae.*

Pro bono Ecclesiae
For the good of the church

Principle used in coming to decisions or applications which are undertaken with a view to the greater good of the well-being of the church. For example, the May 2011 Circular Letter to Assist Episcopal Conferences in Developing Guidelines for Dealing with Cases of Sexual Abuses of Minors Perpetrated by Clerics issued by the Congregation for the Doctrine of the Faith states that "[i]n some cases, at the request of the cleric himself, a dispensation from the obligations of the clerical state, including celibacy, can be given *pro bono Ecclesiae.* See also **Sacramentorum Sanctitatis Tutela**.

Pro forma
For form

As a formality (and often without a real sincere conviction); in a perfunctory manner.

Pro multis
For many/for all

Phrase in the Latin formula of the eucharistic words of consecration that have been the focus of some debate over the proper translation approach. A word-for-word "literalist" theory called "formal correspondence" would have the expression rendered as "for many," while the more idiomatic translation theory called "dynamic equivalence" would argue that the term refers to Jesus' actual meaning in using the expression "for many" as echoing the fourth servant song of Isaiah 53:11-12 and thus was intending to include both Jews and Gentiles and thus effectively all people. The 2011 English translation of the *Missale Romanum (q.v.)* legislated that *pro multis* be changed from "for all" to "for many" in the words of consecration. Regardless of the translation employed, the consecration formula should *not* be understood in such a way that God somehow intends to exclude anyone from the possibility of salvation. See also *Deus donabilis, Pro nobis, Ora pro nobis,* and *Verum Sacrificium.*

Pro nobis
For us

This expression points to, among other things, the soteriological (saving) function of the work of Jesus Christ for us, as well as the intercession of the Blessed Mother and the communion of saints on our behalf. See also *Deus donabilis, Ora pro nobis,* and *Pro multis.*

Pro populo
For the people (both living and the faithful departed)

Expression often used to highlight the role and obligation of the ordained ministers to act in service to the community (i.e., "For the people"), including those members of the communion of saints who have passed from this life (the "faithful departed" who are explicitly mentioned in the eucharistic canons). Thus, in both sacramental theology and canon law the diocesan bishop and the pastor of a parish has a specific duty to celebrate Masses *pro populo*, and if they were to insist on just saying private Masses they would be shirking this important official obligation. For the relevant canons see *C.I.C.* 388 §1; 429; 534 §2; 549; 901, as well as the *Catechism of the Catholic Church* (*CCC*) #1369 and 1371.

Pro rata
In proportion

Often used in English to refer to a per-unit cost or calculation.

Pro tempore
For the time being

For example, something temporary, such as a temporary solution or someone who fills in for another in his or her absence, such as a temporary leader of a group or the President *pro tempore* of the United States Senate (who leads the Senate in the absence of the Vice President, who is the official "President" of the Senate). Sometimes shortened to *pro tem*.

Processus iustificationis
Process of justification

Theological position regarding the process of forgiveness of sins, classically identified with Peter of Poitiers (1205), who in his commentary on Peter Lombard's Sentences (*Sententiarum libri quinque*) articulated four components in this process: contrition, confession, absolution, and satisfaction. See also *Aut satisfactio aut poena*; *Ex attrito fit contritus*; *Ordo salutis*; and *Ubi regnum, ibi reconciliatio*.

Prodere peccatorem, Proditio peccatoris
Revelation of the sin (confessed by a penitent)

Refers to the context of the seal of absolute secrecy governing matters spoken of in sacramental confession. The priest is forbidden to do anything, directly or indirectly, which would reveal either the identity of the penitent or the nature of the sins confessed. Neither can the priest use the knowledge he gains in the confessional in any way "against" the penitent. See also *Cum gravamine poenitentis (paenitentis)* and *Gravamen*.

Professio fidei
Profession of faith

In general, any confessional creed can be taken as a "profession of faith" (e.g., the Apostle's Creed, the Nicene Creed, and so forth), but in recent church history the *Professio fidei* often refers to the 1989 profession of faith issued by the Congregation for the Doctrine of the Faith (CDF) on 9 January 1989, whose English text can be found in *Origins* 18 (16 March 1989): 661ff. This profession of faith is meant to replace the 1967 profession of faith. The text of the profession is essentially a repetition of the Nicene Creed and concludes with three clauses in which the one making the profession affirms his or her acceptance of the church's definitive teachings and traditions. The 1989 profession of faith is the object of Pope John Paul II's *Motu Proprio* (*q.v.*) entitled **Ad Tuendam Fidem** (*q.v.*), which amends the Codes of Canon Law of both the Latin and Eastern Rites to establish the proper legislation (e.g., penalties) to enforce the profession of faith.

Prohibitum quia malum
Forbidden because wrong

Contrast this idea with the opposite notion, *Malum quia prohibitum* (*q.v.*, wrong because forbidden).

Promoveatur ut amoveatur
Let him be promoted so as to remove him

Expression often used in church politics, especially in the Vatican, as a method of getting rid of an individual who has become problematic by "promoting" him to a higher ecclesiastical position, such as a bishop or cardinal, which in turn will facilitate his being moved from his current position into the promotion which is usually in a different location. See also *Persona non grata*.

Propaganda Fide
Propagation of the Faith

Shorthand term for the Vatican Congregation for the Propagation of the Faith, whose mandate is to oversee the church's missionary activity throughout the world.

Proprio motu
See *Motu proprio*.

Proprium
The Proper (as in particular to something)

In Catholic usage this term has two distinct references: in liturgy it refers to the "Propers" of the prayers, i.e., those liturgical formulae which change according to the particular Mass being offered (such as the prayers for a saint's feast day). In moral theology the term refers to the debate over what constitutes the distinction between Christian ethics and general philosophical or humanist ethics. Here the question revolves around just how Jesus Christ and biblical revelation influence ethical norms and the development of Christian character. See also *Sola Scriptura*.

Propter
On account of, because of

Common Latin preposition.

Propter solam procreationem
For the sole purpose of procreation

Traditional norm which rendered the procreative intentionality of the conjugal act as the primary moral determinant. Refers to the procreative intent, which had to be present for the conjugal act to be considered moral. See also *Bonum prolis*.

Prorsus indebitum
Absolutely undeserved

Augustinian phrase that indicated God's salvific grace was totally unmerited and unattainable by humans on their own but that nevertheless expressed God's immense love for sinful humanity (cf. Rom 3:23-25). See also *Massa damnata*.

Providentissimus Deus
Most provident God

Encyclical of Pope Leo XIII on biblical studies, which declared that Scripture was to be the soul of all theology (1893). This notion was confirmed in #16 of Vatican II's Decree on Seminary Training **Optatam totius** (*q.v.*).

Proxima fidei
  Near to the faith

Refers to a doctrine that is held by most theologians to be very probable and able to be defined, but which has never been officially defined. See also *De fide definita.*

P.S.
  Written afterward

Latin abbreviation for *post scriptum*; refers to a short message appended to a text or letter, and generally indicates an afterthought.

Pura potentia
  Pure potency

Important concept in scholastic philosophy and theology which refers to the capacity (potency) of a thing to be changed to an essentially different kind of being, for example, the capacity or potential to change from a living to a nonliving being. *Pura potentia* is passive potency considered apart from any act but is also the principle or capacity by which an essence can receive or be acted upon.

Q

Q.E.D.
That which was to be demonstrated (proven)

Latin abbreviation of *quod erat demonstrandum*, usually appended to mathematical or logical proofs to indicate successful conclusion of the proof of the initial hypothesis. Used to indicate the logical "proof" of any argument or hypothesis. See also *Non liquet* and *Res ipsa loquitur*.

Qua
Who/which (as)

"In the capacity of." For example, Jane *qua* Jane can do little, but Jane *qua* voter can effect change.

Quadragesima
Forty (or fortieth part)

When used alone this word usually refers to the First Sunday of Lent, which is forty days before Easter. In some circles the term can also serve as a synonym for Lent itself as the period of forty days of penance.

Quadragesimo Anno
On the fortieth year (anniversary)

Social encyclical of Pope Pius XI issued in 1931 in commemoration of the for-tieth anniversary of Pope Leo XIII's encyclical *Rerum novarum* (*q.v.*) on labor and capital. Pius XI addressed the economic order and cautioned against the excesses of unrestrained capitalism as well as the dangers of communism.

Quaecumque ea sit
Whatever they may be

Often this expression is teamed with a general principle which is followed, leaving it up to the individual in the concrete situation to determine the best precise means of applying the principle. See also *Aliquo modo* (In some manner or other).

Qualis modus essendi, talis modus operandi
That which is the mode of being determines the manner of operating

Essentially the same notion as *Agere sequitur esse, Modus operandi sequitur modum essendi,* and *Operari sequitur esse* (*q.v.*).

Quam primum
As soon as possible

E.g., in canon law it was traditionally understood that infants should be baptized *quam primum* (as soon as possible) after their birth. However, one always had to interpret this obligation in a reasonable manner. Thus, infants would not necessarily be baptized immediately after their birth (unless they were in danger of death) but instead would normally be baptized at a time convenient for the family to gather in the parish church (which might be several weeks or even months later). In this context, see also *In dubio favores sunt amplificandi, odiosa restrigenda*, which indicates that in matters of doubt favors are given a broad interpretation (or application) and burdensome things a strict (and narrow) interpretation (or application). See also *Odia restringi, et favores convenit ampliari*; *Cessante fine cessat lex*; and *Consuetudo optima legum*.

Quasi-domicilium
Quasi-domicile

Refers to a temporary residence and may be important in certain canonical proceedings for establishing jurisdiction in a matter, such as in a marriage case.

Quasimodo
In the manner

In church circles *Quasimodo* refers to Low Sunday after Easter (also called *Dominica in Albis* [*q.v.*] and, since the pontificate of Blessed Pope John Paul II, Divine Mercy Sunday). The Latin term comes from the introit or opening antiphon of the Mass in Latin, *Quasi modo geniti infantes* (As newborn babes) which comes from 1 Peter 2:2. In literature, *Quasimodo* also refers to the protagonist in Victor Hugo's 1831 *The Hunchback of Notre Dame*. See also *Dominica in Albis*.

Quaestio
Question

Sometimes spelled *questio*, this refers to a question or issue of some ethical or theological importance on which there is more than one current opinion. See also *Inquisitio*, *Quaestio disputata*, and *Status quaestiones*, and, as an example, **Questio de abortu** (*q.v.*).

Quaestio disputata
Disputed question

Term usually used in theology to indicate matters of disagreement among theologians and concerning that for which there has been no definitive pronouncement by the magisterium. An example of a contemporary *quaestio disputata* is whether or not an embryo is infused with an immortal soul at the moment in which the spermatozoa fertilizes the ovum or whether the "ensoulment" occurs at some later time in the development of the embryo, such as when "twinning" is no longer possible (some fourteen days after fertilization). See also *De fide definita*, *Inquisitio*, *Sententia probata*, *Status quaestionis*, and *Theologice certa*.

Quanta cura
How much care

Pius IX's encyclical to which was attached a **Syllabus errorum** (*q.v.*, *Syllabus of Errors*) of the contemporary age, including a condemnation of the idea of freedom of religion (1864) and repeating Pope Gregory XVI's condemnation of indifferentism in religion and the supposed individual's freedom of conscience in choice of religion in his encyclical **Mirari vos** (*q.v.*) (1832). Nevertheless, there is some tension with this position dating from Roman times through Thomas Aquinas, which held contrary views. **Dignitatis humanae**, Vatican II's Declaration on Religious Liberty, ultimately enshrined the position of Thomas Aquinas, who held that no one should ever be forced to act against his or her conscience, and even if this is done the person should resist: "anyone upon whom the ecclesiastical authorities, in ignorance of the true facts, impose a demand that offends against his clear conscience, should perish in excommunication rather than violate his conscience" (Thomas Aquinas, 4 Sent. 38, q. 2, a. 4, Expos. Text). See also **Dignitatis humanae**; **Mirari vos**; *Nisi enim sponte et ex animo fiat, execratio est*; and **Quod aliquantum.**

Querela nullitatus
Asking for (a decree) of nullity (of a judicial sentence)

A complaint of nullity against a juridical sentence, i.e., the expression in canon law which asks for a decree which declares a juridical sentence to be null due to some substantial defect in the sentence, e.g., the incompetence of the sentencing judge in a given case.

Questio de abortu
On the question of abortion

Declaration of the Congregation for the Doctrine of the Faith on Procured Abortion (1974).

Qui bene distinguit bene cognoscit
The one who distinguishes well knows well

Traditional axiom which underscores that one must know the important distinguishing features of an issue or problem in order to understand what the issue is in fact about. This axiom has often been used, for example, in the tradition of moral casuistry in cases such as deciding what constitutes legitimate medical treatments which may have the effect of hastening the patient's death (and which are morally licit) and other instances in which the therapies really involve morally illicit forms of active or passive euthanasia. However, there are certain other situations in which "distinction" is inappropriate, such as in the application of justice (*Lex non distinguit, q.v.*, "Law does not distinguish").

Qui dat finem, dat media ad finem necessaria
The one gives the end (goal) gives also the necessary means to the end

This adage expresses a number of different thoughts. One is that obligations cannot be imposed on people without also making sure they have the means of meeting that duty or obligation. Another concept revolves around the connection between moral intention and the act performed, as expressed in the terms *finis operis* and *finis operantis* (*q.v.*). Finally, it could also be argued that this adage indicates formal cooperation along with material cooperation when one gives the material aid for the commission of an immoral act with a view to sharing the sinful intent—even if one does not carry out the act him/herself. See *Cooperatio in malum* and *Qui vult finem vult media.*

Qui delegat, solvit

> The one who delegates solves (a problem)

Basic principle of good administration, i.e., that no one can be expected to handle all issues and problems, and sometimes the best response is to delegate these to another in order to manage time more efficiently and share burdens. However, some things obviously may not be delegated. See, for example, *Potestas delegata non delegatur.*

Qui dicet de uno negat de altero

> Who says the one negates the other

Basic point of logic and the principle of noncontradiction, namely that if one affirms one proposition to be true then one must therefore deny its contrary. In other words one cannot at the same time affirm both "A" and "Not-A" to be true in the same way at the same time.

Qui potest plus (maius), potest minus

> The one who can (do) more, can (do) less

In general, this axiom means that the one who has the authority to do something greater also has the authority to do something lesser. The *plus/minus* (greater/lesser) could refer to some action required of another, as well as to the granting of favors, permissions, offices, and the like. For example, if a person can grant a permission to another to be absent for a whole week, then it generally follows that he or she could grant the same permission to be absent for a day; or, if you are authorized to spend a million dollars to buy a house, presumably you could also spend less, e.g. half a million. In law, this principle generally means that the one who enjoys discretionary power to require more has as well the power to require less. This axiom has to do more with the flexibility, "elbow room," enjoyed by certain persons in certain situations. For example, in the Code of Canon Law, canon 1599 §2 states that the conclusion of a case occurs when the time limit set by the judge has expired *or* if the judge declares that the case has been sufficiently instructed. Thus, if the judge has the discretionary power to set a time limit for the presentation of proofs (e.g., six months), and if he has the power to extend that time limit, he also has the power to limit or reduce it. Analogously, in civil law one could look at the sentence prescribed for a given crime, with the possibility of a harsher sentence which, say, cannot exceed twice the prescribed punishment, or a more lenient sentence which, say, cannot be less than half the prescribed punishment. If the judge can give a harsher punishment than that prescribed (e.g., up to twice the amount), he or she could also give a more lenient one. This same principle can be used as a moral principle as well. For example, if it is morally licit in a certain situation to perform a certain weightier action (such as a hysterectomy), logically it should be morally permissible to perform a less extreme action (such as simply the removal of a fibroid tumor) if the less extreme action would resolve the problem equally well (or better). A similar expression is *Cui licet quod est plus, licet utique quod est minus*; see also *Potentia iurisdictionis*;

Potestas; *Prima sedes a nemine iudicatur*; *Rex non potest peccare*; and *Summum ius, summa iniuria*.

Qui probabiliter agit prudenter agit
The one who acts according to the probable acts prudently

A literal Latin translation would be cumbersome in English, but both *probabliter* and *prudenter* function as adverbs modifying *agit* (third-person singular of "to act"). This aphorism expresses the position known as probabilism, which holds that in cases of doubt, and if there is a solidly "probable" opinion to support one's decision, then one can decide in favor of liberty even if this would not necessarily be the "safer" or more rigorous course of action. Probabilism has been an accepted moral theory in the Roman Catholic Church since the seventeenth century. See also *Lex dubia non obligat*, *Praesumitur ignorantia ubi scientia non probatur*, and *Ut in pluribus*.

Qui tacit consentire censetur
Qui tacit consentire videtur
Qui tacit consentit
Silence gives consent (Often simply rendered as *Qui tacit*)

Expressions which indicate that if one could speak up and doesn't then this silence would be construed as approval. See also *Argumentum e silentio* and *Ex Silentio*.

Qui tenetur ad finem, tenetur ad media
One who is bound to reach a certain end is bound to employ the means to attain it

Expression of responsibility and duty which notes the connection between the end (or goal) and the concrete means to achieve it. In other words, good intentions are insufficient in themselves but must be matched by corresponding actions. On the other hand, there may be legitimate exemptions from this rule, depending on other circumstances. See also *Deus impossibilia non iubet*, *Impossibilium nulla obligatio*, *Lex non intendit impossibile*, *Nemo ad inutile tenetur*, *Nemo potest ad impossibile obligari*, and *Ultra posse* (or *vires*) *nemo obligatur*.

Qui vult finem vult media
The one who desires the end also desires the means

Term related to *Qui dat finem, dat media ad finem necessaria* (*q.v.*) and which highlights that in moral evaluation of acts the *finis operantis* (*q.v.*) is absolutely crucial.

Quid pro quo
Something for something

Doing/giving something in return for getting something in exchange. See also *Do ut des* and *Ex iustitia*.

Quidquid latine dictum sit altum videtur
That which may be said in Latin seems deep

Somewhat humorous expression meant to debunk the overuse of Latin expressions or to negate giving something added credibility just because it exists in Latin. See also *Mortui vivos docent* and *Traditio*.

Quidquid percipitur ad modum percipientis percipitur

One perceives according to one's own mode of perception

See also *Quidquid recipitur ad modum recipientis recipitur* and *Quidquid solvitur solvitur secundum modum solventis*

Quidquid recipitur ad modum recipientis recipitur

One receives according to one's own mode of reception

Philosophical adage which indicates that a mode of perception and/or understanding is always related to the nature of the being who is doing the perceiving and/or understanding. Thus, it would not be in the mode of a dog to perceive and understand the world in the same way that a human being does, nor would it correspond to the human mode of understanding to have access to some sort of infused knowledge which would bypass or exceed the ordinary capacity of humans to perceive and know. Thus, humans cannot know and perceive completely in the same way that God does. See also *Quidquid percipitur ad modum percipientis percipitur* and *Quidquid solvitur solvitur secundum modum solventis* for related applications of this basic principle.

Quidquid solvitur solvitur secundum modum solventis

That which is solved is solved according to its mode of being solvable

This expression is logically similar to *Quidquid recipitur ad modum recipientis recipitur (q.v.)* and *Quidquid percipitur ad modum percipientis percipitur (q.v.)*, namely that due to basic human nature and its inherent limitations we can only solve problems in a human, and therefore limited, way. One cannot, for example, abolish disease, war, etc., but can only work at resolving these problems in incremental ways and with the possibilities open to us.

Quinque viae

Five ways (or proofs for the existence of God)

Expression which references the five proofs for the existence of God drawn from natural reason unaided by revelation that Thomas Aquinas puts forward in his **Summa Theologiae** (cf. ST I, q. 2), as well as in various other places in his collected writings. Briefly stated, these proofs are based on 1) the unmoved mover, 2) the first caused uncaused by anything prior, 3) contingency, i.e., the necessity of a cause to bring the universe into existence, 4) the argument of degree of greater and lesser being which points to the existence of a greatest or total being, and 5) the teleological argument which points to the purpose or design evident in creation. Thomas indicates that while these arguments are knowable by reason alone they do not of themselves bring about the fullness of faith, which is a theological virtue given by God. At best, then, the *Quinque viae* act as a preamble to faith (*praembula fidei, q.v.*).

Quis ut Deus?

Who is equal to God?

In other words, humans should let God be God and not presume to be equal to

God or even to understand fully God and God's way. See also *Deus absconditus/ Deus revelatus*; *Deus semper maior*; and *Si comprehendis, non est Deus.*

Quo vadis?
Where are you going?

Legendary question put by the apostles to Jesus, and then, according to the apocryphal *Acts of Peter*, the question was asked by Jesus to Peter when the latter was leaving Rome to avoid the Emperor Nero's persecution in AD 64. Also the name of a well-known contemporary Roman travel agency.

Quod aliquantum
With respect to a considerable degree

Papal brief (though some authorities list it as an encyclical) of Pope Pius VI issued on 10 March 1791 that treated many diverse themes, including a rejection of Communion under both species, a call for the pre-eminence of Gregorian chant in church music, and, perhaps most famously, a declaration that it was absolutely unacceptable for Catholics to accept the notions of liberty and equality expressed in the 1789 French "Declaration of the Rights of Man and of the Citizens," adding that the purpose of the Declaration was "to annihilate the Catholic Religion and, with her, the obedience owed to Kings." The pope went on to condemn the notion of religious liberty as a "monstrous right" and an "imaginary dream." Because of the several condemnations found in this papal missive many conservative Catholic groups and websites use it to condemn many of the teachings of Vatican II. See

also *Dignitatis humanae*; *Mirari vos*; *Nisi enim sponte et ex animo fiat, execratio est*; and *Quanta cura.*

Quod Deus conjunxit, homo non separet
What God joins together a human must not separate

Latin version of the famous dictum of Jesus on the indissolubility of marriage (cf. Matthew 19:6 and Mark 10:9). On this biblical basis canon law has consistently held that a marriage that is *ratum et consummatum* (*q.v.*) may not be dissolved, though exceptions based on 1 Corinthians 7:12-15 are granted with the so-called Pauline and Petrine privilege (cf. *C.I.C.* #1141–49). See also *Defensor Vinculi*, *Ligamen*, and *Super rato.*

Quod erat demonstrandum
That which was to be demonstrated

See *Q.E.D.*

Quod in necessitate sunt omnia communia
All things are common (property) in situations of (extreme) necessity

Principle which comes from Thomas Aquinas' *Summa Theologiae* II–II, q. 66, a. 7: "In cases of need all things are common property, so that there would seem to be no sin in taking another's property, for need has made it common." Thomas holds that private property is not an absolute right in itself but only a relative right that must be ceded at times in view of the common good. Thus, in cases of extreme need one could "steal" to feed and clothe oneself or those in one's care without this becoming a moral violation of the Ten Commandments, or to be understood in this situation of dire need as an example of "theft" as condemned in **Veritatis splendor** #13, which states "'The beginning of freedom,' Saint Augustine writes, 'is to be free from crimes . . . such as murder, adultery, fornication, theft, fraud, sacrilege and so forth,'" or again at #81 where Augustine is once again referenced. The grounding of Thomas Aquinas' position is found in the notion of distributive justice which would hold that the goods of creation come from God and are held in stewardship by individual humans. Thus, this notion of distributive justice indicates that total "equality" is not necessarily the most "just" form of distribution, but rather distribution should be governed by relative need and necessity. In this larger view, if there would arise a situation of genuine and dire need this would be seen as *prima facie* evidence of a failure of justice in the distributive sense. "Stealing" in this situation would not be a sin or vice, since the object of the action is not unjustified taking of another's property. There was a debate among moralists as to the boundaries of what constituted genuine "necessity" under this principle, e.g., whether the need had to be "extreme" or merely "grave." While the former position, *In extrema necessitate omnia, societati humanae destinata, sunt communia*, was generally accepted, Pope Innocent XI condemned the latter, which had been expressed in the proposition *Permissum est furari non solum in extrema necessitate sed etiam in grave* (it is permitted to take the necessary goods not only in extreme necessity but also in grave necessity). See

Denzinger #1186 for the pope's condemnation. See also *Altum dominium*; *Epikeia*; *In extrema necessitate omnia, societati humanae destinata, sunt communia*; *Iustitiam subsidiariam*; *Necessitas est lex temporis et loci*; *Necessitas non habet legem*; *Quod non licitum est in lege necessitas facit licitum*; and *Salus publica suprema lex*.

Quod lege permittente fit, poenam non meretur
What the law permits does not merit punishment

It is important to keep in mind that this axiom refers to legal punishment; many things that might be "legal" are still immoral and therefore would be liable to punishment in that sphere. See also *Odia restringi, et favores convenit ampliari*.

Quod non licitum est in lege necessitas facit licitum
That which is not licit in law necessity makes licit

Another expression which indicates the Catholic moral principle that extreme need or necessity can override human law. See also *Necessitas non habet legem, Necessitas non habet legem*, and especially the longer discussion under *Quod in necessitate sunt omnia communia*.

Quod omnes tangit ab omnibus approbetur
That which touches all must be approved by all

Principle of canon law that indicates that legislation which touches everybody will have to be received and accepted in order to be valid. See also

Consensus non facit veritatem, Consuetudo optima legum interpres, Quod ubique quod semper quod ab omnibus creditum est, and *Sensus fidelium.*

Quod omnia appetunt
That which all desire

Refers to the universal nature of the desire for the good inasmuch as it is the one thing desired by all rational beings.

Quod raro fit non observant legislatores
What is rarely done is not observed by legislators

An axiom of practical reason as it applies to law: that which only rarely occurs would not normally be an object of legislative concern. See also *De minimis non curat lex*; *Epikeia*; *In necessariis unitas, in dubiis libertas, in omnibus caritas*; *Lex dubia non obligat*; *Minima non curat praetor*; *Rara con tigribus*; and *Singularia non sunt extendenda.*

Quod ubique, quod semper, quod ab omnibus, creditum est
What has everywhere, always by all, been believed

Principle of Vincent of Lérins (died c. 445) which gives the essential criteria for authoritative tradition to help distinguish truth from heresy and which has its force precisely because it has stood the test of time and place. See also *Consensus non facit veritatem, Consuetudo optima legum interpres, Quod omnes tangit ab omnibus approbetur,* and *Sensus fidelium.*

Quod vide
Which see

See *Q.v.*

Quondam
Formerly

This term can be used in the sense of "former" e.g., to indicate a person who *quondam* ("formerly") was president of a certain school and now is retired.

Q.v.
Which see

Latin abbreviation for *quod vide*, used as a scholarly indication of a cross-reference for further and/or related information on a given topic.

R

Radix Jesse
Root of Jesse

The third of the "O Antiphons" that mark the octave of anticipation or preparation for Christmas Eve, which in itself is the vigil of Christ's birth. See the fuller discussion under *O Adonai*.

Radix Mali
Root of evil

Expression used by Augustine in his *Contra Julianum* (I, 9.42; PL 44, 670) to denote the thoughts sown by Satan into the hearts of Adam and Eve, which in turn led to their committing the original sin of disobedience. Augustine further held that this same original sin and propensity toward evil is passed down by the concupiscence of sexual desire, which is an element of the procreation of all human offspring and thus is responsible for the necessity of washing away original sin if the human is to be reconciled with God. This washing away of original sin is accomplished through baptism in the church's sacramental view or at least through *Fides implicita* (*q.v.*) or the so-called "baptism by desire" (*Baptismus in voto, q.v.*). See also *Extra ecclesia nulla salus* and *Felix culpa*.

Rara avis
A rare bird

A rarity, prodigy, etc. A type of individual not commonly found.

Rara con tigribus
Rarely with tigers

Expression that traditionally was associated to sexual sins that would only rarely occur and so would not be the object of much casuistry or moral study—in other words, even if bestiality might occur, it would be rare indeed that it would happen with a tiger. It is also referenced in post–Vatican II moral theology as a humorous example of the old moral manuals supposed preoccupation with sexual matters. See also *Ex toto genere suo, (In) re venerea, Parvitas materiae in Sexto*, and *Quod raro fit non observant legislatores*.

Ratio entis
Reason of the [human] being

Refers to the power of human reason. See also *Ens rationis, Lex indita non scripta, Lumen naturale, Per modum cognitionis/Per modum inclinationis*, and *Recta ratio*.

Ratio fide illuminata
Reason illuminated by faith

The traditional Roman Catholic position is that human reason is basically sound and trustworthy but that it needs to be illuminated by faith in order to counter the effects of the Fall and original sin. See also *fides ratione illuminata* and *status antelapsarius*.

Ratio legis est anima legis
The reason for the law is the soul of the law

Principle which holds that a rule or law is seen as a means to an end and is not an end in itself. Therefore, in interpreting the law (especially canon law) it is important to understand the overall purpose of the law in order to interpret correctly how the law is to be applied. Cf. canon 17 of the 1983 Code of Canon Law.

Ratio proportionata
Proportionate reason

One of the important justifying factors for committing or tolerating a premoral evil. For example, if a limb is gangrenous it can be amputated in order to save the life of the person, since there is "proportionate reason" for having the amputation. This is an important concept in the principle of the double effect, as well as the moral theory of proportionalism, though "proportionalism" as defined and critiqued in **Veritatis splendor** (*q.v.*) #75 clearly is quite distinct from the use of proportionate reason whose tradition dates back to Thomas Aquinas. See also *Bonum totius*; *Mala moralia* and *mala praemoralia*; *Pars propter totum*; and *Si finis bonus est, totum bonum.*

Ratio studiorum
Plan of studies

Refers to an integrated plan of studies, curriculum, or syllabus. As a proper noun *ratio studiorum* can also refer to the norms governing the curricula of a school or set of schools, such as the *ratio studiorum* of Jesuit high schools.

Ratione censurae/peccati
By reason of the censure [or] sin

Refers to the classification in the old practice expressed, for example, in the 1917 Code of Canon Law (abolished in the 1983 Code), which distinguished reserved sins into two categories: sins reserved because of the nature of the sin itself (*ratione peccati*) and those reserved because of the nature of the censure attached (*ratione censurae*). In the 1983 Code of Canon Law there are very few reserved "sins"—only reserved cases, thus reserved *ratione censurae*.

Ratum
Confirmed (ratified)

For example, in a marriage ceremony the couple has freely given their consent to each other in a proper manner. See also *Ratum et consummatum* and *Super rato*.

Ratum et consummatum
Confirmed and completed

Refers to the marriage bond which was considered irrevocably confirmed upon the proper sacramental exchange of marriage vows and the "consummation" of the marriage though the subsequent conjugal act. However, exceptions based on 1 Cor 7:12-15 are granted with the so-called Pauline and Petrine privilege (cf. *C.I.C.* 1141–49). See also *Affinitas non parit affinitatem*; *Defensor Vinculi*; *Divortium plenum/perfectum*; *Ligamen*; *Non constat de nullitate*; *Potentia coeundi/Potentia generandi*; *Quod Deus conjunxit, homo non separet*; *Ratum*; and *Super rato*.

(In) re venerea
In venereal (sexual) matters

Term used in traditional teachings on sexual ethics which referred to sexual pleasure obtained from a variety of actions, even relatively minor ones such as kissing. A strict interpretation held that any venereal (sexual) pleasure obtained outside of marriage was gravely sinful. See also *Ex toto genere suo*, *Parvitas materiae in Sexto*, *Rara con tigribus*, and *Remedium concupiscientiae*.

Recidivus
Recurring

In moral theology this term usually refers to the type of penitent who confesses but falls into the same sin again repeatedly. The pastoral approach to someone who repeatedly falls into the same sort of sin would necessarily differ from dealing with someone for whom the given sin was a rather singular occurrence. Regrettably, often older moral manuals of moral theology and confessional practice recommended to be withholding sacramental absolution from someone judged to be a *recidivus*, since it was held that this purpose lacked a sufficient purpose of amendment to receive the sacrament. The practical result of this attitude, coupled with a moral rigorism on the part of the confessor, often was that the sacrament was effectively denied to numbers of people who could well have profited from a more merciful and supportive attitude on the part of the confessor. See also *Occasionarii*.

Recognitio
Recognition, approval (after review)

Expression used in Roman Catholic circles to indicate that a document, such as the United States Catholic Bishops Conference document on norms governing sexual offenders, is "recognized" officially by the Vatican and therefore enjoys the force of law. This is a relatively new process and term in ecclesiastical governance. This same Roman *recognitio* is now required by Pope John Paul's 1998 **Apostolos suos** (*q.v.*) of all teaching documents issued by bishops conferences unless the conference were to pass a document unanimously. Some canonists have noted that the use of the *recognitio* creates a bit of an anomaly in jurisdiction, since it seems to create a situation in which one has legal authority (e.g., bishops) but are constrained from using this authority freely and effectively. See also *Nihil obstat* and *Vactio legis*.

Reconciliatio et paenitentia
Reconciliation and penitence

Post-synodal apostolic exhortation of Pope John Paul II On Reconciliation and Penance in the Mission of the Church Today (1984).

Recta ratio
Right reason

The basic moral faculty of discernment. Each human person, through a process of rational reflection, can come to a correct moral understanding of the rightness and wrongness of moral actions, etc. See also *Lex indita non scripta*, *Lumen naturale*, and *Per modum cognitionis/Per modum inclinationis*.

Recursus ad fontes
Return (recourse) to the fonts (sources)

In the case of theology, this might involve the use of Scripture, or some author from among the church fathers, etc. The "fonts" or sources usually would refer to the traditional theological fonts such as Scripture and tradition.

Reddere suum cuique
Give to each his or her own

Basic principle of justice, i.e., rendering to each person what is due to her or him. A slightly different linguistic version of this is *unicuique suum* or, in more abbreviated form, *Suum cuique*. See also *De bono et aequo*, *Ius*, and *Lex non distinguit*.

Redemptionis donum
Gift of redemption

Apostolic exhortation of John Paul II to men and women religious (1984).

Redemptor hominis
Redeemer of humankind

Pope John Paul II's first encyclical of his pontificate, written on the nature of the human person (1979) and promulgated less than five months after his accession to the Chair of Peter.

Redemptoris Custos
Guardian of the Redeemer

Apostolic exhortation on the role of St. Joseph issued by Pope John Paul II in 1989, two years after his mariological encyclical *Redemptoris mater* (*q.v.*) promulgated in 1987.

Redemptoris mater
Mother of the Redeemer

Encyclical of John Paul II On the Blessed Virgin Mary in the Life of the Pilgrim Church (1987), focusing on Mary's role in salvation in her roles in the Mystery of Christ, as Mother of God, and as Mother of the Church. A companion document on the role of St. Joseph, *Redemptoris Custos*, was also issued by John Paul II as an apostolic exhortation two years later in 1989.

Redemptoris missio
Mission of redemption

1990 encyclical of Pope John Paul II On the Mission of the Redeemer and on the essential nature of the Christian mission of evangelization which flows from Jesus' mandate to make disciples of all nations (cf. Matt 28:19-20).

Reductio ad absurdum
Reduction to the (point of the) absurd

Common, though not always methodologically sound, manner of reducing an argument to its supposed absurd conclusion if the premises are carried to their logical (though usually extreme) conclusion. See also *Ne fides rideatur.*

Regiminis
Jurisdiction

See *Potestas regendi.*

Regina Coeli
Queen of Heaven

One of the titles of the Blessed Virgin Mary and the name of a prayer recited in her honor. During the Easter season this prayer is traditionally said at midday in place of the *Angelus* (*q.v.*).

The Latin lines of the prayer are:
> *Regina coeli laetare, Alleluia. Quia quem meruisti portare, Alleluia, resurrexit sicut dixit, Alleluia. Ora pro nobis Deum, Alleluia.*

The English translation is:
> Queen of Heaven rejoice, Alleluia. Because he whom you were worthy to bear, Alleluia, has risen as he said, Alleluia. Pray for us to God, Alleluia.

Regnans in Excelsis
Reigning in the highest (heaven)

1570 papal bull of Pope St. Sixtus V in which he "deposed" England's Protestant Queen Elizabeth I and declared her subjects absolved of the duty of allegiance to her. This action had no immediate political effect other than to increase and legitimize persecution of English Catholics by the Crown.

Regnum Christi
The Reign (Kingdom) of Christ

Name given to the lay branch of the Legionaries of Christ (not to be confused with *Opus Dei*, *q.v.*), a religious order founded in 1941 by the Mexican priest Marcial Maciel Degollado, later discovered to have fathered several children and engaged in other sexual improprieties. Though quite popular during the pontificate of John Paul II (1978–2005), Maciel was removed from priestly ministry by Benedict XVI (2005–) in 2006 to a life of penance until his death in 2008. In 2010 Benedict XVI also delegated a cardinal to oversee the Order and its practices.

Regula fidei
Rule of faith

Concept used by St. Irenaeus of Lyons (c. 130–200) against the Gnostics who claimed knowledge of special revelations available only to a chosen few. According to the idea of the *regula fidei*, the basic criterion for determining the truth of revelation given to the church is that this norm of faith is to be both public and ecclesial rather than private and elitist. Thus, in brief, the *regula fidei* refers to the basic truths of the faith which have been traditionally professed by Christians. See also *Congregatio fidelium*, *Sensus fidelium*, and *Tolle assertiones et christianismum tulisti.*

Relatio (finalis)
(Final) Report

In ecclesial usage this term usually refers to a report drafted either as an introductory document for a larger meeting's consideration (such as the triennial synod of bishops) or as a report from a smaller group back to a larger group, or as a summary report of the whole meeting (i.e., the *relatio finalis*).

Reliquiae peccati
  Residual effects of sin

Traditional maxim which viewed the human person as redeemed in Jesus Christ but still suffering from the residual effects of sin and sinfulness. See *Totus conversus sed non totaliter.*

Remedium concupiscientiae
  Remedy for concupiscence
  (sexual desire)

Traditionally ascribed (e.g., by Augustine and others) to be one of the secondary ends of marriage, i.e., that marriage helped keep unruly sexual passions in check by giving them a licit outlet. See also *Bonum prolis, Bonum fidei,* and *Bonum sacramenti* for the three principal ends of marriage, as well as *Concubitus propter solam procreationem, Debitum, Ius in corpus (corpore),* and *Parvitas materiae in Sexto.*

Requiescat in pace
  Rest in peace

See *R.I.P.*

Rerum novarum
  Of new things

Leo XIII's 1891 encyclical On Capital and Labor, usually considered the first "social" encyclical, which spoke of the necessity of improving the conditions of the working classes, supported their rights to unionize, and rejected both communism and unrestrained capitalism but accepted the notion of private property.

Res
  The/a matter (thing, object); reality

Refers to the essential "matter" or relevant material of a case under discussion, etc. Depending on the context, *res* carries either the meaning of reality itself or an individual entity such as a thing, matter under discussion, etc.

Res analogata
  The "thing" (basis) of the analogy

Expression which refers to the basis of terms put into relation in an analogy. For example, in the analogy "as the relationship of the husband to his wife so is the relationship of Christ to the church," the *res analogata* would be the love that each pair has for the other (and not, for example, an "accidental" term such as gender). In using this kind of analogical expression, it is important to determine clearly the foundational basis for the analogue, lest improper conclusions be drawn (such as since husbands and Christ are both "males" the masculine gender should be somehow seen as superior to the feminine. See also *Analogia entis, Analogia fidei, Analogia Scipturae,* and *Bonum Sacramenti.*

Res et sacramentum
  A (sacred) thing (symbolized) and
  a (sacred) symbol

In scholastic sacramental theology, this term referred to the reality midway between the sacred symbol itself (the sacramental sign) and the grace ultimately conferred by the sacrament. Thus, in baptism, the sacramental sign of pouring the water and saying the words of the trinitarian baptismal formula symbolizes the baptized person's incorporation into the church. This incorporation into the church (the sacred thing symbolized) itself symbolizes sanctifying grace whereby a person becomes a participant in God's divine nature. In the Eucharist, the *res et sacramentum* is the real Body and Blood of Christ, while in the sacrament of Christian matrimony the *res et sacramentum* is the marriage bond which unites the man and woman. The nuance of this expression is further clarified when *res et sacramentum* is distinguished from related terms such as *res sacramenti, res tantum, sacramentum,* and *sacramentum tantum* (*q.v.*). See also *Ex opere operantis, Ex opere operato,* and *Sacramentum.*

Res fidei et morum
A matter of faith and morals

See *De fide vel moribus* for a fuller discussion of this term.

Res frutificat dominum
Property [literally, "the thing itself"] enriches the owner [literally, "lord" or "master"]

Maxim from Roman law which indicates the purpose of private property is discovered in what it does for its owner, thus indicating a rather absolute right of the owner of private property to use as she or he pleases. See also *Bonum utile; Dominium utile; Ius utendi, fruendi, abutendi;* and *Uti et frui.*

Res ipsa loquitur
The thing speaks for itself

Refers to something that is (or at least is perceived to be) self-evident and therefore would not require further proof. However, many things that one person may consider to be absolutely clear and irrefutable are not so judged by others. See also *Facta non praesumuntur sed probantur; In necessariis unitas, in dubiis libertas, in omnibus caritas; Lex dubia non obligat; Onus probandi; Q.E.D.;* and *Tantum valet quantum probat.*

Res iudicata
A judged matter

Term used in canon law which refers to a sentence passed by the competent authority in an ecclesiastical case (cf. *C.I.C.* #1363) and thus cannot be retried by another court. More colloquially, *res iudicata* can refer to a contentious issue which supposedly now has been settled. See also *Res iudicata pro veritate accipitur* and *Roma locuta, causa finita.*

Res iudicata pro veritate accipitur
A matter adjudicated (judicially decided) is accepted as true

A basic principle of law that indicates once a matter has been properly adjudicated with due process (i.e., a *Res iudicata, q.v.*) the decision should be accepted as binding, or "true," in that sense. Of course, mistakes can still be made and due process can be short-circuited, but the legal system could not function well if each and every decision were constantly open to debate and further litigation. See also *Absolutus sententia judicis praseumitur innocens; Actori incumbit onus probandi; Allegatio contra factum non est admittenda; Da mihi factum, dabo tibi ius; Facta non praesumuntur sed probantur; Onus probandi; Roma locuta, causa finita; Tantum valet quantum probat;* and *Testis in uno falsus in nullo fidem meretur.*

Res sacramenti

A (sacred) thing (symbolized) by a (sacred) symbol

This expression is not frequent in scholastic theology and is somewhat ambiguous when it stands alone, since it could refer either to *res et sacramentum* (q.v.) *or res tantum* (q.v.). See also *Ex opere operantis, Ex opere operato, Sacramentalia*, and *Sacramentum*.

Res tantum

Only the (sacred) thing (symbolized)

Expression used in scholastic sacramental theology to refer to the ultimate "matter" of the sacraments, namely the sanctifying grace conferred by the sacramental encounter. Since *res tantum* is the ultimate grace symbolized by the sacrament it is not itself a symbol of anything further, such as in the case of the *res et sacramentum*. The nuances of these expressions are further clarified when they are seen in conjunction with related terms such as *res et sacramentum, sacramentum,* and *sacramentum tantum* (q.v.). See also *Ex opere operantis, Ex opere operato*, and **Sacramentum**.

Responsum ad dubium

Response to the doubt (question)

A formal response given by the appropriate authority to a question (a *dubium* or "doubt") raised about the meaning or interpretation of a certain point. Thus, the *Responsum* can have the effect of clarifying the given point or policy, as well as strengthening its authoritative weight. See also *Dubium* and **Ordinatio Sacerdotalis**.

Restitutio in integrum

Integral (complete) reinstatement

Expression which in canon law denotes the remedy to be had in cases when a canonical sentence is technically valid but is shown to be blatantly unjust and therefore is set aside, restoring the juridical condition which existed prior to (*status quo ante, q.v.*) the giving of the valid, but unjust, sentence. In moral theology, especially in the forum of the sacrament of reconciliation, *restitutio in integrum* refers to the obligation in justice to make amends, pay restitution, etc., in order to repair as completely as possible an injustice caused. Thus, an individual who confesses having stolen something has an obligation to repay or "restore" the thing stolen (or its comparable value) to the rightful owner.

Rex Gentium

King of the Nations

The sixth of the "O Antiphons" that mark the octave of anticipation or preparation for Christmas Eve, which in itself is the vigil of Christ's birth. See the fuller discussion under *O Adonai*.

Rex non potest peccare

The king cannot sin

Expression that can be associated with a divine-right theology of kingship which held that monarchs were so ordained by God and thus answered to God alone for their actions. The expression also can point to the nature of authority, and whoever has the highest or most authority would not normally have his or her decisions questioned. Obviously, this expression does *not* indicate the impossibility of moral failure and serious sin even among hierarchs and monarchs, as history easily illustrates. See also *Potestas*; *Prima sedes a nemine iudicatur*; *Roma locuta, causa finita*; *Si iudicas, cognossce; si regnas, iube*; and *Summum ius, summa iniuria*.

R.I.P.
Rest in peace

Latin abbreviation for *requiescat in pace*, and is a common wish or prayer found on tombstones, memorial cards for the deceased, etc.

Rispondeo
I respond (or answer) . . .

This verb is used by Thomas Aquinas in the development of his arguments to indicate the principle point or core of his teaching on a certain issue. The structure of his method is to pose a thesis statement or "question" and then outline a few principal objections to the proposed thesis. After this he then indicates a transition by the phrase *sed contra* (*q.v.*, "but on the other hand"), which usually indicates a few authorities that hold a counter-position. Next comes the *Rispondeo*, in which Thomas more fully outlines his answer to the question before concluding with a brief reply to each of the "objections" introduced at the beginning of the treatment of the question. This methodology is employed throughout his **Summa Theologiae**.

Risus Paschalis
Easter laughter

Referred to a custom that arose in Bavaria in the fifteenth century in which funny stories were told in the Easter sermon about the devil's futile efforts to keep Christ from descending to hell after his death. Due to perceived abuses of the Word of God in such sermons they were eventually banned by Pope Clement X (1670–76), the German Emperor, and various bishops of Bavaria. See also *Christus Victor*.

Roma locuta, causa finita
Rome has spoken, the case is closed

Traditional axiom, based on Sermon 131 of St. Augustine against Pelagius, by which theological debate is supposedly to be terminated upon a pronouncement by some person or office connected with the Vatican-based magisterium. This principle has been formally enshrined to a certain extent in this half-century in Pius XII's 1950 *Humani Generis* and in John Paul II's 1994 declaration barring discussion of the possibility of women being admitted to the ordained priesthood. See also *Caput mundi*; *Potestas*; *Prima sedes a nemine iudicatur*; *Res iudicata*; *Scriptura sacra locuta, res decisa est*; *Summum ius, summa iniuria*; and *Ultra montes*.

Ruat coelum
(Though) heaven fall (justice must be done)

Singular form of the more oft-used *Fiat iustitia, ruant coeli* (*q.v.*, let justice be done, though the heavens fall), a slogan which indicates that "consequences" should never keep strict "justice" from being done, even if this should be burdensome or occasion negative consequences. "Come what may" might be an equivalent English expression.

S

Sacra Doctrina
Sacred Doctrine

Refers to the truths of the Christian faith, the doctrines and dogmas which must be held and believed by all the faithful. See also *Anathema sit*, *Credenda*, *De fide*, *Sacra Pagina*, and *Sacra Scriptura*.

Sacra pagina
The sacred page

Literally, this refers to Scripture as text, and in the Middle Ages the term was used to indicate the study of Scripture, and a theologian was called a *magister Sacrae Paginae* (*q.v.*), a "master" or expert in the Sacred Text. In spirituality *Sacra pagina* often is associated with a particular passage or text which is read for prayer and meditation. See also *Lectio divina*.

Sacra Scriptura
Sacred Scripture

Refers to the Bible as the authoritative text for Christian theology. See also *Sacra Doctrina* and *Sola Scriptura*.

Sacrae Scripturae Doctor
Doctor of Sacred Scripture

See *S.S.D.*

Sacrae Scripturae Licentiatus
Licentiate in Sacred Scripture

See *S.S.L.*

Sacrae Theologiae Doctor
Doctorate in Sacred Theology

See *S.T.D.*

Sacrae Theologiae Licentiatus
Licentiate in Sacred Theology

See *S.T.L.*

Sacramentalia
Sacramentals

This expression denotes sacred material things, objects, or actions such as Holy Water, wearing of medals, the crucifix, etc., which when used devoutly by believers help increase devotion and piety, as well as remit venial sin. Sacramentals are differentiated from the church's seven sacraments (baptism, confirmation, Eucharist, reconciliation, marriage, anointing of the sick, and holy orders). The efficacy of the latter work *ex opere operato* (*q.v.*), whereas the benefits of the former depend on the interior disposition of the individual using the sacramental (*ex opere operantis*, *q.v.*), sometimes also referred to as *opus operantis*. See also *Ex opere operantis*, *Ex opere operato*, and *Sacramentum*.

Sacramentorum Sanctitatis Tutela
Safeguarding of the Sanctity of the Sacraments

Apostolic letter issued by Pope John Paul II *motu proprio* (*q.v.*) on 30 April 2001. This document dealt with "delicts" or "crimes" of a more serious nature which touched upon the sacraments, especially Eucharist and reconciliation, such as using the sacrament of reconciliation or the place of the confessional to solicit someone for sexual purposes. These sorts of crimes are termed *graviora delicta* and in canon law call for special adjudication and/or penalties. This document was a partial response to the sexual abuse crisis which came to light in the church in the 1990s and established procedural norms for handling of the reporting and follow-up of charges of sexual abuse by priests. For the most part the pope delegated responsibility for these matters to the Congregation for the Doctrine of the Faith. See also *Corpus delicti*, **Crimen sollicitationis**, *Delicta graviora*, **Epistula de delictis gravioribus**, *Graviora delicta*, *In flagrante delicto*, *Pro bono Ecclesiae*, *Secretum pontificium*, *Sub secreto pontificio*, and *Sub rosa*.

Sacramentum
Sacrament, sacred symbol, sign of a sacred thing

Though the Latin word *sacramentum* originally meant anything which obliges a person, such as a "guarantee, oath, or pledge," the term came to be used by the church to refer to the visible signs instituted by Jesus Christ to reveal and communicate God's grace to human beings. Tertullian was the first to use the word to signify the Christian rite or mystery of baptism, and later the term came to refer to any sign or symbol instituted by Christ in some way to give grace. There was much discussion in the Middle Ages about the precise number of sacraments, and finally at the Council of Trent the number of sacraments was defined as being the following seven: baptism, confirmation, Eucharist, marriage, holy orders, reconciliation, and anointing of the sick. See also *Ex opere operantis*, *Ex opere operato*, *Res et sacramentum*, *Res sacramenti*, *Res tantum*, *Sacramentalia*, and *Sacramentum tantum*.

Sacramentum mundi
Sacrament of the world

Title of a well-known post–Vatican II encyclopedia of theology, edited by Karl Rahner (among others).

Sacramentum pietatis
Sacrament (symbol) of piety (religion)

Expression used by St. Augustine, along with *signum unitatis* (sign of unity) and *vinculum caritatis* (bond of charity) in his definition of the Eucharist, given in his *In Ioannis Evangelium tractatus*, 26, 13: CCL 36, 266. Thus, the Eucharist leads to personal sanctification (*pietas*) as well as community unity and reconciliation (*unitas* and *caritas*).

Sacramentum tantum
A (sacred) symbol only

Refers to the external sacramental rite which symbolizes, but is not itself symbolized by anything else. For example, in the baptismal rite the pouring of water (or immersion) and pronouncement of the trinitarian formula is a *sacramentum tantum*. The nuance of this expression is further clarified when *sacramentum tantum* is distinguished from related terms such as *Res et sacramentum, Res sacramenti, Res tantum,* and *Sacramentum (q.v.)*.

Sacrarium
Shrine, chapel

In moral theology this can refer to the sanctity of an individual's conscience. In liturgy it refers to the special sink found in the sacristy whose outlet led directly into the ground (rather than the sewer). Leftover water which had been used for purification in the Mass was to be poured into the *sacrarium*, rather than into a regular sink.

Sacrosanctum concilium
The Sacred Council

Vatican II's Constitution on the Sacred Liturgy (1963) whose major aim was to encourage greater participation of the laity in the Eucharist, which led ultimately to many changes in the liturgy, especially the widespread use of the vernacular in the Mass. These changes, though, were unpopular with some and led Pope Benedict XVI in his 2007 *Motu proprio (q.v.)* **Summorum Pontificum** *(q.v.)* to give broad permission to use the pre–Vatican II Tridentine Rite as a *forma extraordinaria (q.v.)*. See also *Ad orientem, Coetus fidelium, Forma extraordinaria, Missale Romanum, Novus Ordo,* **Universae Ecclesiae**, and *Versus populum*.

Saecula saeculorum
Ages of ages

Common formulaic ending used in liturgical prayers. See also *Gloria Patri* and *Per saecula saeculorum*.

Salus animarum suprema lex
Salvation of souls is the supreme law

Refers to the ultimate aim of the church's canon law, which is for the aid of those in the church to reach salvation. Thus, the principal aim of canon law is not meant to be essentially disciplinary but medicinal or nourishing. See also *Animarum zelus, Cura animarum, Plantatio ecclesiae,* and *Salus publica suprema lex*.

Salus publica suprema lex
The health of the public is the supreme law

The fundamental purpose of law is not to safeguard the power or privileges of the lawgiver but rather is directed to the promotion of the common good. See also *Bonum commune; Epikeia; In extrema necessitate omnia, societati humanae destinata, sunt communia; Iustitiam subsidiariam; Lex iniusta non est lex; Lex lata in praesumptionne periculi communis; Lex semper intendit quod convenit rationi; Necessitas est lex temporis et loci; Necessitas non habet legem; Ordinatio rationis ad bonum commune; Quod non licitum est in lege necessitas facit licitum; Salus animarum suprema lex;* and *Ubi ius, ibi remedium*.

Salvator mundi
Savior of the world

One of the common titles given to Jesus Christ, in which his soteriological import is stressed.

Salve
Hail

Traditional Roman greeting (pronounced in two syllables: *SAL-vay*), and the first word of the Christian Marian hymn *Salve Regina* ("Hail Holy Queen," *q.v.*). See also *Ave*.

Salve Regina
Hail (holy) Queen

Prayer to the Blessed Virgin Mary, often used to conclude the Rosary, Compline, or other prayers. The Latin version of the prayer is as follows:

> *Salve Regina, Mater Misericordiae; vita, dulcedo, et spes nostra, salve. Ad te clamamus, exules filii Evae. Ad te suspiramus, gementes et flentes in hac lacrymarum valle. Eia ergo advocata nostra, illos tuos misericordes oculos ad nos converte; et Jesum, benedictum fructum ventris tui, nobis post hoc exilium ostende. O clemens, O pia, O dulcis Virgo Maria.*

The English translation is:

> Hail holy Queen, Mother of Mercy, our life, our sweetness, and our hope. To thee do we cry, poor banished children of Eve, To thee do we send up our sighs, mourning and weeping in this vale of tears. Turn then most (gracious) advocate thine eyes of mercy toward us; and after this our exile, show unto us the blessed fruit of thy womb, Jesus. Oh clement, oh loving, oh sweet Virgin Mary.

Salvifici doloris
Salvific suffering

Apostolic letter of Pope John Paul II On the Christian Meaning of Human Suffering (1984).

Sanatio in radice
Healing at the root

Sometimes translated as "radical sanation," usually refers to a juridical process which corrects some serious canonical anomaly which would have rendered the sacrament (usually marriage) invalid and thus has retroactive consequences. For example, if a novice entered a novitiate which had not been properly "erected" in the canonical sense, his or her novitiate would be technically "invalid" and the subsequent religious vows not binding. A *sanatio in radice* can correct this legal difficulty without requiring a repetition of the novitiate or vow ceremony. Other common uses of the *sanatio in radice* occur in marriage cases in which there might have been, for example, some defect in form of the celebration of the wedding itself. See also *De Defectibus* and *Divortium plenum/perfectum*.

Sanctorum patrum exempla sequentes
Following the examples of the holy fathers

Used as a succinct expression of the antiquity and the authority of tradition (cf. C. Laternanese I, can. 1, 27 March 1123), and thus lending implicit additional weight to the opinion expressed. "Holy fathers" in this expression would refer principally to the patristic authors (the "fathers" of the church), and not necessarily to popes alone (who are sometimes referred to as Holy Father[s]).

Sanctus
Holy

Common designation for the prayer recited by all during the celebration of the Latin Eucharist at the conclusion of the preface. The text of the entire prayer is *Sanctus, Sanctus, Sanctus, Dominus Deus, Sabaoth. Pleni sunt caeli et terra gloria tua. Hosanna in excelsis. Benedictus qui venit in nomine Domini. Hosanna in excelsis.* ("Holy, Holy, Holy, Lord God of hosts. Heaven and earth are filled with your glory. Hosanna in the highest. Blessed is he who comes in the name of the Lord. Hosanna in the highest").

Sapere aude!
Dare to know

Used as a motto of the Enlightenment, this axiom underscored the necessity to have the courage to make use of the human capacity for autonomous understanding, rather than relying on authority or divine revelation.

Sapienti sat
For the wise no more is necessary (e.g., to be said)

This expression is quite similar to *Verbum sat sapienti* (*q.v.*), a word to the wise is sufficient, a brief indication about some problem or pitfall would be sufficient to a truly prudent individual so that she or he can avoid the danger or handle the problem better than if no warning had been given. See also *In vestimentis non stat sapientia mentis, Ordo sapientiae, Stultis non succuritur,* and *Verbum sat sapienti.*

Sapientia Christiana
Christian wisdom

Pope John Paul II's 1979 apostolic constitution On Ecclesiastical Universities and Faculties. *Sapientia Christiana* ("Christian Wisdom") details the plan of studies plus a number of other norms and rules which govern schools, such as seminaries, which grant ecclesiastical degrees, such as the Master of Divinity (M.Div.), Licentiate in Sacred Theology (S.T.L.), and Doctorate in Sacred Theology (S.T.D.).

Scandalum pusillorum
Scandal of the weak

Type of scandal which comes from actions, which though in themselves are "lawful" and not immoral nevertheless have the appearance of evil and therefore may disturb those with more "delicate" or "weak" consciences and perhaps cause these people to sin. St. Paul's advice to the early Christian community on abstaining from meat sacrificed to idols (1 Corinthians 8) would be a good example of being sensitive to the problem of *scandalum pusillorum.* See also *Male sonans* and *Piarum aurium offensiva.*

S.C.G.
Summary against the Gentiles (non-believers, heretics)

Abbreviation which designates the **Summa Contra Gentiles** (*q.v.*) of St. Thomas Aquinas.

Schola
School

This Latin term has a wide range of possible meanings. However, depending on the context, and when used without an accompanying adjective, *schola* usually refers to the choir which sings at liturgies. See also *Schola cantorum*.

Schola brevis
Brief school

Refers to a short lecture and customarily to the tradition of having only a brief introductory lecture on the first day of class of a term.

Schola cantorum
School of singers

Usually refers to the choir in liturgies and sometimes also to choir practice or to a school for training of the singers of liturgical chant. See also *Cantatorium*, *Liber Gradualis*, and *Schola*.

Schola theologorum
School of theologians

Refers to the range of opinions one might find in various "schools" of theological thought. Thus, a *schola theologorum* may refer to an eminent theologian and his or her disciples, or those that ascribe to that particular theological opinion or methodology. The expression could also refer to the general role of theologians as a source of teaching authority in the church.

Scientia media
Middle knowledge

Refers to a theory held in the late Middle Ages which sought to explain how God could know what individual humans would actually do in freedom in any particular circumstance, yet still leaving the human person to act in freedom. This theory sought to safeguard both the idea of God's complete omniscience, providence, and predestination and the concept of human freedom and moral responsibility for an individual's actions and state of his or her soul before God. See also *De Auxiliis*.

Scientia naturalis
Natural science

This expression has a variety of meanings. Generally it is used to describe philosophy, especially the philosophy of nature. This expression is also used in moral theology as a way of referring to the natural law understood as a "natural" knowledge (or process of understanding, rational reflection, etc.). Thus, according to the theory of *scientia naturalis*, humans, since they are by nature rational beings, possess a certain innate knowledge or tendency by which, without further instruction and help, they can recognize their true nature and act in a manner which conforms to that nature, i.e., in accord with the natural law.

Scientia sexualis
Sexual knowledge

A phrase used by French philosopher Michel Foucault in his 1978 *History of Sexuality* to denote the Western approach to the study of sex focusing on knowledge leading to power over sex, as contrasted with the *ars erotica* (*q.v.*) which Foucault characterized as the Eastern approach to sex as primarily an art form.

Scintilla conscientiae
Spark of conscience

Expression that speaks of the innate sense of conscience to determine right and wrong as well as to provide a sense of guilt for evil actions committed. This term is also related to the term *synderesis* (coming from the Greek συντήρησιν) which is usually translated as conscience, though this term is today largely agreed to be either a mistranslation on the part of St. Jerome in his composition of the Latin Vulgate and/or a manuscript corruption in medieval manuscripts of Jerome's commentary for the *bona fide* Greek word *syneidêsis* (συνείδησις).

Scriptura sacra locuta, res decisa est
Sacred Scripture has spoken, the matter is decided

Adage, common among Protestants, that indicates that once it can be demonstrated that Scripture has "spoken" about a certain matter of faith or practice, that matter is not open to further debate, change, or development. In terms of a fundamentalistic type of approach to authority, this maxim is similar to *Roma locuta, causa finita* (*q.v.*). See also *Scriptura sacra sui ipsius interpres* and *Sola scriptura*.

Scriptura sacra sui ipsius interpres
Sacred Scripture interprets itself

Theological axiom often tied with Protestant Reformation's affirmation of *sola Scriptura* (*q.v.*), which holds that the Bible is self-interpreting and therefore needs simply to be read, applied, and followed. This axiom is also used in Protestantism to counter the claims of the Roman Catholic *magisterium* (*q.v.*)

to be the authentic interpreter of the Scriptures. However, Thomas Aquinas used this expression to indicate that one part of Scripture could be used to interpret or clarify another part of Scripture. See also *Depositum fidei*.

Scripturam ex Scriptura explicandam esse
Scripture is to be explained from Scripture

Essentially a variant form of the principle of *Scriptura sacra sui ipsius interpres* (*q.v.*).

Secretum pontificium
Pontifical secret

Confidentiality clause governing certain church documents, the violation of which would carry ecclesiastical penalties. One recent example concerns the secrecy with which notification of sexual abuse claims are to be made to the Congregation for the Doctrine of the Faith as outlined in the 2001 documents *Epistula de delictis gravioribus* (*q.v.*) and *Sacramentorum sanctitatis tutela* (*q.v.*). See also *Corpus delicti*, **Crimen sollicitationis**, *Delicta graviora*, **Epistula de delictis gravioribus**, *Graviora delicta*, *In flagrante delicto*, **Sacramentorum sanctitatis tutela**, *Sub secreto pontificio*, and *Sub rosa*.

Secunda pars
The Second Part

Usually refers to the second major section of St. Thomas Aquinas' **Summa Theologiae** (*q.v.*), which deals with the human person, human acts, moral habits, theological and moral virtues, etc.

The *Secunda pars* is further subdivided into two other sections, the *Prima Secundae* (*q.v.*) and the *Secunda Secundae* (*q.v.*). See also *Prima pars* and *Tertia pars*.

Secunda Secundae
Second of the second

Usually refers to the second section of the *Secunda pars* (*q.v.*) of St. Thomas Aquinas' **Summa Theologiae** (*q.v.*), which deals with the particular aspects of human acts, the theological and moral virtues, etc. The *Secunda secundae* is often abbreviated as II–II or IIa–IIae.

Secundo loco
Second place

Refers to something which, though not in the primacy of a certain position, is closely associated with it and therefore enjoys a certain amount of influence based on that relationship. Thus, while sterilization is not the same as homicide, it is so closely associated with the sanctity of human life that it should not be done.

Secundum
Along, after, according to

Common Latin preposition derived from *sequor*, meaning "to follow." *Secundum* does *not* mean "second" or "secondary."

Secundum naturam
According to nature

Refers to the proper functioning of any natural power, such that its proper use should be in accord with its proper end. Thus, the faculty of speech is for communication of the truth, and truth-telling would be *secundum naturam* of the power of speech, whereas lying would be against the proper end of the power of speech and therefore *contra natruam* (*q.v.*) and therefore sinful in itself. *Secundum naturam* is often used in traditional sexual ethics and refers to a sexual act which is supposedly done in accord with the natural order. Acts done *secundum naturam* would depend upon further conditions to determine their moral value. Thus, heterosexual relations between a married couple would be *secundum naturam* and lawful due to the bond of marriage; heterosexual relations between unmarried persons would be *secundum naturam*, but sinful (fornication) because the partners were not married to each other. Other sorts of acts, such as homogenital sexual expression, would be *contra naturam*. See also *Condicio sine qua non*, *Contra naturam*, *Secundum rationem*, and *Sequi naturam*.

Secundum quid
According to something (else)

Expression which is used to indicate a qualifier that must be considered in order to find the correct meaning in a given context. This expression is often contrasted with *simpliciter* (*q.v.*), which refers to something in an unqualified sense. See the example given of a *virtus secundum quid* and a *virtus simpliciter* presented in the *Simpliciter* entry. See also *Materia circa quam* and *Sine modo*.

Secundum (rectam) rationem
According to (right) reason

Refers to the principle that it is "according to human reason" (which is taken to refer to the meaning of humanity itself) that the moral meaning of individual acts is found. The entire natural law is understood to be promulgated *secundum rationem*. For example, in sexual ethics, even though all heterosexual relations would be considered to be "according to nature" (*secundum naturam, q.v.*), but taking into account the nature of humanity itself in regards to the nature of marriage as a social institution, marriage would be further judged to be both monogamous and indissoluble, *secundum rationem*, i.e., a further requirement which comes not from the "nature" of the sexual organs *per se* (*q.v.*) but from reasoned reflection on the institution of marriage "according to reason." See also *Condicio sine qua non* and *Secundum naturam*

Securus iudicat orbis terrarum
Secure is the judgment of the whole world

Expression of Augustine, which indicates that we can rely on the judgment of the whole world as a guarantee of orthodoxy in matters of the faith of the universal church. After Vatican I's definition of papal infallibility Blessed John Henry Cardinal Newman insisted that the validity of the council would depend upon its reception by the *orbis terrarum* (*q.v.,* the whole world). See also *Congregatio fidelium, Ecclesia docens/Ecclesia discens*, the entries under *Magisterium, Sensus fidei, Sensus fidelium*, and *Solus consensus obligat*.

Sed contra
But on the contrary

Refers to the part of an argument in which one introduces a reason contrary to the objections just given. Usually, but not always, the *sed contra* states the position of the author. For example, Thomas Aquinas would list first several "objections" at the beginning of his discussion of an article to be proved, and then after enumerating these objections he would begin his elaboration of the proof for his position with the formula *sed contra*, usually followed by the *rispondeo (q.v.)* or "response" in which Thomas' own position is further amplified. Following the *sed contra* and *rispondeo*, Thomas Aquinas would then move on to reply to each of the objections in turn which had been enumerated at the beginning of the discussion.

Sede impedita
Impeded see

Refers to a situation in which a bishop is blocked, or impeded in some way, from functioning in his diocese (i.e., his "see"), for example, due to war or political persecution. The Code of Canon Law establishes some provisions for the governance of the diocese under such conditions. See also *Cum iure successionis, Sede vacante*, and *Sede vacante nihil innovetur*.

Sede vacante
Vacant seat

In technical ecclesiastical terms a *sede vacante* refers to a church office, such as that of the pope or a bishop, which is temporally vacant. Colloquially, though, the expression can refer to any office which is temporarily unfilled. In the case of the pope the *sede vacante* is ended when a new pope is chosen by a conclave of cardinals eligible to vote in a papal election (i.e., under eighty years of age). A number of legal provisions are established in canon law which regulate certain circumstances that arise in a *sede vacante* (cf. canons 416–30). This expression is also used by some ultraconservatives who refuse to accept the legitimacy of Vatican II and contend that the papacy has been "vacant" since the death of Pius XII in 1958. See also *Coetus Internationalis Patrum, Cum iure successionis, Habemus Papam, Sede impedita,* and *Sede vacante nihil innovetur.*

Sede vacante nihil innovetur
During a vacant see nothing is to be changed

Traditional canonical principle (cf. *C.I.C.* #428 §1) which states that when an ecclesiastical see is vacant (*sede vacante, q.v.*) no significant change is allowed (though obviously minor changes essential to the running of the see would be allowed). See also *Cum iure successionis* and *Sede impedita.*

Sedia gestatoria
Portable chair

Refers to the portable throne carried on the shoulders of a number of bearers and upon which the pope sat as he was borne in and out of liturgies and public audiences. The *sedia gestatoria* enabled the gathered crowds to see the pope more easily and was used up to and through the pontificate of Pope John Paul I (died 1978).

Semina virtutum
Seeds of virtue

Natural moral inclinations, such as a sense of justice, love of truth, friendship, courage, etc., which can be nurtured until they became true habits of virtue. See also *Habitus.*

Semper et pro semper
Always and in each instance

Refers usually to a norm or rule that would be binding in all cases without exception due to any circumstances. In moral theology, negative precepts (i.e., prohibitions) are considered to bind in each and every case. Thus, "do not murder" would bind *semper et pro semper.* Positive precepts, such as "help the poor," bind *semper* (always) but not *pro semper* (in each instance), as there are many instances in which someone may not be able to be engaged in the direct work of helping the poor (for example, when one is studying, recreating, sleeping, etc.). The expression relating to positive precepts is *Semper sed non pro semper (q.v.).*

Semper fidelis
Always faithful

Motto of the United States Marine Corps and title of a well-known military march by John Phillips Sousa.

Semper idem
Always the same

Episcopal motto of Cardinal Alfredo Ottaviani (1890–1979), conservative head of the Vatican's Holy Office (today the Congregation for the Doctrine of the Faith) prior to and during Vatican II, and opponent to most of the theological reforms of Vatican II. This motto has been taken over to refer to a rigid conservative mindset which finds any change to be suspect. Thus, the view of *Semper idem* would be to maintain things as they are. See also *Hic sunt dracones* and *Status quo.*

Semper Paratus
Always prepared

Motto of the United States Coast Guard.

Semper sed non pro semper
Always but not in each and every instance

Expression of positive duties like "pray always" or "feed the poor" which are universally valid but which are not necessarily binding at each and every moment of one's life (such as the moments devoted to reading this definition!). See also the related term for negative duties which *always* are binding, *Semper et pro semper*, and also *Caritas non obligat cum gravi incommodo* as well as *Generaliter.*

Semper, ubique, et ab omnibus
Always, everywhere, and by all

Criteria of orthodoxy and "constancy of tradition," proposed by Vincent of Lerins in the fifth century, i.e., that which had always been held, by all believers, and in all places.

Senatus Populusque Romanus
The Senate and the People of Rome

See *S.P.Q.R.*

Sensum, non verba spectamus
It is the sense and not the words that is observed

In other words it is not necessarily the literal meaning of a formulation that is determinative but rather the composite sense that gives the truer guide to its meaning—especially in matters of legal interpretation. See also *Ad literam*; *Consuetudo optima legum interpres*; *Epikeia*; *Exceptio firmat regulam*; *Lex dubia non obligat*; *Lex valet ut in pluribus*; and *Odia restringi, et favores convenit ampliari.*

Sensus ecclesiae
Sense (meaning) of the church

Refers to the nature of the church, which is found in individual church gatherings but which also in some sense transcends any specific situation, group, or culture. In this sense the church expresses its universal or "catholic" dimension. See also *Sensus fidei, sensus fidelium.*

Sensus fidei, sensus fidelium
Sense of the faithful

Expression of the sensitivity and capacity of all the faithful, who through their baptism share in the gifts and guidance of the Holy Spirit, to appreciate and discern the practical meaning revelation and the Christian faith has in the contemporary world. This term can refer to both the subjective aspect associated with the believers' sense of their faith (i.e., the gift of faith) and to the elements of the faith itself which the believers believe and profess (e.g., belief in the asumption of the Blessed Virgin). See also *Congregatio fidelium*; *Consensus non facit veritatem*; *Consuetudo optima legum interpres*; *Ecclesia discens*; *Quod omnes tangit ab omnibus approbetur*; *Quod ubique, quod semper, quod ab omnibus, creditum est*; *Regula fidei*; *Securus iudicat orbis terrarum*; *Sensus ecclesiae*; *Sentire cum ecclesia*; *Solus consensus obligat*; and *Tolle assertiones et christianismum tulisti.*

Sensus literalis
Literal sense

This term refers to the literal (and/or literary) sense or meaning of Scripture which is directly expressed by the authors of the biblical texts (who are understood as writing under the aid of divine inspiration). Properly understood, *sensus literalis* is not to be confused with "literalism" since the determination of the context and genre of a given text is absolutely necessary in order to determine its true "literal/literary" sense (e.g., is the text history or legend, a hymn, prayer, proverb, etc.).

Sensus plenior
Fuller sense

Refers to the hermeneutical affirmation that a classic text (here traditionally understood as the Scriptures) contains meanings that go beyond the literal sense or meaning explicitly intended by the original human author for the specific cultural-historical audience of the period in which the text was written. Thus, the Scriptures can always yield new and deeper meanings which may come up in new and different situations or which are realized through ongoing study and/or reflection and meditation.

Sententia facit ius
The sentence (penalty) makes for justice

Legal principle, especially important in canon law, which holds that ultimately even punitive measures have a medicinal quality aimed at helping cure the malefactor while restoring or upholding basic justice which in turn will safeguard the *bonum commune* (*q.v.*). See also *Dura lex sed lex*; *Lex iniusta non est lex*; *Odia restringi, et favores convenit ampliari*; *Ordinatio rationis ad bonum commune*; *Salus publica suprema lex*; *Sententia incerta non valet*; and *Ubi ius, ibi remedium.*

Sententia incerta non valet
An uncertain sentence (penalty) is not valid

An ambiguous judicial sentence or penalty is not considered binding. This is a sentiment similar to *Lex dubia non obligat* (*q.v.*). See also *Dubium iuris vel facti*; *In dubio favores sunt amplificandi, odiosa restrigenda*; *In dubio pars tutior sequenda*; *Non est imponenda obligatio nisi certo constet*; *Sententia facit ius*; and *Ubi ius incertum, ibi ius nullum.*

Sententia probata
An approved ("probable") position ("sentence")

One of the theological "notes" indicating a theological position which, while not formally defined or pronounced upon by the magisterium, was still held as "probable" by the majority of theologians that it enjoyed a very high presupposition of truth and could be freely taught and believed. See also *Credenda, De fide, Ex Cathedra*, and *Tenenda.*

Sentire cum ecclesia
Thinking (or judging) with the church

Refers to being in communion theologically with what the church believes and teaches. It is seen as an important mark of fidelity on the part of believers, especially those entrusted with the ministry of teaching. See also *Congregatio fidelium*; *Consensus non facit veritatem*; *Ecclesia dicens*; *Quod ubique, quod semper, quod ab omnibus, creditum est*; *Regula fidei*; *Securus iudicat orbis terrarum*; *Sensus fidei*; and *Sensus fidelium*.

Sequela Christi
Following of Christ

Refers to the basic Christian stance of discipleship, in which the believers are called upon to follow Jesus Christ. See also *Imitatio Christi* and *Via Dolorosa*.

Sequi naturam
To follow nature

Principle which holds that one ought to conform one's being and actions to "nature." However, this principle should not be understood as an absolute correspondence with biological nature but rather with the rational aspect of human nature. Understood in this sense, the axiom is closely related to *secundum naturam* (*q.v.*). Thus, *sequi naturam* should be seen as conformity with the essential rational nature of human beings, i.e., an orientation to the good, truth, etc., and the aspect of to "conform to" or follow that human nature.

Seriatim
In series, one after another

For example, when used to denote publication brought out in a series.

Servitium debitum
Debt of service

Military obligation, sometimes termed "knight-service," that a vassal owed his feudal lord or king. See also *Debitum*.

Servus Servorum Dei
Servant of the servants of God

Title used to describe the Roman pontiff and often shortened to *Servus Servorum*. It was used in AD 591 by Pope Gregory the Great (590–604) at the time the bishop of Constantinople assumed the title of Ecumenical Patriarch and has been in general usage since the papacy of Pope Gregory VII (1073–85). See also *Munus Petrinium*, *Primus inter pares*, and *Vicarius Christi*.

Si comprehendis, non est Deus
If you (fully) comprehend, it is not God

Augustine *Sermo 117, PL 38, 663*

Refers to an aspect of God which admits that full knowledge of God would surpass all human concepts and theological formulations which are intrinsically limited by the partiality of human knowledge. See also *Deus absconditus/Deus revelatus*; *Deus semper maior*; and *Non ut explicetur, sed ne taceretur*.

Si Deus non daretur
If God does exist, he doesn't belong [to us]

Statement of a theological hypothetical and usually refers either to conclusions drawn about what life would be like if there were no God or, more polemically, as a charge leveled against those who may profess belief in God but who seem to act or hold other positions that appear to be so secular, agnostic, or even atheistic that these would counter the professed belief in God. It was used in this latter context, for example, by Joseph Cardinal Ratzinger [later Pope Benedict XVI] in his "Address to Catechists and Religion Teachers" given at the Jubilee of Catechists, 12 December 2000.

Si finis bonus est, totum bonum erit
> If the end is good, all will be good

Can be rendered as "all's well that ends well," but always refers to the relation of a morally good end used to judge the anterior actions required to arrive at that particular end. See also *Bonum totius*, *Mala moralia* and *mala praemoralia*, *Pars propter totum*, and *Ratio proportionata*.

Si iudicas, cognossce; si regnas, iube
> If you are judging, be aware; if you are reigning, act

Expression that points out the primary obligations of those in the ruling class: judges must inform themselves fully about the facts of the case before them, while executives or rulers have the obligation to act. See also *Facta non praesumuntur sed probantur*; *Onus probandi*; *Potentia iurisdictionis*; *Potestas regendi*; *Potestas regiminis*; *Praesumitur ignorantia ubi scientia non probatur*; *Summum ius, summa iniuria*; and *Testis in uno falsus in nullo fidem meretur*.

Si vis pacem, para bellum
> If you want peace, prepare for war.

Ancient aphorism which indicates that the best defense would be a good offense, or that deterrence based on strong military preparedness would be the best guarantor of peace. An opposing view could be obtained by replacing "war" with "peace" throughout: *Si vis pacem, para pacem*. See also *Bellum iustum*, *Ius ad bellum*, *Ius in bello*, and *Ius post bellum*.

Sic
> Thus

Sic is used in references and citations in written works to indicate an apparent error, such as a misspelling, in the original text being cited. *Sic* should not be used in excess or to highlight anachronistic expressions or spellings. For correct usage see an accepted manual of style, such *The Chicago Manual of Style*.

Sic et non
> Yes and no

Refers to the dialectic method of philosophical reflection on a matter so as to reach the truth. Expression used by Peter Abelard (1079–1142), and also the title of one of his principal works.

Sic et simpliciter
> Thus and simply

Simply, in a straight-forward manner, simply put, with no need of further description or argumentation. See also *Totaliter*.

Sic transit gloria mundi
  Thus passes the glory of the world

Traditional maxim, found in Thomas à Kempis' *Imitation of Christ*, which highlights the ephemeral nature of created things, especially worldly honors and pleasures. Liturgically, this expression is recited while a piece of flax is burned in the installation of a new pope. See also *Imitatio Christi* and *Devotio moderna*.

Sigillum
  Seal (of confession)

Term which refers to the absolute secrecy of the confessional and the prohibition of the confessor to divulge either directly or indirectly either the identity of the penitent and/or the sins she or he has confessed. See also *Privilegium fori.*

Sigla
  Signs

Often used as the title or reference to a list of abbreviations employed in a scholarly work.

Signum unitatis
  Sign of unity

See *Sacramentum pietatis.*

Similtudo Dei
  Likeness to God

Sometimes this expression is used synonymously with *imago Dei* (*q.v.*) to indicate humanity's creation in the image of God (cf. Genesis 1:26) or to refer to the original human nature which was lost due to original sin. See also *Imago Dei.*

Simpliciter
  Simply, candidly, frankly, straightforward, unqualified

Common Latin adverb, and when used in theological discourse means that the expression or concept should be interpreted in a straightforward manner, without any nuances or qualifications one can find elsewhere, especially in canon law which will put forward a proposition and then qualify it with a *nisi* (*q.v.*) clause listing exceptions. In other instances, something described *simpliciter* can be contrasted with the same term described *secundum quid* (*q.v.*) in a qualified sense. Thus, a *virtus simpliciter* would be a full and unqualified virtue directed toward an unqualified good, whereas a *virtus secundum quid* would be a virtue in a qualified sense, such as the skill of a locksmith which would be directed toward the "good" of getting me back into my house when I forgot my keys or toward an evil end if used to assist in a robbery. See also *Generaliter*, *Sine modo*, and *Totaliter.*

Simul iustus et peccator
  Being at the same time redeemed (righteous) and sinful

Classic Lutheran axiom of theological anthropology, which holds that the human person is at one and the same time a sinner (sinful) and yet redeemed through the grace of Jesus Christ. Even when justified, the human being remains a sinner. See also *Pecca fortiter*, *Sola gratia*, and *Totus conversus sed non totaliter.*

Sine
Without

Common Latin preposition.

Sine culpa
Without fault or blame

This expression is used theologically to refer to those who through no fault of their own are not responsible for some error in judgment, or to respond to the message of the Gospel. **Lumen gentium** (*q.v.*) #16 expresses this concept in these words: "Nor does Divine Providence deny the helps necessary for salvation to those who, without blame [*sine culpa*] on their part, have not yet arrived at an explicit knowledge of God and with His grace strive to live a good life." Such individuals were sometimes termed *Ignorantes* (the ignorant ones) and were judged to be acting without blame (*culpa*) since their ignorance was "invincible" and could not be overcome by their own efforts. See also *Culpa*; *Extra ecclesia nulla salus*; *Ignorantes*; *Ingnorantia invincibilis*; *Limbus*; *Mens rea*; *Nulla poena sine culpa*; *Radix Mali*; and *Ubi non est culpa, ibi non est delictum*.

Sine die
Without a day (being specified)

Ecclesiastical equivalent of sending something back to committee as a way of killing it. A document that is remanded *sine die* usually will never be promulgated. However, this principle is not always true. An earlier version of **Veritatis Splendor**, John Paul II's 1993 encyclical on fundamental moral theology, had been remanded *sine die* in 1991 but eventually was reworked and officially promulgated.

Sine ira et studio
Without anger or partiality

Refers to objective discourse or academic-type inquiry into a certain topic, done without anger or prejudice.

Sine modo
Without limit

This expression can be used both positively and negatively, e.g., to love God whole-heartedly (a good) or to love pleasure *sine modo*, which would be a violation of reason and virtue. See also *Secundum quid*, *Simpliciter*, and *Totaliter*.

Sine prole
Without issue

Refers to those who have no children. Often used legally to refer to someone who dies without leaving children as heirs, but is also used to refer to marriages which are childless. See also *Bonum prolis* and *Generatio prolis*.

Sine qua non
Without which nothing (can be done)

Often used as a shorthand expression for an indispensable condition or item. See also *Conditio sine qua non*.

Singularia non sunt extendenda
Singular things (e.g., exceptions) are not extended

While the law can treat exceptions and unique cases, these "singular" cases should not be extended to other situations or become a general rule. This concept is balanced by another legal aphorism, *Exceptio firmat regulam* (*q.v.*). See also *De minimis non curat lex*; *Epikeia*; *Lex valet ut in pluribus*; *Odia restringi, et favores convenit ampliari*; and *Quod raro fit non observant legislatores*.

Societas perfecta
Perfect society

Theological view that the church, as a human society, has the characteristics, structures, and institutions of any autonomous or sovereign society, i.e., all the means within it to achieve its purpose. In this sense, *perfecta* carries the connotation of being "complete" or "whole" and *not* that the church is completely without sin or failure. Sometimes this term is used in distinction from seeing the church as a *Communio* (*q.v.*). See also *Perfectus* and *Speculum iustitiae*.

Socius
Companion

Designation used often in some religious orders to refer to the principal assistant to the superior, such as the *socius* to the Director of Novices or to the Provincial.

Sola cum seipsa
Alone with itself

Expression that usually refers to a subjectivist view of reality, e.g., of conscience that looks just to the person him/herself to determine what is right or to be done. This expression is contrasted with the church's usual understanding of the sanctuary of conscience expressed in the aphorism *solus cum solo* (*q.v.*), which refers to the individual being alone with God in conscience and in that privileged forum trying to discern what is to be done or what God is asking of the person.

Sola experientia facit theologum
Only experience makes the theologian

Attributed to Martin Luther, and refers to the necessity of lived experience as a critical source and resource for doing theology.

Sola fide
Faith alone

Along with *Sola Scriptura*, *Sola gratia*, *Solus Christus*, and *Soli Deo gloria* (*q.v.*), this was one of the five basic principles which Martin Luther used to ground his theology, in contrast to what he considered to be the false reliance of Roman Catholicism upon tradition, as well as a justification based on works or merit, which he believed was another principal heresy of Roman Catholicism. See also *Fides fiducialis*, *Pecca fortiter*, *Simul iustus et peccator*, and *Totus conversus sed non totaliter*.

Sola gratia
Grace alone

Along with *Sola Scriptura*, *Sola fide*, *Solus Christus*, and *Soli Deo gloria*, this was one of the five basic principles of traditional Reformation theology. *Sola gratia* held that God's gratuitous gift of grace was totally unmerited and also could never be "earned" through good works or pious exercises. Therefore, the human person was called to acceptance of this grace through faith alone.

Eventually, Protestant theology would elaborate five *sola* principles. See also *Fides fiducialis, Pecca fortiter, Simul iustus et peccator, Sola gratia, Solus Christus*, and *Totus conversus sed non totaliter*.

Sola Scriptura
Scripture alone

Along with *Sola fide, Sola gratia, Solus Christus*, and *Soli Deo gloria*, this was one of the five basic principles of traditional Reformation theology. *Sola Scriptura* referred to the primacy of God's revelation in the Sacred Scriptures as the touchstone for all theology and ethics. Thus, Luther rejected moral casuistry based on the natural law and also appealed to tradition rather than Scripture alone for validation of any theological position. See also *Homo unius libri* and *Proprium*.

Soli Deo gloria
To God alone the glory

Along with *Sola Scriptura, Sola fide, Sola gratia*, and *Solus Christus*, this was one of the five basic principles of traditional Reformation theology. Since it is God's grace alone which saves us through Jesus Christ, the Protestants held that glory should be given only to God, and *not* to the saints or members of the hierarchy, etc. The *Soli Deo gloria* principle was used especially in Calvinist theology and is somewhat akin to the motto of the Society of Jesus (Jesuits), which is *Ad maiorem Dei gloriam* (*A.M.D.G., q.v.*): "to the greater glory of God." See also *Curet primo Deum, Fides fiducialis, Pecca fortiter, Simul iustus et peccator, Sola fide, Sola gratia*, and *Totus conversus sed non totaliter*.

Sollicitudo omnium Ecclesiarum
Solicitude (Care) for all the churches

Title of two quite different papal documents. The first, issued by Pope Pius VII on August 7, 1814, restored the Society of Jesus (Jesuits), which had been suppressed by the papal brief of Pope Clement XIV **Dominus ac redemptor** (*q.v.*) issued July 21, 1773. The second document was an apostolic letter issued by Pope Paul VI June 24, 1969, and dealt with papal representatives to various nations, international organizations, and local churches.

Sollicitudo Rei Socialis
Solicitude (care) for social matters

Encyclical of John Paul II On Social Concerns, including the international economy, issued in 1988 to commemorate the twentieth anniversary of Pope Paul VI's 1967 social encyclical **Populorum Progressio** (*q.v.*).

Solus Christus
Christ alone

Along with *Sola Scriptura, Sola fide, Sola gratia*, and *Soli Deo Gloria*, this was one of the five basic principles of traditional Reformation theology. It is ultimately Jesus Christ who saves us, not our own good works. See also *Fides fiducialis, Pecca fortiter, Simul iustus et peccator, Sola fide, Sola gratia*, and *Totus conversus sed non totaliter*.

Solus consensus obligat
Only consensus obliges

Basic principle of democratic process that indicates that it is the majority decision in a disputed proposal that determines which course of action is to be followed. However, in the Catholic tradition majority rule is *not* that which determines authoritative leadership, nor can a majority position determine the rightness or wrongness of a moral proposition. See also *Magisterium, Munus, Orbis terrarum, Sensus fidelium*, and *Securus iudicat orbis terrarum.*

Solus cum solo
Alone with the alone

Refers to the fundamental stance of each person who ultimately must stand alone before God, who alone is the absolute. See also *Coram Deo* and *Sola cum seipsa.*

Spe salvi
In hope we are saved

Title of Pope Benedict XVI's second encyclical issued on November 20, 2007. See also **Caritas in Veritate**; *Caritas in veritate in re sociali*; **Deus caritas est**; *Ubi caritas*; *Deus ibi est*; and *Ubi societas, ibi ius.*

Specialissimo modo
In a most special manner/mode

This expression was often used in the 1917 Code of Canon Law to refer to special provisions to more general norms, such as the reservation of certain cases or penalties to a higher authority such as the pope or a bishop. An example was remission of the *latae sententiae (q.v.)* penalty of excommunication for a physical attack on the pope which was reserved *specialissimo modo* to the Holy See itself, whereas the penalty for attacking clerics of a lesser order such as bishops and car-

dinals were reserved also to the Holy See, but in *special modo* (in special manner, sometimes also rendered as *modo speciali*). Moving down the ecclesiastical ladder, attacks on priests and religious were able to be remitted by the local bishop. Thus, the distinction between *specialissimo modo* and *special modo* was helpful in judging the perceived relative gravity of the crime or delict (to use the technical canonical terms).

Speculum iustitiae
Mirror of justice

One of the Marian titles associated with the Immaculate Conception, and also a metaphor used for the church, which should "mirror" perfect justice to the world. This metaphor has also been employed to indicate why the church would not allow certain things, such as divorce, which secular legal orders recognize and accept. See also *Societas perfecta.*

Spiritus Gladius
Sword of the Spirit

The expression comes from Ephesians 6:17, in which Paul gives his famous allegory of armor and calls the Word of God the sword of the Spirit. The sword is often used in depictions of Paul, as contrasted with the keys of the kingdom, which are associated with Peter. *Spiritus Gladius* is used also to denote certain catechetical groups which focus on faith formation.

S.P.Q.R.
The Senate and the People of Rome

Latin abbreviation for *Senatus Populusque Romanus*, which referred to the legal power and authority of the Roman Republic. This expression is still used by the city of Rome.

S.S.D.
Doctor of Sacred Scripture

Latin abbreviation for *Sacrae Scripturae Doctor*, which refers to the terminal degree in biblical studies, granted by a pontifical ecclesiastical faculty which is governed by the ecclesiastical statutes of **Sapientia Christiana** (*q.v.*).

S.S.L.
Licentiate in Sacred Scripture

Latin abbreviation for *Sacrae Scripturae Licentiatus*, which refers to the penultimate degree in biblical studies, granted by a pontifical ecclesiastical faculty which is governed by the ecclesiastical statutes of **Sapientia Christiana** (*q.v.*). The *S.S.L.* "licenses" or credentials one to teach in a pontifical or ecclesiastical faculty.

ST
Summa Theologiae
Summary of theology

Common abbreviation for the **Summa Theologiae** (*q.v.*) of St. Thomas Aquinas. The abbreviation ST is often followed by a set of section divisions which specify the exact location of a text. Thus, ST I–II, q. 94, a. 1 would signify Article 1 of Question 94 of the *Prima secundae* (*q.v.*) of the **Summa Theologiae**.

Stabat Mater Dolorosa
The sorrowful mother stood

Refers to the first words of a thirteenth-century Latin poem and hymn to the Blessed Mother in honor of her enduring the suffering and death of her son at the foot of the cross. In English the opening lines of this hymn are "At the cross her station keeping, stood the mournful Mother weeping." This hymn is often called simply the *Stabat Mater*. See also *Mater Dolorosa*.

Stabiliter existens
Existing as a stable group

See *Coetus fidelim* for an example of how this term might be used.

Status antelapsarius/postlapsarius
State (of human beings) before (*ante*) / after (*post*) the Fall

Antelapsarius refers to the original and sinless state of the first parents, which after their fall (*postlapsarius*) was lost for all of their human descendants due to their commission of original sin. In moral theology and social ethics, this distinction is often used to justify a certain amount of moral compromise. Thus, due to human sinful nature it is necessary to allow for private property and the laws which govern its use.

Status quaestionis
State of the question

In general this term refers to the point at issue in developing some position. In theological circles this would often refer to a debated point in theology, etc., in which the *status quaestionis* gives the main opinions concerning the particular issue. See also *Quaestio disputata, Sententia probata*, and *Theologice certa*.

Status quo
Situation as it is

Refers to the situation as it currently stands. Often used to refer to a situation which does not change, even though it may be desirable to effect some change. See also *Semper idem*.

Status quo ante
Situation beforehand

Expression which denotes the situation (*status quo*) prior to another given point in time. E.g., in canon law the *status quo ante* can refer to the situation which existed prior to the handing down of a juridical sentence. See also *Restitutio in integrum*.

Statuta sunt stricte interpretanda
Laws (statutes) are interpreted strictly

Legal aphorism that indicates that human laws (cf. *Ius positum*) are to be interpreted narrowly and according to the letter of the law. For the balancing hermeneutical principle of legal interpretation, see *Odia restringi, et favores convenit ampliari*. See also *Ad literam*, *De minimis non curat lex*, *Epikeia*, *Lex valet ut in pluribus*, and *Quod raro fit non observant legislatores*.

S.T.D.
Doctorate in Sacred Theology

Latin abbreviation for *Sacrae Theologiae Doctor*, which refers to the terminal degree in theological studies, granted by a pontifical ecclesiastical faculty which is governed by the ecclesiastical statutes of **Sapientia Christiana** (*q.v.*).

S.T.L.
Licentiate in Sacred Theology

Latin abbreviation for *Sacrae Theologiae Licentiatus*, which refers to the penultimate degree in theological studies, granted by a pontifical ecclesiastical faculty which is governed by the ecclesiastical statutes of **Sapientia Christiana** (*q.v.*). The *S.T.L.* "licenses" or credentials one to teach in a pontifical or ecclesiastical faculty.

Stricte mentalis
Strict (doctrine of) mental (reservation)

One opinion in the casuistry debate on *Mentalis restrictio* (mental reservation, *q.v.*) and *locutio contra mentem* (*q.v.*), which held that one was allowed effectively either to equivocate or tell only partial truths for proportionate reason as long as the full truth would be told in the mind to God. E.g., someone could reply aloud "I know not" to a question that sought information to which the interlocutor had no legitimate right as long as the respondent added silently a qualifier such as "I know not *what to tell you*," which would then make the statement "true" *Coram Deo* (*q.v.*) to God as the Author of all Truth.

Stultis non succuritur
A fool is not helped

Though seemingly hard-hearted at first glance, this expression usually connotes that a foolish person, because of his or her lack of wisdom, is not open to being helped and thus ends up trapped in the consequences of one's foolishness. See also *Ordo sapientiae* and *Verbum sat sapienti*.

Suaviter in modo, fortiter in re
Smoothly in manner, firmly in matters of substance

Means to be diplomatic, but at the same time to not yield on essentials.

Sub
Under, toward, at

Common Latin preposition.

Sub conditione
Under condition

Refers to certain conditions, or the conditional nature of an action. For example, in case of doubt about whether baptism has been administered validly, a second baptism is administered "conditionally" in case the first baptism in fact was not performed in a valid manner.

Sub gravi
Under grave weight

Traditional expression used to denote sinful matter that was considered grave, or a precept whose end or object was critical to maintaining friendship with God as our human *Summum bonum* (*q.v.*). This expression was used primarily in one of two senses in the traditional manuals of moral theology. In one sense, *sub gravi* was understood to refer to some "law" which if transgressed would involve the commission of mortal sin. Thus, attendance at Sunday Mass was taught as obliging *sub gravi*, i.e., under the pain of mortal sin. However, other theologians used this expression as a warning of some potential grave danger which should be avoided and therefore pointed to the importance of a certain matter (such as not missing participating in the Sunday Eucharist) without neces-

sarily concluding that if one deliberately missed a Sunday celebration she or he would be guilty of mortal sin as such. This term is contrasted with *Sub levi* (q.v.). See also *Ex toto genere suo (grave)*, *Graviter et dolose*, *Materia levis (gravis)*, *Parvitas materiae in Sexto*, and *Sub poena*.

Sub levi
Under (the aspect of being) less important (or trivial)

Expression contrasted with *Sub gravi* (*q.v.*) that denotes something—often of a moral nature—that really has little importance or which would be subject to a lesser penalty. Punishment for many venial sins, as contrasted with the loss of God's friendship due to mortal sin, would be an example of *sub levi*, as would an ecclesiastical penalty for an infraction of a precept of lesser import. This concept could also be important in battling scruples, since the pathology of scruples is to see serious sin where there is none or to exaggerate the importance of a minor failing into a major fault. A related expression is *Materia levis (gravis)* (*q.v.*). On the other hand, certain sins—especially of a sexual nature—were always considered to be objectively grave, as expressed in the axiom (*Nulla* [No]) *Parvitas materiae in Sexto* (*q.v.*). See also *Sub poena*.

Sub poena
Under penalty

In ecclesiastical circles, this usually refers to the prohibition of something "under the pain" of serious sin or excommunication. See also *Ferendae sententiae*, *Latae sententiae*, and *Sub levi*.

Sub rosa
   Under the rose

In strict confidence or secretly (the rose being a symbol of secrecy, which was sometimes carved above the confessional to signify the absolute secrecy of the seal of confession). See also *Sub secreto.*

Sub secreto
   Under secrecy

Often refers to an ecclesiastical document that is given to a particular person for some official reason but which is not to be released to the public or its contents divulged. See also **Crimen sollicitationis**, *Crimen pessimum, Corpus delicti, Delicta graviora,* **Epistula de delictis gravioribus**, *Graviora delicta, In flagrante delicto,* **Sacramentorum sanctitatis tutela**, *Secretum pontificium, Sub secreto pontificio,* and *Sub rosa.*

Sub secreto pontificio
   Under pontifical secret

See *Secretum pontificium* for the discussion of this term.

Sub verbo
   Under the word

See *S.V.*

Subsistit in
   Subsists in

These two Latin words refer to a sharp debate which has occurred since the close of Vatican II over the precise meaning and intention of the council's formulation found in **Lumen gentium**, the Dogmatic Constitution on the Church, regarding the nature of the Church of Jesus Christ, the Roman Catholic Church, and other Christian Churches. Is the Church of Jesus Christ exclusively coterminous with the Roman Catholic Church, such that one is fully the other and vice versa, or does it mean that while the Roman Catholic Church fully subsists in, or is found in, the Church of Jesus Christ the latter also includes room for the other Christian Churches, at least to some extent? **Lumen gentium**, paragraph 8, states the following: "This Church [established by Jesus Christ] constituted and organized in the world as a society, subsists in [*subsistit in*] the Catholic Church, which is governed by the successor of Peter and by the Bishops in communion with him, although many elements of sanctification and of truth are found outside of its visible structure." A very good summary of this whole discussion can be found in the theological writings of Rev. Francis A. Sullivan, SJ, who taught ecclesiology for many decades at the Pontifical Gregorian University in Rome. A recent article of his which revisits this discussion can be found under the title *"Quaestio Disputata: Further Thoughts on the Meaning of* **Subsistit In**," *Theological Studies* 71 (March 2010): 133–47. See also **Dominus Iesus, Lumen gentium**, *Elementa ecclesiae, Extra ecclesia nulla salus,* **Mystici Corporis**, *Plantatio ecclesiae,* and **Unam Sanctam**.

Sui generis
   Of its own kind

Refers to a "one of a kind"—something or someone unique—whose characteristics militate against its being classed in a group to which it might otherwise seem to belong.

Sui iuris
In his or her own right (i.e., independent)

In law this refers to someone of legal age and of sound mind and therefore competent to handle his or her own affairs. It can also refer to a body or organ that functions by its own right. For example, the synods of bishops of the Eastern Catholic Churches function *sui iuris* as synods and do not depend on Rome for the "right" to exist, whereas the synods of bishops in the Latin Rite would depend on recognition from Rome.

Summa
The main part (or summary)

The closest English cognate is "summary" or "complete treatment," and thus, for example, the **Summa Theologiae** (*q.v.*) of St. Thomas Aquinas. Some other possible translations for *summa* would be "compendium, sum total, comprehensive exposition of main issues."

Summa Casuum Conscientiae
Summary of Cases of Conscience

Moral theology manual, popular in the seventeenth century, which presented sample confessional cases using casuistry to illustrate the relevant moral principles involved in giving pastoral advice and making appropriate judgments about the type and gravity of sins confessed in the sacrament of penance. See also *Casus conscientiae*.

Summa Contra Gentiles
Summary against the Gentiles (non-believers, heretics)

Commonly abbreviated **SCG**, this work of St. Thomas Aquinas was designed as a summary of all the heresies known to him.

Summa iustitia in se
Highest justice in itself

Expression which refers to God since God is the principle of highest justice. This expression was used extensively in theologies of justification and salvation, as well as indicating that it is in God's very nature always to act for the best, and therefore he will always remain faithful to the covenant established with humankind. See also *Ordo rectitudinis* and *Summum bonum*.

Summa Theologiae
Summary of theology

Title used by many manualists to refer to their texts on theology, but unless otherwise noted, e.g., the *Summa theologiae* of St. Antoninus of Florence (1389–1459), one can presume the work in question is St. Thomas Aquinas' masterpiece (commonly abbreviated ST), and intended by him to be a summary and introduction of the main points of the study of theology. See also *Prima pars*, *ST*, *Secunda pars*, *Tertia pars*, *Prima secundae*, and *Secunda secundae*.

Summae confessariorum
Summaries of confession

Texts which originated in the thirteenth century to present material for the training of priests on the nature of various sins, often arranged in alphabetical order, without much systematic overview or development of a theology of sin and forgiveness. Rather, they listed various norms of law to be applied in the confessional to cases brought by the penitents. See also *Casus conscientiae, Libri paenitentiales, Summa Casuum Conscientiae,* and *Summae confessorum.*

Summae confessorum
Summas (summaries) of confessors

Generic title given to the various moral and canonical manuals devoted to the training of priests in the hearing of confessions. This genre began to emerge around the beginning of the thirteenth century as a guide to penitential praxis. See also *Casus conscientiae, Libri paenitentiales, Summa Casuum Conscientiae,* and *Summae confessariorum*

Summorum Pontificum
[The care] of the supreme pontiff

Motu proprio (q.v.) of Pope Benedict XVI on the Roman liturgy prior to the reform of 1970 issued on 7 July 2007. This piece of papal legislation gave every priest the rite to celebrate the pre–Vatican II Latin Tridentine Liturgy as an "extraordinary form" *(forma extraordinaria, q.v.)* without getting special permission from the diocesan bishop, as had been the case under the three previous popes (Paul VI, John Paul I, and John Paul II). This document was further explained by the instruction **Universae Ecclesiae**. See also *Ad orientem, Cappa magna, Coetus fidelium, Forma extraordinaria, Missale Romanum, Novus Ordo,* **Sacrosanctum concilium**, **Universae Ecclesiae**, and *Versus populum.*

Summum bonum
The highest good

Following St. Thomas Aquinas, we would say that the *summum bonum* possible for humans is union with God in the enjoyment of the beatific vision (*Visio beatifica, q.v.*), and this is also the ultimate end or goal for all humans. Since God is the sum of all perfection it is God then toward which all beings move to attain their proper completion. See the other entries under *Bonum,* especially *Bonum utile, Bonum suum,* and also *Capax Dei* and *Uti et frui.* See also *Exitus et reditus, Finis ultimus,* and *Nihil amatum nisi praecognitum.*

Summum ius, summa iniuria
The highest authority (i.e., the nation-state) is capable of the gravest injustice

Traditional axiom of Roman law; also can indicate that an overly strict enforcement of a law is capable of causing great harm. There is also a subtle play on the words in Latin, *ius* (justice) and *in-iuria* (injustice, or injury) which suggests that a perfect application of the law can also lead to real and actual injustice in certain concrete applications. This aphorism also indicates that human laws and lawgivers ultimately are subjected to a higher moral order (and in this sense suggests the role of the natural law). See also *Altum dominium, Ens rationis, Lex aeterna, Lex indita non scripta, Lex naturae, Mutatio legis odiosa, Ordo rationis, Per modum cognitionis/Per modum inclinationis, Prima sedes a nemine iudicatur, Recta ratio,* and *Rex non potest peccare.*

Super rato
On being ratified

Reference in canon law to a marriage which has been properly performed (*ratum, q.v.*) but not (yet) sexually consummated and therefore can be validly dispensed. See also *Quod Deus conjunxit, homo non separet* and *Ratum et consummatum.*

Suppositum
Subsists (subject)

Refers to the philosophical concept of the principle of subsistence by which a thing exists in itself, or which has its own distinctiveness or individuation. See also *Accidens, Essentia, In se, Per accidens,* and *Per Se.*

Supra
Above, beyond

Common Latin preposition. This word is also often used in scholarly writing to refer to something stated earlier in the text, as in *vid. supra* (see above), i.e., look to a place earlier in the text.

Sursum corda
Lift up (your) hearts

In the Latin Eucharist this phrase is found in the introductory dialogue of the preface to the eucharistic canon, which occurs between the presider and the congregation. However, in Protestant theology this phrase is important as an explanation of the union which exists between the participants in the Lord's Supper (*coena Domini, q.v.*) and the resurrected Jesus Christ. In distinction to the Roman Catholic stress on the Real Presence of Christ in the consecrated bread and wine, Protestant theology stresses the spiritual union of the believers with the Risen Christ celebrated in the Lord's Supper.

Susurrus
Muttering, whispering, speaking in a low sound

This expression denotes a particular form of defamation or detraction in which someone speaks evil of another with the intention of sowing discord between that person and another. In moral theology this action was considered to be a graver sin than defamation or detraction, since not only did the offended individual suffer the loss of honor but of friendship as well.

Suum cuique
To each his or her own

As a principle of justice, this is the same as *Reddere suum cuique* and *Unicuique suum.*

S.V.
Under the word

Latin abbreviation for *sub verbo,* i.e., in an encyclopedia, lexicon, or dictionary, discussion of a particular topic such as "birth control" might be found under the heading indicated *s.v.* "contraception."

Syllabus errorum
Syllabus (Compendium) of errors

Title of the collection of modern propositions, such as freedom of conscience in religion, democracy, and socialism, which were condemned by Pius IX in his 1864 encyclical **Quanta Cura** (*q.v.*).

T

Tabula dierum liturgicorum
Table of liturgical days

This is the collection of liturgical feasts in the church and indicates their relative rank or importance, which in turn has a bearing on certain liturgical rubrics, prescriptions, prohibitions, and dispensations. The *Tabula* also lists local solemnities, such as the principal patron of the place, anniversary of the dedication of a particular church, titular saints, founders or principal patrons of religious orders or congregations, and so on. See also *Ad libitum* and *Ordo*.

Tabula rasa
A slate scraped (clean)

Usually refers to a person with a mind like a "blank slate," which is free from preconceptions, information, etc. Negatively, this would suggest someone not well educated or informed, but positively it can indicate someone innocent and/or free from prejudices and biases.

Tantum ergo
See *Pange Lingua*.

Tantum quantum
So much as

Ignatian principle in which, for example, a certain material object or good is used *tantum quantum* in as much as, or so far as, it aids in achieving a certain (spiritual) end and no more. Cf. the First Principle and Foundation of St. Ignatius of Loyola's *Spiritual Exercises* 23. In short, the principle of *tantum quantum* points to the prudent use of created things and guards against turning them into ends in themselves, rather than treating them in the proper sense as the means to a greater end.

Tantum valet quantum probat
It as valid insofar (or as much as) it is proven

Epistemological axiom that indicates that a proposition can be taken to be "true" only insofar as, or as much as, the truth of the proposition can be demonstrated or proven. In other words, merely saying "X" is "true," does not make the proposition true in itself—even if a significant extrinsic authority were to make this claim. Truth depends not on extrinsic authority for its intrinsic truthfulness but on the nature of the proposition itself. Thus, if in a case that a certain proposition were long held to be "true" (e.g., that the sun revolved around the earth), if later and more compelling evidence were marshaled to question the truth of this long-held proposition, then the axiom *Tantum valet quantum probat* suggests that superior evidence would have to call into question the long-held view. See also *Facta non praesumuntur sed probantur*; *In necessariis unitas, in dubiis libertas, in omnibus caritas*; *Lex dubia non obligat*; *Non liquet*; *Onus probandi*; *Praesumitur ignorantia ubi scientia non probatur*; *Res ipsa loquitur*; and *Testis in uno falsus in nullo fidem meretur*.

Te Deum
(We praise) you God

Opening words in Latin of a traditional hymn of praise to God. As a prayer the *Te Deum* is recited on Sundays and major feasts in the recitation of the Liturgy of the Hours (the Breviary), as well as other solemn moments of thanksgiving. Thus, a liturgical service at which the *Te Deum* is sung may be used to close an assembly or meeting, the end of the year, or some other similar event or moment.

Te totum applica ad textum; rem totam applica ad te
Apply your whole self to the [scriptural] text; apply the whole thing [the meaning of the text] to yourself

Saying of Johannes Albrecht Bengel (1687–1752), the scholar widely regarded as the founder of New Testament textual criticism. One should study the biblical texts thoroughly and completely (the process of exegesis) and then apply the meaning of the biblical

texts to one's whole life (the process of hermeneutics).

Tempora Sacra
Sacred time

This expression refers to the church's liturgical calendar which, unlike the civil calendar, does not aim primarily to mark the chronological progression of the days, weeks, and years, but rather commemorates primarily the important events in the life of Christ. Thus, the liturgical year begins with the First Sunday of Advent and concludes with the celebration of Christ the King, rather than beginning on January 1 and ending on December 31.

Tempus fugit
Time flies

Common adage which expresses how quickly time seems to pass. See also *Dum tempus habemus operemur bonum*.

Tenenda/Tenendum
Things to be held (pl.)/Thing to be held (sing.)

Refers to doctrines that are to be held by the Christian faithful as pertaining to the faith itself when they are proposed as such in an authoritative manner by the magisterium. *Tenendum* was the term employed in Vatican I's 1870 formal definition of papal infallibility (cf. *DS* 3074). There is, however, an important distinction between doctrines that are to be "held" (*tenenda*) from those which are to be believed (*credenda, q.v.*). See also *Articulus stantis et cadentis ecclesiae*, *Credenda*, *De fide definita*, and *Ex Cathedra*.

Terminus a quo
> The starting point from which (for an action/motion)

Refers to the motivation out of which an action or motion is performed, or the end out of which the action or motion operates, e.g., according to St. Thomas Aquinas, charity's starting point is an already existing union with God. See also *Terminus ad quem.*

Terminus ad quem
> The (ultimate) end to which (of an action/motion)

Refers to the motive which governs an action or any motion, e.g., according to St. Thomas Aquinas, charity seeks union with God as its *terminus ad quem.* See also *Terminus a quo.*

Terra firma
> Solid land

Usually refers to earth or to land as opposed to the sea. After a long voyage it is good to be back once again on *terra firma.* Metaphorically, this expression refers to anything that is firmly grounded and therefore stable and trustworthy.

Terra incognita
> Unknown land

Usually refers to a place or a subject about which one knows little or nothing, or when one is embarking on something that likely will involve consequences difficult to predict in advance.

Tertia pars
> Third part

Usually refers to the third major section of St. Thomas Aquinas' **Summa Theo-** *logiae* (*q.v.*), which deals with Jesus Christ. See also *Prima pars* and *Secunda pars.*

Tertio Millenio Adveniente
> Coming of the Third Millennium

Apostolic letter of Pope John Paul II issued on 10 November 1994 that convoked the special synod for Asia, which was subsequently held in Rome from 19 April to 14 May 1998.

Tertium quid
> A third entity

Literally, a "third something," and refers to something which is related to two other things but which is distinct (and to a degree independent) of these other two things. For example, the exercise of the magisterium involves the pope and the college of bishops. The Roman Curia is an arm of the pope, but could come to see itself as a *tertium quid* or distinct entity so that the understanding of the magisterium would expand to include three entities (pope, college of bishops, *and* the Roman Curia) where only two had existed before (the pope and the college of bishops). This example is offered by Archbishop John R. Quinn in his 1996 Oxford address, "The Exercise of Primacy," which discusses the role of the Roman Curia. The text is reprinted in *Commonweal* 123 (12 July 1996): 11–20.

Testem benevolentiae
> Benevolent witness

1899 Apostolic letter of Leo XIII to James Cardinal Gibbons of Baltimore, in which the vaguely defined heresy of "Americanism" was condemned.

"Americanism" supposedly involved positions attributed to Isaac Hecker (a former Redemptorist who went on to found the Paulists and who died in 1888). These erroneous positions supposedly included religious indifferentism, a skeptical attitude toward vowed religious life, and a resistence to acceptance of the church's external authority.

Testimonium veritati
Testimony to the truth

The highest form of giving testimony to the truth is through action, i.e., in "doing the truth," and thus corresponds to living morally.

Testis in uno falsus in nullo fidem meretur
A witness that is mistaken (false) in one instance does not merit confidence in anything

Basic legal concept concerning the reliability of witnesses in a contest issue. If the witness should prove mistaken or false in one instance this would lead one to surmise that this particular witness should not be considered trustworthy overall. See also *Absolutus sententia judicis praseumitur innocens*; *Actori incumbit onus probandi*; *Allegatio contra factum non est admittenda*; *Da mihi factum, dabo tibi ius*; *Facta non praesumuntur sed probantur*; *Onus probandi*; and *Res iudicata pro veritate accipitur.*

Testis non est iudicare
A witness does not act as judge

Basic legal principle that acknowledges that the roles of a witness in a legal case and the judge are quite different. While the witness may speak to evidence, ultimately it is the role of the judge to give a final decision. See also *Absolutus sententia judicis praseumitur innocens*; *Da mihi factum, dabo tibi ius*; *Facta non praesumuntur sed probantur*; *Onus probandi*; and *Res iudicata pro veritate accipitur.*

Textus receptus
The received text

Usually this refers to the text which has come down to the present, and which therefore designates a text which is traditionally accepted as being authentic. For example, in Scripture studies the *textus receptus* is the canonical version of the biblical text found in the Bible, even though scholars recognize that this text may not report the very words of Jesus or serve as a reliable historical account of some event narrated in the Bible. The Greek text of the New Testament established by Erasmus (1466–1536) is also often called the *Textus receptus*. See also *Ipssissima verba.*

Theologia cordis/Theologia mentis
Theology of the heart/theology of the mind

Distinction made in a theological approach which speaks principally either to the affective dimensions (*theologia cordis*) or to the speculative dimension (*theologia mentis*).

Theologia crucis/theologia gloriae
Theology of the cross/theology of glory

Two fundamental christological themes, stressing either the suffering and crucifixion of Christ as the means of our salvation or the resurrection and glory of Christ as the eschatological signs of our salvation.

Theologia moralis
Moral theology

Traditional reference to moral theology as a distinctive "scientific" branch of theology that was concerned with the rightness and wrongness of human actions, and also often used as the title for manuals on the subject when they were written in Latin (i.e. before Vatican II).

Theologia viatorum
Theology of [for] the way[farers] or pilgrims

Refers to the reality that all of theology will be necessarily incomplete and provisional in nature, since it deals with God who is always more than we are able to conceive and therefore will remain somewhat of a mystery to us. Once we reach heaven our pilgrimage on earth will be completed and we shall have a fuller (yet not absolutely complete) knowledge of God. See also *Deus semper maior*; *Deus absconditus/Deus revelatus*; and *Si comprehendis, non est Deus*.

Theologice certa
Theologically certain

Similar expression to *Sententia probata* (*q.v.*), namely one of the theological "notes" indicating a theological position which, while not formally defined or pronounced upon by the magisterium, was still held as "probable" by the majority of theologians and therefore enjoyed a very high presupposition of truth and could be freely taught and believed. *Theologice certa* ("theologically certain") ranked below *Proxima fidei* (*q.v.* "nearly certain to belong to the faith") but was higher than *Pia opinio* (*q.v.* "pious opinion"). None of these theological notes, though, were to be held as a defined article of the faith (*de fide definita*). See also *Credenda*, *De fide*, *Depositum fidei*, *Diffinimus*, *Ex cathedra*, *Obsequium religiosum*, *Pia opinio*, *Proxima fidei*, and *Tenenda*.

(A) Thoro
From the marriage bed

See *Divortium a thoro*.

Timeo hominem unius libri
I fear the person of one book

Attributed to Thomas Aquinas, the phrase raises caution about people that hold to just one "source" for their ideas and opinions. Even if the "book" in question be exemplary (such as the Bible or Thomas' own **Summa Theologiae**), this dictum advises us to exercise a greater curiosity and wider research stance toward new and/or unfamiliar ideas.

Titulus
Title (privilege, right)

In ecclesiastical circles a *titulus* generally refers to some title of dignity, rank, or office, or reason or basis for something, as well as the rights and privileges associated with that particular *titulus*. For example, a doctoral biretta may be worn by those who possess a doctoral degree from a pontifical institution. *Titulus* also is used to refer to the church building in Rome which is assigned to an individual cardinal. Thus, every cardinal has his "titular" church, such as Santa Susanna in Rome is the titular church of the Cardinal Archbishop of Boston (and the parish run by the Paulists for the American Catholic community resident in Rome).

Tolerati
Tolerated

See *Vitandus*.

Tolle assertiones et christianismum tulisti
Take away the assertions and you take away Christianity

Dictum attributed to Martin Luther which highlights the articles of faith that are necessary to maintain if one hopes to maintain Christian identity. In other words, Christianity cannot capitulate to popular opinion or political correctness for its enduring validity and vitality. See also *Consensus non facit veritatem*; *Quod ubique, quod semper, quod ab omnibus, creditum est*; *Regula fidei*; *Securus iudicat orbis terrarum*; *Sensus fidei*; *Sensus fidelium*; and *Sentire cum ecclesia*.

Tot miraculis quot articulis
There are as many miracles as there are articles

When the devil's advocate arguing against the canonization of the *Doctor Angelicus* (*q.v.*), Thomas Aquinas complained that the Thomas' cause for canonization should not go forward since there was a lack of post-mortem mira-

cles. A cardinal replied that there were as many miracles in his life (*tot miraculis*) as there are articles in his **Summa Theologiae** (*quot articulis*). By extension, this aphorism highlights that sanctity and worth can be measured in many ways, even in the seemingly "ordinary" production of scholarly works.

Totaliter
Absolutely, totally

Often used in theological or canonical terms to indicate something that has a total, absolute, or complete effect, e.g., a plenary indulgence granted *totaliter* for the full remission of temporal punishment due to sin. See also *Generaliter*, *Simpliciter*, *Sine modo*, and *Toties quoties*.

Totaliter aliter
Totally other

Totally different argument, topic, etc., which does not apply to this case, topic, etc.

Toties quoties
So often as

Shorthand expression often linked to the gaining of indulgences as often as the prescribed conditions were fulfilled, even on a daily basis. This notion was important in the theology which allowed an individual who gained an indulgence to apply it vicariously to a soul in purgatory. By extension, this term can be used to indicate the effect of any action which meets its prescribed conditions for completion. See also **Incarnationis Mysterium**, *Per modum suffragii*, and *Totaliter*.

Totus conversus sed non totaliter
   The human person is a total convert but not totally

Refers to the traditional understanding that although human persons are redeemed by God's transformative grace, they are still vulnerable to the power of sin, self-love, and self-deception. See also *Reliquiae peccati*, *Simul iustus et peccator*, and *Sola gratia*.

Totus tuus
   (I am) all yours

Papal motto of John Paul II (1978–2005), which signifies his total dedication to God and to the church.

Traditio
   Tradition

Understood theologically to refer to doctrines, practices, and beliefs which have been handed down through the ages in the church. In terms of "authority" for a number of theological and moral teachings of the church, the very fact that this position has been held for a long time is taken as *prima facie* (though not absolute) evidence of its truth. Some examples of the use of church tradition to uphold current teaching would include contraception, the indissolubility of marriage, the prohibition of the ordination of women, and so on. See also *Mortui vivos docent*, *Nihil consuetudine maius*, *Nihil novi sub sole*, *Predicatio ecclesiastica*, and *Quidquid latine dictum sit altum videtur*.

Trans
   Across

Common Latin preposition and component of many English words, such as "transport" (i.e., literally, "to carry across").

Translatio studii
   Carrying over (translation) of studies (i.e., learning)

Concept of using ancient learning in a process of reading and commentary.

Translator traditor
   The translator is the traitor (literally, one who "surrenders" or "hands over")

Aphorism with a play on words in Latin which highlights the difficulty of providing an absolutely faithful translation from one language into another. Often the translator includes his or her own biases in producing a translation.

Triduum
   Three days

The expression usually refers to a certain three day period, such as the Easter Triduum of Holy Thursday to Evening Prayer of Easter Sunday (also termed the *Triduum Sacrum* or Sacred Triduum), or, more generally, to a three-day retreat.

Trivium
   Trilogy

Refers to the classic educational curriculum of ancient Rome which divided studies into three major fields: grammar, rhetoric, and dialectic. This approach to study influenced education in the Middle Ages and Renaissance as well and provided the interpretive tools and methodology for the study of classical literature, as well as the study of Scripture and the patristic authors. See also *Sacra Pagina.*

Tu es Petrus

You are Peter (and upon this rock I will build my church)

Latin for the beginning of Jesus' renaming of Simon as Peter (Greek for "rock") and commissioning him as the cornerstone of the church given in Matthew 16:18. This verse is reproduced in Greek at the base of the dome in the Basilica of St. Peter's in Rome. This expression is often used in a shorthand fashion to indicate the apostolic succession from Peter down to the present in the person of the pope, as well as affirmation of fidelity to the Roman pontiff. See also *Coetus fidelium, Nulla Veritas sine Traditione,* and *Ubi Petrus ibi ecclesia.*

Tuas libenter

Joyfully yours

1863 Letter of Pius IX to the Archbishop of Munich in which the term "ordinary magisterium" was first used in an official document of the church. The letter was occasioned by a meeting of Catholic theologians held in Munich in which an opinion was expressed that Catholics were bound to hold only those truths of the faith which had been formally defined. See also *Credenda, De fide definita, Ecclesia discens, Ecclesia militans, Ex cathedra, Fides implicita,* **Lumen gentium**, *Magisterium, Munus, Obsequium religiosum, Officium, Potestas docendi, Sensus fidelium,* and *Tendenda.*

Tuum

Yours

See *Meum* ("mine").

Tyrannus in titula; Tyrannus in regimine

Tyrant (who has usurped the) title (of office); Tyrant in (legitimate) power

Two expressions related to the moral discussion of the possible legitimacy of tyrannicide, the killing of an unjust tyrant for the common good. A *tyrannus in titula* would be one who unjustly usurped the ruling office from the legitimate ruler, while the *tryannus in regimine* would be one who is abusing his or her otherwise legitimate power of rule to severely harm those being governed. See also *Hostis humani generis.*

U

Ubi caritas, Deus ibi est
> Where there is love (or charity),
> there is God.

Classic expression of the connection between God, love, and human community. See 1 John 4:17 for the *locus classicus* of this principle in the New Testament, though the whole of the letter is important to understand the connection between God, love, and a rightly ordered human community. See also **Caritas in Veritate**; *Caritas in veritate in re sociali*; **Deus caritas est**; and *Ubi societas, ibi ius.*

Ubi cessat ratio legis, cessat ipsa lex
> Where the reason for the law
> ceases the law itself ceases

Essentially the same idea as *Cessante fine cessat lex (q.v.)* and *Cessante ratione legis cessat ipsa lex (q.v.).* In other words, law does not exist for itself but always in service to some larger end and the *bonum commune (q.v.).* See also *Lex semper intendit quod convenit rationi, Ordinatio rationis ad bonum commune, Ordo publicus*, and *Salus publica suprema lex.*

Ubi deficiunt equi trottant aselli.
> Where there is a shortage of
> horses, the donkeys (asses) trot

Traditional axiom meant to indicate that in the absence of individuals of ability those with lesser gifts will come to the fore.

Ubi ius, ibi remedium
> Where there is justice there must
> be a means of aid

Every system of justice must also involve means to treat or resolve injustices. This concept underlies the medicinal nature of judicial sentences which go beyond mere retributive justice and aim at helping to cure that which leads to the breakdown of justice in the first place. See also *Salus publica suprema lex; Sententia facit ius; Sententia incerta non valet; Ubi ius incertum, ibi ius nullum*; and *Ubi societas, ibi ius.*

Ubi ius incertum, ibi ius nullum
> Where justice is uncertain, there
> is no justice

Axiom which underscores the importance of a system of justice for human society and which indicates that "uncertainty" about justice prevailing in one instance points to a basic lack of justice over all. See also *Lex dubia non obligat; Lex dubia lex nulla; Lex iniusta non est lex*; *Ordinatio rationis ad bonum commune*; *Salus publica suprema lex*; *Sententia facit ius*; *Sententia incerta non valet*; *Ubi ius, ibi remedium*; and *Ubi societas, ibi ius*.

Ubi non est culpa, ibi non est delictum

Where there is no culpability there is no crime (delict)

See also *Absolutus sententia judicis praseumitur innocens*; *Actus non facit reum nisi mens sit rea*; *Lex dubia lex nulla*; *Lex iniusta non est lex*; *Mens rea*; *Nulla poena sine culpa*; *Onus probandi*; *Ordinatio rationis ad bonum commune*; *Sententia incerta non valet*; *Sine culpa*; and *Ubi ius incertum, ibi ius nullum*.

Ubi Petrus, ibi ecclesia, ibi Deus

Where Peter is, there is the church, there is God

The original expression seems to come from St. Ambrose but is now commonly used as an ultramontane expression which suggests that the pope, as successor of Peter, virtually comprises the essence of the church. Therefore, the pope's will or teaching is virtually identical to that of the entire church. This maxim is the motto of the ultra-conservative group Catholics United for the Faith (C.U.F.). See also *Coetus fidelium*; *Ecclesia non moritur*; *Missale Romanum*; *Munus Petrinium*; *Novus Ordo*; *Nulla Veritas sine Traditione*; **Summorum Pontificum**; *Tu Es Petrus*; *Ubi Veritas, Deus ibi est*; **Universae Ecclesiae**; and *Vicarius Christi*.

Ubi regnum, ibi reconciliatio

Where the kingdom [of God] is, there is reconciliation

Aphorism which underscores the nature of God's kingdom as embodying forgiveness and reconciliation. See also *Processus iustificationis*.

Ubi societas, ibi ius

Where there is society there is justice (e.g., system of law)

Classic social principle recalled by Pope Benedict XVI in his social encyclical **Caritas in Veritate** (Charity in Truth) issued on 29 June 2009. This principle means that society requires a system of just laws to function ethically, and the pope added that this justice must ultimately be grounded in love. This social doctrine, the pope says, is expressed in the Latin aphorism of *caritas in veritate in re sociali* (charity in truth in social matters). See also **Caritas in Veritate**; *Caritas in veritate in re sociali*; **Deus caritas est**; *Ubi caritas, Deus ibi est*; *Ubi ius, ibi remedium*; and *Ubi ius incertum, ibi ius nullum*.

Ubi Veritas, Deus ibi est

Where the truth is, there God is

Indicates the primacy of the objective order and its intrinsic relation with God. This axiom could be used as a corrective to something like what could be an exaggerated dogmatism of groups that claim their connection with some political or ideological wing gives them a sure guarantee of moral or theological supremacy. See also *Nulla Veritas sine Traditione*; *Ubi Petrus, ibi ecclesia*; and *Veritas omnia vincit*.

Ultra montes
> Beyond the mountains (i.e., the
> Alps)

Expression that gives rise to the English "Ultramontanism," which stresses the ecclesial power of Rome against that of the parts of the church on the other side of the Alps. See also *Caput mundi* and *Roma locuta, causa finita.*

Ultra posse (or vires) nemo obligatur
> No one is obliged to do more than his or her ability (or strength) allows

In moral theology this expression relates to the notion of moral impossibility, which is somewhat different from physical impossibility. What is physically impossible is fairly clear, but the Christian tradition also holds that one is not morally obliged to do that which is particularly burdensome or "heroic" (of course presuming that no sin would be involved). Determining just what is morally impossible though is often rather difficult. See also *Agere sequitur esse, Deus impossibilia non iubet, Humano modo, Impossibilium nulla obligatio (est), Lex sequitur esse, Lex semper intendit quod convenit rationi, Lex spectat naturae ordinem, Nemo potest ad impossibile obligari, Nemo tenetur ad impossibile, Operari sequitur esse,* and *Qui tenetur ad finem tenetur ad media.*

Unam Sanctam
> One holy

Bull of Pope Boniface VIII issued in 1302 which addressed the question of the interrelationship of the spiritual and temporal spheres of power. Boniface VIII formally declared "that it is absolutely necessary for the salvation of all people that they submit to the Roman Pontiff" (*DS* 875). This papal bull is often referenced to rebut the claim made by some that there have never been any substantive changes in teachings of the ordinary magisterium over the centuries. See also *Extra ecclesia nulla salus* and *Semper idem.*

Unicuique suum
> To each his or her own

Foundational principle of justice (*ius*) with essentially the same meaning as *Reddere suum cuique* and *Suum cuique* (*q.v.*).

Unicum
> The only (unique) instance

This expression refers to something found just once, or at most rarely, in a given text or treatise. For example, in Thomas Aquinas' treatise on the ends of human acts in the ST I–II, q. 1, a. 3, ad. 3, he uses just once the term *finem proximum* (*finis proximus, q.v.,* proximate end) and so it would be textually problematic to conclude from this single usage that Thomas meant that the meaning of moral actions (their "species") comes directly and solely from a consideration of the "proximate end." See also *Locus classicus* and *Ut in pluribus.*

Unitatis redintegratio
> Reintegration of unity

Vatican II's Decree on Ecumenism (1964) which is especially noted for its expression of the hierarchy of truths (*Hierarchiam veritatem, q.v.*), which noted that "when comparing doctrines with one another, they should remember that in Catholic doctrine there exists a "hierarchy" of truths, since they vary in their relation to the fundamental Christian faith" [*UR* 11].

Universae Ecclesiae
Universal church

Instruction issued 18 May 2011 by the Pontifical Commission "Ecclesia Dei" on the application of **Summorum Pontificum**, the 2007 *Motu Proprio (q.v.)* of Pope Benedict XVI which in turn dealt with a broadening of the permission to celebrate the Tridentine Mass as an "extraordinary form" (*forma extraordinaria*) of the Eucharist, which would no longer require a bishop's permission. See also *Ad orientem, Cappa magna, Coetus fidelium, Forma extraordinaria, Missale Romanum, Novus Ordo*, **Sacrosanctum concilium**, **Summorum Pontificum**, and *Versus populum*.

Uno itinere non potest veniri ad tam grande secretum
One cannot come to (i.e., understand) such a great mystery by only one road

Symmachus (Roman rhetorician, c. 345–402)

Arguing for the necessity of a plurality of religions. This position was cited and condemned by Joseph Cardinal Ratzinger (later Pope Benedict XVI), the then Prefect of the Congregation for the Doctrine of the Faith (CDF), in the latter's discourse given to the Asian bishops in Hong Kong in March 1993 ("Christ,

Faith and the Challenge of Cultures," *Origins* 24 [30 March 1995]: 679–86).

Urbi et orbi
To the City and the World

Refers to Rome and the world, and thus to something intended for the widest possible diffusion, rather than restricted to a particular location. Certain papal documents are proclaimed *Urbi et orbi*, and the pope traditionally gives a number of apostolic blessings (including his very first as a new pope) *Urbi et orbi*. See also *Habemus Papam* and *Orbis terrarum*.

Usque ad
Continually, all the way, up to (and including), as far as

This expression is also rendered as one word, *adusque*. It is usually found in other expressions such as *Amor Dei usque ad contemptum sui (q.v.)*: "the love of God that leads even up to (*usque ad*) contempt of self.

Usus
Use (noun)

Depending on the context this term can have a variety of meanings, such as usage or right to usage, custom, benefit, occasion, etc.

Usus Antiquior
Older (as in historical or traditional) use

Expression used to denote especially traditional practices in the church, such as liturgy, which helps show the organic development and unity of the present practices as traced back to the past. The expression (or its alternate, *forma antiquior, q.v.*) is also used by some to denote the Tridentine Mass that was celebrated in Latin up to the end of Vatican II. This expression also serves as a title for an academic journal that focuses on the study of the historical, philosophical, theological, and pastoral aspects of the Roman liturgical rite as it developed over the centuries. See also *Ad orientem, Cappa magna, Coram Cardinale/Coram Episcopo, Coetus fidelium, Forma Antiquior, Missale Romanum, Novus Nulla Veritas sine Traditione, Ordo, Quidquid latine dictum sit altum videtur*, **Sacrosanctum concilium**, **Summorum Pontificum**, *Tu Es Petrus*, **Universae Ecclesiae**, and *Versus populum*.

Usus legis
Use of the law

Important concept in Protestant theology, especially that of Luther and Calvin. Luther spoke of two primary uses of the law: first, the civil use of law, which by threat of punishment acts to restrain sin; and second, as a "teacher of sin" law acts to break down the human tendency to self-righteousness and self-justification and thus prepares the sinner to receive God's saving grace. Calvin also proposed a third use of the law, to indicate the will of God and to exhort the faithful to obedience. See also *Indicativa oboedientiae* and *Sola gratia*.

Ut
(See explanation which follows)

This Latin word is used very frequently in combination with other words and is impossible to translate into one or two English words. As an adverb *ut* means "how," "in what way"; as a conjunction it has an even wider range of meanings: "as," "although," "when," "while," "in order that," "granted that," "inasmuch as," and so on. Since *ut* has so many different meanings and nuances it will be important to determine exactly how it functions in a given phrase in order to ascertain the phrase's meaning. Some common examples of the usages of *ut* follow below.

Ut cognoscant te
That they recognize (know) you

Expression sometimes used as a motto for Christian educational institutions, namely that part of the school's mission is to enable its students and the world to know God better.

Ut in paucioribus
In a few cases

Exceptions, though, do not necessarily make a rule or precedent.

(Valet) Ut in pluribus
Valid/applies in most cases

Important distinction in the understanding and application of concrete moral norms that was articulated by Thomas Aquinas in his treatise on the natural law (cf. ST I–II, q. 94, a. 4), in which he notes that applications of the natural law which are an exercise of what he calls "practical right reason" will differ at times according to circumstances and knowledge. Thus, a concrete norm or law that holds *ut in pluribus* serves as a generally useful principle, but, as Thomas Aquinas noted, these should not be treated as if they bound absolutely in every case. For example, we have an obligation to preserve life, but this is a "law" (*lex*) that is *valet ut in pluribus*, and therefore there may be legitimate circumstances in which life support systems are terminated. See also *Ad literam*; *Cessante fine cessat lex*; *Ex facto ius oritur*; *Odia restringi, et favores convenit ampliari*; *Quod omnes tangit ab omnibus approbetur*; *Sensus fidelium*; *Sensum, non verba spectamus*; and *Unicum*.

Ut infra
As below

Scholarly phrase meaning "see below."

Ut supra
As above

Scholarly phrase meaning "see above."

Ut unum sint
That they may be one

Words which come from the Latin Vulgate's translation of John 17:23, in which Jesus prays to the Father that the disciples may become one just as Jesus and the Father are one. These words usually are associated with the prayer and hope for the restoration of complete Christian unity. **Ut unum sint** is also the title of John Paul II's encyclical on ecumenism (1995).

Uti et frui
Use and enjoyment

Distinction from St. Augustine, taken over especially by John Calvin in his theology, in relating the means to the end on the use of created things. We are to *use* the mean, but to *enjoy* the end (and the ultimate end is God). The end sanctifies the means, and thus creation is seen as a good in itself. Thus, God saves the world, not saves us out of the world. But on the other hand, only God is to be "enjoyed" for God's Self, whereas the created things in the world are to be used as means to our proper end. See also *Bonum utile*; *Dominium utile*; *Ius utendi, fruendi, abutendi*; *Res frutificat dominum*; and *Summum bonum*.

V

Vacatio legis
    Vacation (or "vacating") of the law

Usually a set period between the promulgation of a law or rule and the date on which the law takes effect. During this period the new law does not yet bind, and thus this is important for the legal application of penalties. See also ***Acta Apolostolicae Sedis***, *Donec aliter provideatur*, *Hucusque vigens*, *Ius vigens*, *Lex non obligat nisi promulgata*, and *Recognitio*.

Vademecum
    Go with me

Refers to a small companion guide, manual, or reference to a certain subject. A *vademecum* would be small enough to be carried in one's pocket and therefore connotes a handy reference work, rather than a painstaking analysis of a subject.

Vagus
    Wanderer

In canon law a *vagus* is a person without a fixed residence. Certain provisions are made for the pastoral care of such individuals (cf. *C.I.C.* 383).

Vale
    Farewell

Latin expression roughly equivalent to the English "Goodbye." See also *Ave*, *Ave atque vale*, and *Salve*.

Valet ut in pluribus
    Valid/applies in most cases

Important distinction in the understanding and application of concrete moral norms which indicates that certain norms may be generally true, but there also could be valid exceptions. See also *Ut in pluribus*.

Vanitas vanitatum, omnis vanitas
    Vanity of vanities, all is vanity

Latin rendition of the well-known phrase from Ecclesiastes 1:2, indicating that all earthly realities are ultimately empty ("vanity").

Varia lectio
    Variant reading

Expression used to refer to the fact that in different manuscripts of ancient texts there may be certain small differences in words, phrases, or passages. Such a difference would be a *varia lectio*.

Vehemens horror
    Vehement horror

Concept referring to the subjective fear or loathing of a certain procedure, e.g., an amputation, such that it would constitute such a personal burden as to render the otherwise "ordinary" procedure "extraordinary" due to the subjective burden entailed. This is a traditional criterion going back at least to the sixteenth century and would be important in contemporary discussion on advance health care directives and end-of-life decisions to forego medical treatment.

Veni, Creator Spiritus
Come, Creator (Holy) Spirit

An invocation for the aid of the Holy Spirit, but more commonly these words refer to the traditional prayer and hymn which is read or intoned in certain liturgical celebrations, such as ordinations and feasts associated with the Holy Spirit. See also *Veni, Sancte Spiritus*.

Veni, Sancte Spiritus
Come, Holy Spirit

An invocation for the aid of the Holy Spirit, especially in the special "sequence" hymn recited or sung immediately prior to the proclamation of the Gospel for the Pentecost liturgy. This prayer is one of only four medieval sequences that were preserved in the reform of the *Missale Romanum (q.v.)* published in 1570. The other three are the *Victimae Paschali (q.v.)* for Easter, the *Lauda Sion (q.v.)* for *Corpus Christi (q.v.)*, and the *Dies Irae (q.v.)* for the Requiem Mass. See also *Veni, Creator Spiritus*.

Verba volant, scripta manent
Spoken words fly away, written words remain

Thus, an exhortation to commit one's teachings to paper, or perhaps a version of "publish or perish." *Scripta* here does *not* mean Sacred Scripture but merely the written word.

Verbi Sponsa
Bride of the Word

Instruction On the Contemplative Life and on the Enclosure of Nuns issued on 13 May 1999 by the Congregation for Institutes of Consecrated Life and for Societies of Apostolic Life. The instruction both gives the theological background for the understanding of the contemplative life and proposes various norms for the maintenance of monastic enclosure for orders of contemplative nuns.

Verbum Dei
Word of God

Refers to divine revelation in general and the Scriptures in particular. An important role of the church is to respect, safeguard, and minister to the Word of God. See also ***Dei Verbum***.

Verbum sat sapienti
A word to the wise is sufficient

Often abbreviated as *verbum sat sap*, this adage indicates that a brief warning about some problem, danger, delicate situation, etc., should be sufficient to a truly prudent individual so that she or he can avoid the danger or handle the problem better than if no warning had been given. See also *Sapienti sat* and *Stultis non succuritur*.

Veritas
Truth

See also *In vino veritas*; *Particula veri*; *Ubi Veritas, Deus ibi est*; and *Vincit veritas*.

Veritas omnia vincit
Truth conquers all things

Expression that is essentially the same idea as *Veritas vincit*, indicating that in the end truth will out. See also *In vino veritas*; *Particula veri*; *Ubi Veritas, Deus ibi est*; and *Veritas*.

Veritatis splendor
Splendor of the truth

John Paul II's 1993 encyclical on fundamental moral theology.

Versus populum
Toward the people

Expression used primarily in a recent liturgical dispute surrounding the "proper" direction that the eucharistic presider and people should face during the Eucharist, i.e., toward the people (as is the current practice) or *ad orientem* (*q.v.*), in which both the presider and the congregation face in the same direction (ideally toward the east). See the longer discussion under *Ad orientem* as well as *Coetus fidelium*, *Forma extraordinaria*, *Missale Romanum*, *Novus Ordo*, **Summorum Pontificum**, and **Universae Ecclesiae**.

Verum Sacrificium
True Sacrifice

I.e., the sacrifice of Jesus Christ in the Eucharist. The expression dates back to Augustine and is lifted up in Trent's definition of the Mass as a true sacrifice, which Jesus offered once for all (cf. *Pro multis*) on earth and now eternally in Heaven, while Christians unite their own sacrifice to that of Christ which likewise is celebrated in the Eucharist. See also *Victimae Paschali*.

Vestigia Trinitatis
Vestiges (traces) of the Trinity

Refers to a theological affirmation that since God's revelation occurs in many forms, certain hints, clues, or traces of the doctrine of the Trinity can also be found outside of Sacred Scripture, e.g., in creation.

Veterum Sapientia
Ancient wisdom

Apostolic constitution of Pope John XXIII, issued on 22 February 1962, shortly before the beginning of Vatican II, in which the pope confirmed the importance of Latin as the language of the church and the medium of seminary instruction, since Latin was not subject to the weaknesses of vernacular languages which were tied to individual cultures. "Latin by its nature is perfectly adapted to promoting every form of culture among every people. It does not give rise to jealousies, is impartial with all, is not the privilege of anyone and is well accepted by all."

Vetus Testamentum
Old Testament

Refers to the Old Testament of the Bible. See also *In Vetere Novum (Testamentum) latet, et in Novo Vetus patet* and *Novum Testamentum*.

Via
Way

Can be used both concretely, in the sense of a path or road (e.g., the *via crucis*), and figuratively, in the sense of a method or approach (e.g., *via empirica*). See also *In via* and *Viator*.

Via affirmationes
Way of affirmation

Affirmation in this phrase is understood as the opposite of negation and is *not* meant to be understood in the sense of giving someone positive encouragement, support, or feedback. In classical theology, the *via affirmationes* is essentially the same as the *via eminentiae* (*q.v.*). See also *via negativa*.

Via crucis
The way of the cross

Can be understood literally, in the sense of the Stations of the Cross, or figuratively, as the necessity of taking up one's individual cross in order to follow Christ.

Via Dolorosa
Sorrowful way

Usually refers to the Stations of the Cross in Jerusalem which retrace Jesus' path to Calvary. This term can also refer to the difficulties involved in the Christian life of discipleship. See also *Imitatio Christi* and *Sequela Christi*.

Via eminentiae
The way of eminence

As distinguished from the *via negativa* (*q.v.*), the *via eminentiae* is used to derive, for example, the positive attributes of God by considering these attributes in their most perfect or ideal form. Thus, wisdom, when predicated of God, would become omniscience, power would become omnipotence, and so on. See also *via positiva*.

Via empirica
The empirical way (method)

Analytical methodology which begins with an investigation of the nature of an object as it exists and then moves on to a consideration of its relationship to its directionality, ultimate end, or to other terms. In ecclesiology, the *via empirica* studies the church by beginning with the church as it exists and then moves on to consider its relationship to Christ (rather than starting with Christ and Christology and moving to a consideration of the nature of the church).

Via illuminativa, purgativa, unitiva
The illuminative, purgative, and unitive way(s)

Important concept in traditional ascetical theology that distinguishes various approaches and stages of the spiritual life. The journey often begins with the *via purgativa*, which stresses doing away with one's sins and faults and emphasizes penance, mortification, and self-control. The *via illuminativa* aims at developing a life of virtue, both "moral" and "theological" (i.e., faith, hope, and charity). The *via unitiva* stresses union with God and openness to the Spirit and the Spirit's gifts.

Via media
Middle way

Often the surest path between two extremes or opposing camps is a path that aims to navigate between them, i.e., a *via media*. Thus, *via media* can imply moderation and/or diplomacy. However, in the nineteenth century *via media* was used to describe the position of some Anglicans as a way between Protestantism and Roman Catholicism.

Via moderna
  Modern (new) way

Theological school of thought that was associated with William of Ockham and a number of other theologians in the fourteenth and fifteenth centuries which held that the economy of salvation depends solely on God's free and arbitrary will and that humans were required to love God and keep God's commandments. Such obedience, though, did not merit justification, but this depended solely on God's free will to save an individual or not.

Via negativa/negationis
  The way of negation

In description or definition of a certain term or concept, sometimes a *via negativa* approach is used in which what the term is *not* is what is described, so as to mark off certain parameters of what is not included or meant by such a term. In theology, a *via negativa* approach highlights the dissimilarity between God and creatures, whereas a *via positiva* stresses human dignity by emphasizing the similarity human beings have with God as created in God's own image (cf. Genesis 1:26 and *imago Dei* and *similtudo Dei*).

Via positiva
  The positive way

In theology this expression usually refers to the positive way of knowing God which relies on the real similarity between creatures and the Creator (God), making it possible to use for God words and ideas drawn from creatures, such as being good, beautiful, powerful, wise,

and so on. See also *Via emientiae* and *Via negativa.*

Viator
  One on the way

This term can refer to a pilgrim or someone on a journey (sometimes rendered as *homo viator*) and metaphorically to Christians (*viatores*, plural), who as members of the pilgrim church are on their way to God. ***Lumen gentium*** (*q.v.*), Vatican II's Dogmatic Constitution on the Church used "Pilgrim Church" as one expression to refer to the nature of the church as being a people "on the way." See also *In via* and *Via.*

Vicarius Christi
  Vicar of Christ

One of the principal titles associated with the pope in his role as successor of Peter, namely, the head of the church who stands in the place of Christ until the end of the world when Christ will return in the Last Judgment. See also *Munus Petrinium*; *Primus inter pares*; *Servus Servorum Dei*; *Tu Es Petrus*; and *Ubi Petrus, ibi ecclesia, ibi Deus.*

Victimae Paschali
  Paschal Victim

Sequence prayer recited after the Epistle on Easter Sunday and throughout the octave, which gives a call to praise Christ, the Lamb of God, and recounts the key work of salvation history with the reconciliation of humans with God and the triumph over death. The prayer was reputedly composed by Wigo of Burgundy, who was the court chaplain to Conrad II and Henry III in the eleventh century, and is one of only four medieval sequences that were preserved in the reform of the *Missale Romanum* (*q.v.*) published in 1570. The other three are the *Veni Sancte Spiritus* (*q.v.*) for Pentecost, the *Lauda Sion* (*q.v.*) for *Corpus Christi* (*q.v.*), and the *Dies Irae* (*q.v.*) for the Requiem Mass. See also *Verum Sacrificium*.

Vide infra, supra
See below, above

Often used in scholarly articles to indicate a reference to what has gone before (or is to come after) in a given text. *Vide* is sometimes abbreviated *vid.*, as in *vid. supra*. See also *infra* and *supra*.

Videantur auctores probati
Consult the "approved" authors

In disputed theological questions, one was counseled to consult the opinions of recognized experts in the field. However, in certain circles of contemporary moral theology this principle is being applied in such a way that only "authors" of a certain school of thought are considered "approved" and therefore "orthodox."

Videlicet
Clearly, evidently, namely

See *Viz*.

Vincit veritas
Truth conquers

The idea is that eventually the truth will come out and carry the day. Another rendition of this aphorism is *Veritas omnia vincit* (*q.v.*, Truth conquers all

things). See also *In vino veritas*; *Particula veri*; *Ubi Veritas, Deus ibi est*; and *Veritas*.

Vinculum caritatis
Bond of charity

See *Sacramentum pietatis*.

Vinculum matrimonii
Bond of matrimony

Though *vinculum* could also be translated as "noose" or "chain," in the theological and canonical sense the *vinculum matrimonii* refers to the presumed indissoluble nature of a sacramental marriage. Thus, in annulment proceedings one of the juridical participants is the "defender of the bond," whose role is to argue for the preservation of the matrimony (and therefore, supposedly, generally indisposed to the granting of an annulment). See also *Debitum, Ratum et consummatum, Vinculum sacrum*, and *Vis et metus*.

Vinculum sacrum
Sacred bond

Term which refers to the marriage bond, which once ratified and completed is considered to be binding until the death of one of the partners. See also *Debitum, Ratum et consummatum*, and *Vinculum matrimonii*.

Virginitas in Partu
Virginity in parturition (act of giving birth)

Refers to the doctrine that Mary remained a physical virgin even during the actual giving of birth to Jesus. This expression would indicate that somehow Mary's hymen was miraculously preserved during the birth process. However, in a less physicalist understanding the expression can be taken to refer to Mary's virginity both before and after the birth of Jesus.

Viri probati
Proven (tested) men

Expression used in the contemporary discussion of priestly celibacy to refer to older men who are married but yet might be considered potential candidates for priestly ordination if the requirement for mandatory celibacy were to be waived. In this conjunction, see also *Cura animarum*.

Vis et metus
Violence and fear

In canon law the presence of grave fear of extrinsic violence can function as a nullifying impediment to the contract of matrimony or to the imposition of certain *latae sententiae* (*q.v.*) penalties (cf. *C.I.C.* 1323 and 1324). See also *Vinculum matrimonii.*

Visio beatifica
Beatific vision

Being in complete union with God in heaven after death, i.e., seeing God "face-to-face." This is the ultimate happiness and the end to which human nature, endowed with grace, strives as its highest good (*Summum Bonum, q.v.*). See also *Beati.*

Visio Dei
Vision (seeing) of God

Final and ultimate vision of God. Essentially means the same as *Visio be-*

atifica (*q.v.*). See also *Audio Dei* and *Summum bonum.*

Vita
Life

When used without additional metaphors, or when abbreviated as *vitae* from *curriculum vitae* (*q.v.*), this term can refer to the highlights or résumé of a person's professional life.

Vita aeterna
Eternal life

Eternal life as participation in the divine life is the ultimate destiny and goal of all humans. See also *Visio Dei.*

Vita apostolica
Apostolic life

Often used interchangeably with *vita evangelica* (*q.v.*), this term refers to a life of discipleship ministry and service, often associated with a disdain for worldly goods and honors.

Vita communis est mea maxima penitentia
Community life is my greatest penance

Saying attributed to the Jesuit scholastic St. John Berchmans, who maintained community life was his greatest trial in his efforts to religious perfection. Some, though, have wondered if the community also found living with this ascetical saint likewise to be a "penance."

Vita evangelica
Evangelical (gospel) life

Essentially the same concept as *Vita apostolica* (*q.v.*).

Vitandus/vitandi (pl)
One (those) to be shunned.

Expression related to the canonical penalty of excommunication imposed on individuals. There were two types of people excommunicated: *vitandi* and *tolerati*. The presence of the former (*vitandi*) in a church service, for example, was strictly forbidden; if a *vitandus* tried to remain he or she would have to be forcibly removed. *Tolerati*, on the other hand, while also excommunicated from the church, were allowed to hear Mass, for example. This distinction rests on an earlier division of the censure of excommunication into "major" and "minor" excommunication. Major excommunication was handed down by the Holy See to an individual who was then publicly denounced as *vitandus* and therefore to be shunned by all the faithful in religious gatherings.

Vitia capitalia/Vitia principalia
Capital vices (or sins) / Principal vices

Expression dating back to Pope St. Gregory the Great (540–604 CE) who formulated a list of "capital" sins or vices. "Capital" here comes from the Latin *caput* (head), since these sins were considered to be the primary roots of all other sins. The other sins stemming from these were sometimes called *filiae* (sons and daughters, or children). The acronym *SALIGIA* is derived from the first letters in Latin to enumerate these seven vices: *Superbia* (pride or vainglory), *Avaritia* (greed, avarice, or covetousness), *Luxuria* (lust), *Invidia* (envy), *Gula* (gluttony), *Ira* (anger), and *Acedia* (sloth).

Viva voce
Live voice

Refers to something done or presented "orally," as in a *viva voce* (oral) exam.

Viz.
Clearly, evidently, namely

Latin abbreviation for *videlicet*, which is used in written English to express the idea of "namely" or "to wit."

Vocatus atque non vocatus, Deus aderit
Called or not called, God is there

Latin translation by Erasmus of a Delphic oracle and which attests to the omnipresent nature of God. This saying was also adopted by C. G. Jung as his personal motto, which he had carved over the doorpost of his house at Kusnacht.

Volens, nolens
Wanting it (to be so) or not

"Willy-nilly" might be the best colloquial English translation. See *Nolens, volens*.

Volitum nihil, nisi cognitum
Nothing is desired unless it is known

In other words, only something which is known (even if falsely or partially) can be the object of desire or choice.

Volo, non valeo
I am willing, (but) I am not able

Indicates a certain divided mind, such as knowing in one's heart that a certain course of action should be pursued, yet one still finds resistance to embarking upon this course of action.

Voluntarium directum/indirectum
Voluntarium in se/in causa
Directly/Indirectly willed (action); Voluntary in itself; Voluntary in cause

These two terms were used interchangeably, and their meaning depends on a careful consideration of the moral object of an action, especially in situations involving the principle of the double effect in which a single action has two or more foreseen effects, one of which is intended and "good" and the other which is tolerated even though it is "bad." Classic cases which illustrate this principle are medical scenarios such as amputation of a limb to stop the progress of gangrene and save the life of the individual. In such a case, the removal of the limb is not "directly" willed but only indirectly willed (though clearly chosen). This would be an example of the *Voluntarium indirectum* or *Voluntarium in causa*. On the other hand, if there were no extenuating circumstances such as the risk of life but one were to amputate the limb out of malice, then the will would be *Voluntarium directum* or *Voluntarium in se* and in this case immoral. Or, if the limb were amputated to treat something like a hangnail, then even though the motive by itself (the *Voluntarium directum*) would seem to be good, nevertheless the lack of proportionate reason for causing so much damage would make this act likewise immoral. See also *Ea* (*eorum*) *quae sunt ad finem, Finis operis, Finis operantis, Genus morum, Intentio, In-* *trinsice malum, Licet corrigere defectus naturae, Obiectum actus, Pars propter totum,* and *Praeter intentionem.*

Voluntas
Will (desire)

Important concept in morality, as the will or desire for one's action is foundational to performing and evaluating those actions. See also *Liberum arbitrium.*

Voluntas Dei
The will of God

That which is the will of God is considered to be good because God, as the all-powerful Creator, has ordained or willed it so. If the issue in question relates to something which can be performed by human beings, this should then be done (or not done, if it is proscribed by the will of God). See also *De potentia Dei ordinata.*

Votum
Vow, prayer, desire, vote

This Latin term can have a wide range of meanings depending on its context. Besides the meanings given above *votum* can also refer to a recommendation, opinion, evaluation, sought by a competent ecclesiastical superior before rendering a decision in a certain case. Another range of meanings refers to *votum* as a vow, prayer, or desire. In this context see also *Ex voto.*

Vox populi, vox Dei
The voice of the people is the voice of God

Common aphorism of the principle of democracy, yet this principle also can be abused. For related expressions both pro and con see the following: *Consensus non facit veritatem, Consuetudo optima legum interpres, Contra vim non valet ius,* and *Conventio est lex.*

W

---

*NB: There is no "W" in classical Latin; "V" is used instead.

X

**NB: Very few words begin with "X" in Latin, and most of these are proper names of persons or places, or terms derived from Greek.

Y

**NB: There is no "Y" in classical Latin; "I" is used instead.

Z

**NB: Relatively few words begin with "Z" in Latin, and most of these are proper names of persons or places, or terms derived from Greek.*

* * * * * * * *

Bibliography of Other Works

Latin Dictionaries

Deferrari, Roy J. *A Latin-English Dictionary of St. Thomas Aquinas, Based on the* Summa Theologiae *and Selected Passages of His Other Works*. Boston: St. Paul Editions, 1960.

Diamond, Wilfrid. *Dictionary of Liturgical Latin*. Milwaukee: Bruce Publishing Company, 1961.

Ehrlich, Eugene. *Amo, Amas, Amat and More: How to Use Latin to Your Own Advantage and to the Astonishment of Others*. New York: Harper & Row, 1985.

Guterman, Norbert, comp. *The Anchor Book of Latin Quotations*. New York: Anchor Books (Doubleday), 1966, 1990.

Muller, Richard A. *Dictionary of Latin and Greek Terms: Drawn Principally from Protestant Scholastic Theology*. Grand Rapids: Baker Book House, 1985.

Stelten, Leo F. *Dictionary of Ecclesiastical Latin*. Peabody, MA: Hendrickson Publishers, 1995.

Latin Grammars

Collins, John F. *A Primer of Ecclesiastical Latin*. Washington, DC: The Catholic University of America Press, 1985.

Henle, Robert J. *Latin Grammar*. Chicago: Loyola University Press, 1945, 1958.

Theological Dictionaries and Encyclopedias

Bretzke, James T. *A Handbook of Moral Terms*. Washington, DC: Georgetown University Press, 2013.

Childress, James F., and John Macquarrie, eds. *The Westminster Dictionary of Christian Ethics*. Philadelphia: Westminster Press, 1987.

Davies, J. G., ed. *The New Westminster Dictionary of Liturgy and Worship*. Philadelphia: Westminster Press, 1986.

Dwyer, Judith A., ed. *The New Dictionary of Catholic Social Thought*. Collegeville, MN: Liturgical Press, 1994.

Fink, Peter E., ed. *The New Dictionary of Sacramental Worship*. Collegeville, MN: Liturgical Press, 1990.

Green, Joel B., ed. *Dictionary of Scripture and Christian Ethics*. Grand Rapids: Baker/Brazos Press, 2011.

Komonchak, Joseph A., and others. *The New Dictionary of Theology*. Wilmington, DE: Michael Glazier, 1987; Collegeville, MN: Liturgical Press, 1990.

Latourelle, René, and Rino Fisichella. *Dictionary of Fundamental Theology*. New York: Crossroad, 1995.

McBrien, Richard P., ed. *The HarperCollins Encyclopedia of Catholicism*. San Francisco: HarperSanFrancisco, 1995.

McFarland, Ian A., et al. *Cambridge Dictionary of Christian Theology*. Cambridge: Cambridge University Press, 2011.

O'Collins, Gerald, and Edward Farrugia. *A Concise Dictionary of Theology*. Rev. and exp. ed. New York: Paulist Press, 1991, 2000.

Rahner, Karl, ed. *Encyclopedia of Theology: The Concise* Sacramentum Mundi. London: Burns & Oates, 1975.

Rahner, Karl, and Herbert Vorgrimler. *Theological Dictionary*. Edited by Cornelius Ernst. Translated by Richard Strachan. New York: Herder & Herder, 1965.

Roberti, Francesco, and Pietro Palazzini, eds. *Dictionary of Moral Theology*. Translated from the second Italian edition under the direction of Henry J. Yannone. London: Burns & Oates, 1962.